Supervisor's SCRIPT BOOK

RAYMOND DREYFACK

PRENTICE HALL
Englewood Cliffs, New Jersey 07632

Library of Congress Cataloging in Publication Data

Dreyfack, Raymond
    The supervisor's script book / Raymond Dreyfack.
        p. cm.
    ISBN 0-13-460114-9 — ISBN 0-13-476052-2 (pbk.)
    1. Supervison of employees—Problems, exercises, etc.
    2. Personnel management—Problems, exercises, etc. I. Title
    HF5549.12.D7   1996
    658.3'02—dc20   96-13792
                                                       CIP

© *1996 by Prentice Hall, Inc.*

Printed in the United States of America

10 9 8 7 6 5 4 3 2 1

ISBN 0-13-460114-9 (C)   ISBN 0-13-476052-2 (P)

ATTENTION: CORPORATIONS AND SCHOOLS

Prentice Hall books are available at quantity discounts with bulk purchase for educational, business, or sales promotional use. For information, please write to: Prentice Hall Career & Personal Development Special Sales, 113 Sylvan Avenue, Englewood Cliffs, NJ 07632. Please supply: title of book, ISBN number, quantity, how the book will be used, date needed.

 PRENTICE HALL
Career & Personal Development
Englewood Cliffs, NJ 07632
A Simon & Schuster Company

On the World Wide Web at http://www.phdirect.com

Prentice Hall International (UK) Limited, *London*
Prentice Hall of Australia Pty. Limited, *Sydney*
Prentice Hall Canada, Inc., *Toronto*
Prentice Hall Hispanoamericana, S.A., *Mexico*
Prentice Hall of India Private Limited, *New Delhi*
Prentice Hall of Japan, Inc., *Tokyo*
Simon & Schuster Asia Pte. Ltd., *Singapore*
Editora Prentice Hall do Brasil, Ltda., *Rio de Janeiro*

INTRODUCTION

How the *Supervisor's Script Book* Will Save You Time and Boost Your Supervisory Effectiveness

As a supervisor, you run into problems, disagreements, and misunderstandings daily, often when they're least expected. They involve subordinates and superiors, fellow supervisors, and customers. The faster these situations are resolved, the faster your department can get back to normal productive operation. *The trick is to keep problems from erupting into profit- and career-defeating actions.* The time element can be critical. Experience proves that when the iron cools off it may be too late to strike.

> **CASE IN POINT:** A key man in the department unexpectedly requests a wage boost you're unable to grant. What to do? What can you say that will keep him from quitting?

> **CASE IN POINT:** A fuming red-faced employee charges an assistant with sexual harassment. What can you say to calm her down, prevent her from filing suit, and permit you to deal with her rationally?

> **CASE IN POINT:** An irate customer complains he was rudely mistreated by a subordinate. What words can you use in an effort to save the account? What should you tell the employee to get him back on the ball?

In-house and field experience testifies that it's unwise to put off such problems for days, or even hours, while you dope out a strategy to apply. By then action might be taken that could hamper and stall operations, or injure you and the company.

What's the best tactic to take? Clearly, the action *not* to take is to guess at the right strategy, or respond off the top of your head. Fortunately, the solution is as close as the end of your arm. Instead of putting off pressing problems for hours or days, you can solve them immediately. Instead of wracking your brain, you can reach out for the *Supervisor's Script Book* and turn to the subject in question for the sure-fire, pretested, what-to-say answer. Word for word. *Specifically geared to the situation at hand.* Face to face—or phone to phone as the case may be—with your chances of messing it up and getting yourself in an embarrassing bind microminimized.

Management gurus like Peter Drucker and Tom Peters agree that supervisors are most vulnerable to misjudgment and error when caught off guard. Experts stress that surprises are fun—but only at celebrations or birthdays. They have no place in the workplace. It is the mission of the *Supervisor's Script Book* to ensure that you will always be prepared whenever problems erupt. Covering the gamut from morale and performance problems to avoiding grievances and managing change, this reference will prepare you to respond *within moments* to whatever contingency might arise. Take this example: A valued, financially hard-pressed employee is disgruntled because employees in another department are getting more overtime than she is. Hard pressed yourself for good people, the last thing you need is for her to shop around for another job and resign. So how do you deal with the problem?

Simply enough. You say, "Give me a few minutes to complete this report I'm working on, Mary Ann. I'll get back to you just as soon as I can."

Then, turn to Chapter 5, Dialogue 2 on time issues. There, word for word, you review the dialogue: Mary Ann's beef, the researched and pretested response. Then within ten or fifteen minutes, you summon Mary Ann to your desk to *talk out* the problem so that it will be resolved as much as possible to both her, and your own satisfaction. Could anything be more neatly tailored to your needs than that?

The *Supervisor's Script Book* is a supervisory management tool no supervisor can afford to be without. Its easy-to-use index helps you put your finger on the ideal tested and proven word-for-word strategy for the 30 basic management issues that account for over 90% of problems and misunderstandings—with subordinates, your boss, other supervisors, and customers—that occur daily in the nation's offices, warehouses, and plants. Swiftly. Expeditiously. Before harm can be done.

Raymond Dreyfack

CONTENTS

Introduction
iii

Chapter 1
STRENGTHENING TEAMWORK
1

Dialogues

v

Chapter 2
UPGRADING PERFORMANCE
13

Dialogues

Chapter 3
REINFORCING LEADERSHIP PRINCIPLES
25

Dialogues

Chapter 4
OVERCOMING RESISTANCE TO CHANGE
37

Dialogues

Chapter 5
DEALING WITH TIME ABUSE
49

Dialogues

Chapter 6
DELEGATING MORE EFFECTIVELY
60

Dialogues

viii • Contents

Chapter 7
MULTIPLYING PRODUCTIVITY
72

Dialogues

Chapter 8
DEALING WITH PROBLEM EMPLOYEES
83

Dialogues

Chapter 9
KEEPING COSTS UNDER CONTROL
93

Dialogues

Chapter 10
ENCOURAGING INITIATIVE
102

Dialogues

Chapter 11
BOOSTING MORALE
113

Dialogues

Chapter 12
DEALING WITH ATTITUDE PROBLEMS
124

Dialogues

Chapter 13
MAKING MORE EFFECTIVE DECISIONS
132

Dialogues

Chapter 14
MAKING MEETINGS PAY OFF
141

Dialogues

Chapter 15
WINNING AND KEEPING RESPECT
152

Dialogues

Chapter 16
IMPROVING HUMAN RELATIONS
163

Dialogues

Chapter 17
SOLVING PROBLEMS MORE EFFECTIVELY
173

Dialogues

Chapter 18
IMPROVING CUSTOMER SERVICE
185

Dialogues

Chapter 19
SAFEGUARDING EMPLOYEE HEALTH AND WELL-BEING
196

Dialogues

Chapter 20
TIGHTENING PLANT AND OFFICE SECURITY
208

Dialogues

Chapter 21
TRAINING AND DEVELOPING PEOPLE
218

Dialogues

Chapter 22
HIRING AND FIRING PEOPLE
229

Dialogues

Chapter 23
GRIEVANCE AVOIDANCE
239

Dialogues

Chapter 24
APPLYING DISCIPLINE CONSTRUCTIVELY
250

Dialogues

Chapter 25
DEALING WITH SEXUAL HARASSMENT
260

Chapter 26
GETTING NEW HIRES OFF ON THE RIGHT FOOT
272

Chapter 27
SETTING HIGH PERFORMANCE AND ETHICAL STANDARDS
283

Dialogues

Chapter 28
PROMOTING HEALTHY AMBITION
295

Dialogues

Chapter 29
COMMUNICATING MORE EFFECTIVELY
306

Dialogues

Chapter 30
COMPENSATING EMPLOYEES
316

Dialogues

Index
327

chapter one

· · · · · · · · · · · · · · · · ·

STRENGTHENING TEAMWORK

What do teamwork and cake have in common? For either to work right, their ingredients must blend. Bite into a cake in which a single ingredient is wrong—too much, too little, poor quality—and it won't taste right. Same thing with a work group or department in an office, warehouse, or plant. Here the "ingredients" aren't flour, sugar, or milk. They're people. All it takes is one difficult person, one poor team player who doesn't blend harmoniously, to mess up the mix. One of your most crucial tasks as a supervisor is to make sure that the blend is harmonious.

DIALOGUE ONE

Complaints have been coming through that Alice in Data Processing gives co-workers a hard time getting the information they need.

Talking It Out

Supervisor - Alice, what's this I hear about you refusing to give Frank Peterson the third-quarter report on the special deal sales?

1

Employee - (waffling) Oh, I didn't refuse to give it to him; I was just too busy at the time.

S. Was that also the case when Mary asked you to spend a few minutes with her to explain how you worked up the end-of-the-month commission statements?

E. Well. . .

S. Let's level with each other. Too many complaints have been filtering through that you're not cooperating with co-workers as much as you should. Are they unjustified? I want to hear your side of the story.

E. (embarrassed) I don't know. I guess maybe some of the time. . .

S. Alice, excuse me for interrupting, but you're one of the department's smartest and most valued employees. Holding back information is like blocking the flow of oil from a pipeline. It keeps people from doing their jobs. It hurts the department, and it hurts you most of all.

E. I don't want to hurt anyone. But some of those questions are so dumb I lose patience.

S. That's because you're bright and have so much more experience. I run into the same problem myself. People ask me for information I feel they should know for themselves. But it's my responsibility to cooperate and share information. That's everyone's responsibility. It's what teamwork is all about.

E. (lowers her eyes)

S. Let me ask you a question. How would you feel if someone was too busy or impatient to give you information you needed?

E. (reluctantly) I wouldn't like it.

S. Of course you wouldn't. And chances are you wouldn't think very well of that person either. In fact, you might have it in for him or her as they say. Right?

E. I guess I would.

S. Okay, enough said about that. I'm sure you're familiar with the Golden Rule. But there's something else you should think about. This may sound silly, but I've run across some people who harbor the notion that giving away knowledge or information is like giving away career Brownie points. The more they keep to them-

selves the more valuable they will appear to the boss. You don't think that way, do you?

E. Oh, no!

S. I didn't think so. Because it works just the opposite: The more you help train, develop, and qualify co-workers, the more useful you will be, and the greater your chance for advancement. Doesn't that make sense to you?

E. Yes, it does.

S. Good. Let's face it. The more you cooperate with your fellow employees and pitch in when they need help, the better they'll like you, and root for your success and well-being. It's human nature. And I can tell you from experience, Alice, in business the more friends and allies you cultivate, the happier and more successful you'll be.

• • • **TALKING POINTS** An old Chinese proverb states: "One hand washes the other." It applies in the family, the community, on the job. The more effectively you hammer this concept home to your people, the better their teamwork response will be. The goal is to create awareness. It's never been known to fail. Getting these points across to Alice is sure to make her a better team player.

DIALOGUE TWO

A group leader functions as a one-person team. He tries to run the whole show himself.

Talking It Out

Supervisor - Bill, if you've got a few minutes I'd like to have a heart-to-heart talk. There's a question or two I would like to have answered.

Employee - Yeah, sure.

S. No sweat, but have you made any headway with that bottleneck at the Receiving Desk that's been throwing the operation behind schedule?

E. Uh, no. I've been planning to work on it first chance I get.

S. What about your group's participation in the suggestion program? I don't have to tell you you're way down near the bottom of the list.

E. I know. That's been bugging me.

S. And how are you coming along on that Attendance Evaluation Report which was supposed to be ready last week?

E. I've been trying to get to it. But I've been so busy lately I don't have time to breathe. I put in fourteen hours of overtime last week.

S. I know. That's one of the reasons I welcome this opportunity to sit down with you. Correct me if I'm wrong, but I'd lay 10–1 odds that Grace hates those long hours even more than you do.

E. No argument there. She complains I don't spend enough time with the kids.

S. I can appreciate the gripe; I've been through that mill myself. Bill, let me give you my feedback based on years of experience. If you play your supervisory cards right, my guess is you'll be able to eliminate a lot of that overtime and make your job more productive and enjoyable in the process.

E. (his interest aroused)

S. Let me ask you one other question. What's the difference between a supervisor, whether he's in charge of three people or thirty, and a line or staff employee?

E. A supervisor has more responsibility. Also, he's supposed to know more about the job.

S. Absolutely. But there's another key difference as well. It's up to the guy in charge to do the major thinking and planning for his group. Don't you agree?

E. Yeah, I guess so.

S. Bill, from what I've observed, you're usually so busy racing from work station to work station putting out fires, fixing machines, solving work problems, or working up reports that there's little else you have time for. Am I right?

E. I suppose so. But that's my job, isn't it?

S. I'm glad you said that. It's where we disagree. The facts speak for themselves. Even with all the overtime you've been putting in, you

still don't have enough time for the thinking and planning that it's your job to do.

E. (worried frown) I know. Sometimes there aren't enough hours in the day.

S. There'd be more than enough if you made it your business to provide the time. There would be fewer complaints from your people about the work being boring, and from Grace and the kids about your not spending time with them.

E. I see what you're getting at, but half the time if I don't do the job myself, it's not done right. Take that stamping machine I fixed this morning, I'm the only one who could have done it. And the rejects report—I knocked it off in two hours. It would have taken Harry or Mae all day.

S. Is that because they're stupid?

E. No, it's because they don't have my skill or experience.

S. That's the point. How are they ever going to get the skill and experience if you don't give them the chance to acquire it? Bill, the evidence proves that a really effective group functions as a team, not as a one-man operation. It's fine to strive for perfection, but a good slogan to hang over your desk is: SUPERMAN DOESN'T WORK HERE. The reason you're in charge is because you're smarter, better qualified, more efficient, and more experienced than the people who work for you. Your challenge as a supervisor isn't to do the job yourself because you're best at it. It's to qualify your people to do the job *they're* being paid for. Doesn't that make sense?

E. Yeah, I guess it does.

S. Take my word for it. Bill, the good news is that if you function as a team *leader* instead of a one-man team, you'll wind up running a happier and more productive operation. You'll be creating a cushion of time for the real supervisory work. You'll be building your own management skills for the next step up the ladder. And as a bonus you'll be giving Grace and the kids a real break for a change.

• • • **TALKING POINTS** It's not by accident that the *Participatory Team Approach* is one of the hottest buzz phrases around. Under this concept members in the group pitch in to think and act on their own. To the best of their ability, they solve work problems and decisions themselves. When they need guidance they call the head person for help. Under the Participatory Team Approach, the supervisor isn't the "boss," he or she is the leader.

DIALOGUE THREE

An employee balks at an assignment on the grounds that it's not her job.

Talking It Out

Supervisor - Phyllis, do you have a few minutes? I'd like you to learn how to work up the Weekly Status Report so you'll be able to cover for Jo Ann when she goes on vacation, and fill in at other times too. The procedure isn't difficult. I think you have the smarts to master it quickly.

Employee - (frowning) I have more than enough work already. Besides, it isn't my job.

S. What makes you say that?

E. Well, if you check the job description manual you'll see that my classification doesn't call for that kind of work.

S. That never occurred to me. I thought you would welcome the opportunity because of the benefits involved.

E. (warily) What benefits?

S. There are several. Don't you ever get bored doing the same kind of work much of the time?

E. Sure, because of all the repetition. But repetition is part of the job.

S. I agree. And a certain amount is unavoidable. But as studies prove, one of the best antidotes to boredom is change. It cuts down repetition and makes the job more interesting. Doesn't that make sense?

E. Yes, I guess it does.

S. Not only that, diversification makes you a more important part of the team. The more different jobs you can perform, the more valuable you are to the company, and the better your chance for merit increases and job advancement. That's why industrial engineers

push the concept of job variety. It's good for the organization, good for the department, and best of all for the employees.

E. *Well, if you put it that way. . .*

S. It's the only way to put it. Think about your own experience. Doesn't it make you feel good when your in-basket is overloaded and Ellen pitches in to help you to chop down the backlog?

E. *Sure.*

S. Well, think about it, Phyllis. You wouldn't have gotten that help if Ellen refused to pitch in on the grounds that it wasn't her job. It's a simple fact of business life: The more you know, the more you grow. Every job skill you acquire is a deposit in your career bank. Now if you don't want me to go over the Status Report with you, I can choose someone else.

E. *Oh no, I'll do it. I didn't realize what was involved.*

• • • **TALKING POINTS**   Abundant evidence shows that the more skills a team acquires, the stronger the team. The main underlying value of the *Participatory Team Approach,* or *Quality Circles,* as the Japanese call it, is the ability of the work team to interact and interchange as the need occurs. This not only makes the team more productive, but makes the work experience more enjoyable as well.

DIALOGUE FOUR

Teamwork between Mary and Frieda leaves a great deal to be desired because Mary, the senior and more experienced employee, doesn't like Frieda and hates to work with her.

Talking It Out

Supervisor - Take a look at this job sheet, Mary. The quality and quantity of the work is below standard.

Employee - That's because you assigned Frieda to work with me. I can't help it. I just don't get along with her.

S. **Why is that?**

E. *(reluctantly) I don't like to talk about people behind their backs.*

S. **I respect you for that. But one way or another I want to get to the bottom of this. I'm not looking to blame anyone. What I need is to reach an understanding that will result in better cooperation and teamwork between the two of you.**

E. *I don't know if that's possible. Our personalities just clash.*

S. **Is that due to an incident that occurred in the past?**

E. *Maybe, partly at least.*

S. **How would it be if I brought the two of you together so that you could talk it out and shake hands? Do you think that might work?**

E. *(skeptically) I don't know. Maybe.*

S. **Okay, Mary, thanks for leveling with me. I'm going to have a chat with Frieda and see how she feels about it.**

(After talking with Frieda, the supervisor concluded that teamwork—and the department—would be best served by making other arrangements, keeping Mary and Frieda apart to the maximum degree possible.)

• • • **TALKING POINTS** Realities of life being what they are, not all people can be made to work harmoniously with all other people. Differences in age, temperament, political orientation, and personal prejudices must be taken into consideration. This by no means implies that a supervisor must, or should, tolerate bigotry. But from a teamwork consideration it makes good practical sense to put people together who enjoy the rapport it takes to make them work harmoniously.

DIALOGUE FIVE

Grumpy ill-tempered Joe is a more or less satisfactory worker. The problem is that he too often bad-mouths his supervisor, co-workers, the company, and its officials.

Talking It Out

Supervisor - Joe, I read an interesting article in the paper the other day. It was about a merchant in Iraq who referred to Saddam

Hussein, the country's leader, as "a ruthless dictator who ought to be deposed." The following day the poor guy was found dumped in a ditch with his throat cut. That's pretty harsh punishment just for expressing dissatisfaction with a political ruler. Don't you agree?

Employee - Sure, but given the situation in that country, the guy was a jerk. He should've known when to keep his mouth shut.

S. (laughs) That's a funny statement coming from you.

E. What do you mean?

S. (consulting his notes) The latest news from the grapevine is that you've been going full steam in the bad-mouthing department yourself. The word I get is that you were bruiting around in the lunch room that Mr. Benson's an incompetent boob who should be mopping the washroom instead of running a company. Am I quoting you accurately?

E. (flushes) I don't know; I might've said something like that. But it's true; I don't think he's a good President.

S. You're entitled to your opinion. But it may surprise you to know that Mr. Benson worked his way up from a routine field sales job. Do you think an incompetent boob could have done that?

E. Well, maybe I was exaggerating, but. . .

S. Excuse me for interrupting, but I also got word from Mr. Kraft, one of our important customers, that you said you thought our Model 15B engine was a piece of junk. He wonders what kind of team spirit exists here if our employees berate the company's products.

E. (flush deepens)

S. (consults his notes) I also hear from a group leader that you've been raking *me* over the coals and some of your co-workers as well. Joe, if everything about this company and its people is so terrible, how come you continue to work here? Why don't you find another company that isn't populated with morons and incompetents?

E. (sullen and downcast) I didn't think my personal, private comments would get back to you.

S. That tends to happen when you make your personal, private comments public. Joe, you're lucky you don't live in Iraq. You might wind up in a ditch. But I can tell you this: If your bad-mouthing of

employees in general and customers in particular continues, you may not wind up in a ditch, but the one place you most certainly won't wind up is here. Take care. This information is now a part of your personnel record.

• • • **TALKING POINTS** Team spirit and loyalty go hand in hand. No team, be it a corporation, department, or work group, can afford the luxury of an employee who berates the organization, its people, or products. If someone like Joe works for you the alternatives should be clear: Either take strong measures to straighten him out, or *get* him out at your earliest opportunity.

DIALOGUE SIX

Phil's problem is that he treats employees in other sections and departments as if they're the enemy.

Talking It Out

Supervisor - Phil, how do you feel about the team approach to the job?

Employee - (hesitantly) It's a good idea.

S. I agree. But what does it mean to you?

E. I guess you might say all for one and one for all. Working together with the people on your team. Cooperating.

S. Right on! I couldn't have said it better myself. But let me ask you another question: *Which* team are you talking about?

E. (frowns) I'm not sure I understand that question.

S. Okay, I'll explain. An organization, any business that employs more than a handful of people, is composed of several teams. Take this company: We have a number of departments; most of them break down into sections. In Production you have assembly, the machine shop, the supply room, finishing, and inventory control. The general office consists of billing, accounts receivable, accounts payable, payroll, and so on. Each of these groups is a team. Are you with me?

E. Yeah. Teams within teams.

S. Exactly. So, when you refer to the team approach, which team are you talking about?

E. I guess most of all my own team, the people I work with. That's the team that concerns me.

S. Good answer, but I wonder if you may be missing a main point of the team approach. The truth is that no matter how many teams there are, the key to effective teamwork is how well *all* the teams work together to meet the goals of the *parent* team. That's the organization itself whose job it is to produce quality products, meet the needs of its customers, and operate at a profit. Does that make sense?

E. Sure, but why. . .

S. (smiling) Why am I bending your ear about all this? Good question. The reason is simple. Phil, you're one of our most valued employees. But complaints have been coming through that, while you're always ready to pitch in and cooperate with people from your own group, when someone from another section or department needs your help you sometimes give him or her a hard time.

E. (frowning) If I do I don't do it consciously.

S. Maybe that's the problem. I'll give you an example or two. When Mary in Accounts Receivable needed to know the status of the Johnson Brothers account, you made her wait two days for the information even though she told you she was in a hurry for it and called you two or three times. When Ben in Data Processing asked you to explain how you arrived at the percentages on the Consolidation Report, you told him you were too busy to do it.

E. (lowers his eyes)

S. I don't like to be critical, Phil. You're an important part of the machinery that makes your own personal team function smoothly. But beyond that, it's the cooperation and coordination of each individual team that makes the *parent* team succeed. All for one, one for all. Everyone working together. Teams within teams.

E. (nodding thoughtfully)

S. It's a funny thing about teamwork. It has a boomerang effect. When you work with people the cooperation bounces back, and they work with you. If you give them a hard time, they become your opponents. That's bad for business, and it's bad for people.

Business is competition. But it's not *internal* competition, except as a friendly contest to chalk up the best work record. The real competition is with *external* forces. Each company vying against others in the field to make the best products, win the most customers, provide the best services, and chalk up the most profits.

E. (still thoughtful)

S. Keep that in mind, Phil, the next time Ben or Mary come to you with a problem or request for information.

E. I'll try.

• • • **TALKING POINTS**   People want and need to be part of the group, to be accepted and appreciated by their teammates. But sometimes group loyalty becomes confused with the broader mandates of organizational loyalty. Employees take an us-against-them approach on a narrow tunnel-visioned basis. When that occurs, the sooner you expand the horizon with organizational performance and profit goals in mind, the more effectively teamwork will prevail.

chapter two

• • • • • • • • • • • • • • • • • •

UPGRADING PERFORMANCE

Performance—how well employees do their jobs—stems from a combination of knowledge, natural and developed abilities, experience, and most of all motivation. It is no secret or surprise that supervisors and managers in most cases are better motivated than line and staff personnel. In the typical office or plant it is clear to the men and women running the show what they have to gain or lose from the performance level achieved. The trick is for the leaders to get the message across to the led that they too have an important personal stake in the quality of work they produce. The top-rated supervisor is the man or woman who: 1) Can spot and develop the potential good performer; 2) Pinpoint and improve the poor performer; 3) Qualify and help motivate all employees to perform at their best.

DIALOGUE ONE

Lathe operator Ed is a family man whose performance over a three-month period declined from good to marginal. Nor is he the only one in his group who is sliding.

Talking It Out

Supervisor - (Ed's record in front of him) Let's sit down and see if we can get to the root of your sliding performance.

Employee - (glum, doesn't deny allegation)

S. Ed, your potential is outstanding. We both know that. You're bright. You have the required experience. You know the work as well as anyone in the department. So the conclusion is obvious. Something must have happened to change you from a good to mediocre performer. It's to both our advantages to find out what it is and see what can be done about it. What can you tell me?

E. I don't know. I'll try to do better.

S. You said that last time. If anything, your work's declined further. More mistakes, less productivity. Do you have personal problems at home?

E. No, nothing like that.

S. Anything wrong with your health?

E. No. I had a checkup recently. Everything's okay.

S. Thank God for that. What about the work you're assigned? Any problems there?

E. (hesitating) No. The work's okay.

S. (pressing) come on, Ed, something's bugging you, I can see it in your eyes. Level with me and I'll level with you.

E. (wavering)

S. Let's have it, Ed. A problem can't be resolved until you get it out in the open.

E. (reluctantly) Well, things aren't the same around here as they used to be.

S. Used to be? When?

E. Before Charlie was promoted and Vince put in charge of our group?

S. What have you got against Vince?

E. It's nothing personal.

S. Well that's good. I don't have to tell you, Ed, Vince is the hardest working guy in the department.

E. (shrugs) Maybe he works too hard.

S. What do you mean by that?

E. *Charlie monitored the work like he was supposed to, to make sure it got out on time. But if there was no problem he left us alone to do our jobs. Vince breathes down our backs all the time. He checks on us every step we take. He treats us like we can't think for ourselves. It makes us feel like we're back in sixth grade.*

S. **You say "us." I take that to mean you're not the only one who feels this way.**

E. *That's right. Most of the people I talk to feel the same way.*

S. **Thanks for leveling with me, Ed.**

• • • **TALKING POINTS**   Declining performance is like a red flag signaling the need for some hard, thoughtful spade work. It may take a little prodding to get people like Ed to open up, but once you dig down to the root cause for the decline, the action followup will be indicated. In the above situation, the supervisor wisely interviewed others in the group who echoed Ed's reaction. This, as we shall see, called for a heart-to-heart talk with Charlie's replacement, Group Leader Vince, to get his side of the story.

DIALOGUE TWO

Vince, as indicated in Dialogue One, is a newly appointed and inexperienced group leader. He suffers from lack of confidence and insecurity. This causes him to distrust his subordinates as well. He thus feels that if he doesn't dot every *i* and cross every *t* himself the job won't be done properly.

Talking It Out

Supervisor - When were you appointed Group Leader, Vince?

Employee - Five months ago, why? Is there a problem?

S. **It seems that way. On the one hand, we both know you wouldn't have gotten the promotion if you weren't the one best qualified for it. But the facts speak for themselves. The operation's productivity has been falling since you took over. That's normal for a while when a new supervisor comes on board. But what bothers me is that the slide seems to be persisting.**

E. *I know, that's been bugging me. I've been working my butt off. . .*

S. I know you have. You're one of the hardest working guys in the department. So it's apparent that busting your butt isn't the answer. Let's see if we can find out what is. Do you have any ideas?

E. Frankly no. I wish I had. All I know is that the group isn't the same since I took over.

S. That's the beef I get from a few of your people. They complain you're monitoring the work so closely it makes them feel like sixth graders. They feel stifled, which undermines morale. When morale declines so does performance. It's never been known to fail. Do you think there's any merit to these gripes?

E. (worried) I don't know. I try to make sure that the job is done right.

S. I know you do. That's very much to your credit. But even the best of intentions can be overdone. I've got a suggestion, Vince: Ease up a bit. Charlie's a good model to go by. Try to put more trust in your people to do their jobs right. Encourage them to think for themselves. Then let's see how it works out. Fair enough?

E. Sure. Thanks for the advice.

• • • **TALKING POINTS**   Supervisors stimulate or stifle performance depending on their style and approach. Ideally, a supervisor leads subordinates, offering guidance when it's needed. He or she allows them to function like adults. Pride and self-respect are as much fuel for the human spirit as gasoline is for a car. When you water down pride and respect, you water down performance as well.

DIALOGUE THREE

Ethel is smart, conscientious, and a quick learner. Her problem is that she lacks the self-confidence to do her best work.

Talking It Out

Supervisor - Ethel, I have good news and bad news. You've been preparing the Weekly Army Sales Report for five months now. The good news is that it's been perfect every month running, not a single

error or comma out of place. **The bad news is that it takes you five hours to complete when it should take you three or four at most.**

Employee - I work as fast as I can.

S. **I know you do. I've observed you from time to time and I appreciate your conscientiousness. That's not the problem. Let me ask you a question: Do you check the report before entering the final figures?**

E. Oh yes. I check it twice.

S. **Why twice?**

E. Well, I want to make one-hundred percent sure that it's accurate.

S. **I can't argue with that. But tell me, in the five months you've been doing the report, how often, on the second check, have you found an error?**

E. (frowns) I think once, when I first started doing it.

S. **Once in five months. That's pretty darned good. In fact it's remarkable. Tell me something else: What do you think would happen if an error slipped through?**

E. Oh, I shudder to think of it.

S. **(smiles) I don't shudder at all. We're all human, Ethel. We all make mistakes from time to time. I'm not saying accuracy isn't important. But one error in five months isn't the end of the world. Someone would question the mistake and it would be corrected. The building wouldn't come down. No heads would roll.**

E. (tentatively returns smile)

S. **Do you know something, Ethel? On a scale of one to ten, at the present time you rank nine-plus and are well on your way to ten. You're bright, conscientious, and eager to learn. No supervisor could ask for more. Do you mind if I make a suggestion?**

E. Not at all.

S. **Relax. Don't worry so much. Check your work carefully, but one check is enough. You're doing fine. Don't be afraid of an error or predict dire consequences if one should occur. (smiles) If you make a mistake, come to confession and I'll forgive you. Fair enough?**

E. (her own smile broadening) Okay. Thanks a lot.

• • • **TALKING POINTS** Lack of confidence and the insecurity it generates, like motivational insufficiency, undermines performance. The best favor you could do for yourself as a supervisor is to identify the good people in your operation whose self-confidence needs bolstering. Mark Twain once said, "I can live for two months on a good compliment." Be generous with pats on the back where merited. Encourage your good people to keep up the good work. Keep in mind that people who are short on confidence are usually long on anxiety. Like Ethel, they're apt to check, double-check, and even triple-check their work unnecessarily. All that accomplishes is to waste time and undermine performance.

DIALOGUE FOUR

Ned is a mediocre employee. Worse yet, he can't be trusted to do his job unless watched.

Talking It Out

Supervisor - Ned, this isn't the first time I had to talk to you about the job you're doing.

Employee - I work as hard as most of the other people in the department.

S. That's news to me. You do your work when you're watched. But if I don't happen to be around your work is below standard.

E. That's not so.

S. It isn't? Then explain this to me: Two days ago you filled 14 orders from 8:00 A.M. until lunchtime. Yesterday you filled 9 orders in the same period. How do you account for the difference?

E. Simple. Yesterday's orders were bigger.

S. We both know that's not so. I checked the orders out in both cases. They were roughly in balance. I'll give it to you straight, Ned. The difference exists because two days ago I was on hand to oversee the operation. Yesterday I was at a meeting all morning.

E. (tightlipped sullen response)

S. Ned, I have to tell you you're treading on dangerous ground if you're interested in keeping this job. I'm issuing an official warn-

ing and entering it in your file. That's the second entry this month. One more and you're on the street. Do I make myself clear?

E. Yeah.

• • • **TALKING POINTS**   There's a time to reason with people who don't toe the line and a time to hang tough. Unless you take a hard line with employees like Ned, you encourage others to duplicate their performance. The disciplinary procedure in such cases is straightforward and blunt. First offense, reason with the employee and try to persuade him to reform. If this doesn't work, use firmer reasoning and a second chance if it seems merited. If the unacceptable behavior persists, issue a warning and make sure it is documented. Next time, issue another warning accompanied by a suspension if need be. Finally, if reform doesn't occur, the old heave-ho is in order.

DIALOGUE FIVE

What do you do about the employee who feels she has nothing to gain by shaping up and improving?

Talking It Out

Supervisor - Ellen, I think we both agree on one thing. You're a smart lady.

Employee - (smiles brightly) Why thank you, sir.

S. (returns smile) But sometimes I can't help wondering if you put your brains to full use.

E. What do you mean?

S. Well, here, let's take a look at your performance record for the past six months. Comparing your output qualitatively and quantitatively with other employees in your group, your performance ranks among the bottom half. I think we both agree that you could do a lot better than that if you wish. I'll show you the evidence of that if you like.

E. I'll take your word.

S. Thanks. You don't seem too concerned about it. Why?

E. (shrugs) Why should I be? It's a routine job. I get the same crummy pay-check for the same boring job no matter how hard I work. Why should I knock myself out? Where will it get me?

S. Good question. No one's asking you to knock yourself out. Knocking yourself out is one thing; applying yourself conscientiously is another. Let me answer your question with one or two of my own. You complained about the job being boring. How would you like more interesting assignments, like the Commission Statement, the Rejects Report, or the EOM Franchise Sales?

E. Are you kidding? I've been requesting those jobs for months. I have yet to see one of them.

S. Did you ever wonder why not? Think about it a moment. Who deserves the preferred assignments? People at the bottom half of the list, or the ones at the top half?

E. Well. . .

S. Okay, let's talk about money. I imagine you could use more money, right?

E. Ha, ha, ha. The last time I got an increase. . .

S. Thanks for making my point. Would you like to see the list of the people in this department who got increases and promotions in the past two or three years?

E. My name wasn't among them.

S. That's exactly my point. Don't you ever wonder why?

E. (resigned sigh) I know. Bottom half of the list.

S. You got it, Ellen, but that's only one side of the coin. Since you're on the *top* half of the list in intelligence and experience, I see no reason why some of those goodies shouldn't be going to you. But let's not cry over spilled milk. There's always tomorrow. We have to face the reality that if you want your fair share of the goodies, you have to *earn* them.

• • • **TALKING POINTS** Any employee who thinks *earning* the goodies isn't worthwhile is, like Ellen, in need of a rude awakening. The evidence exists in every organization and every department. Business has one thing in common with war: To the victor belongs the spoils. It's your job as a supervisor to make that abundantly clear. In business the victor is the person who works hard to perform well. The spoils are a whole assortment of goodies that range from job satisfaction and self-respect to the material rewards that derive from success.

DIALOGUE SIX

Bob is a disgruntled employee. He's restless and bored because he feels the assignments he gets are below his level of competence.

Talking It Out

Supervisor - Let's have it, Bob: What's bothering you?

Employee - Well, since you ask, it's the work. The work orders I'm getting are driving me up a wall.

S. Why is that?

E. They're too simple, no challenge. That jig I was assigned this morning, for example. A high-school kid in Shop could throw it together in an hour or two. Or the shelving I worked on all last week. My 12-year-old kid could've done it.

S. Hey Bob, I'm no mind reader. I had no idea you felt this way. Why didn't you tell me?

E. I'm telling you now.

S. You've only been with the company for four or five months. I never would have suspected it if I didn't decide to have a chat with you because you appear so disgruntled. Let's look at the Job Schedule together. Tell me which jobs you think you can handle.

E. (reviews the schedule) All of them, except maybe this combination rotating jig and that manifold contraption. In fact, most of them are kid stuff.

S. (nods thoughtfully) I'm glad I sat down with you. Let me give this some thought.

S. (comes back to Bob the next day) I've been talking with Chuck Madden. He can use a man like you. How would you like to transfer to Special Projects?

E. Are you kidding? I'd love it, so long as I don't lose my seniority.

S. No reason you should. I'll try to set it up and get back to you.

• • • **TALKING POINTS**   There's no question that your best employees are your most creative and talented staff. But in order to keep creative people willingly and enthusiastically on their toes, you have to keep them interested and motivated. The more creative the individual, the less tolerance he or she has for repetitive routine that fails to challenge initiative or imagination. As frustration increases one or two things will occur: a hunt for greener pastures followed by resignation, or a performance decline stemming from apathy. Superior employees like Bob must be kept stimulated if you expect to keep them percolating productively.

DIALOGUE SEVEN

Arlene takes criticism personally. Instead of using it to learn and improve, her mind focuses on answers designed to defend herself.

Talking It Out

Supervisor - Arlene, we have to talk about the way you handle customer calls on the order board.

Employee - Why? What did I do wrong?

S. You didn't do anything wrong. I didn't summon you here to blame you for anything. It's just that I have a few suggestions with possible improvement in mind.

E. What kind of suggestions?

S. Well, for one thing, when customers you know from your previous business with them call, it would be a customer-relations plus if you would greet them cheerfully with a welcoming smile in your voice, the way you would greet an old friend. "Good *morning* Mr. Jones, it's great to hear from you again." Or words to that effect. Do you know what I'm talking about?

E. (defensive) I'm friendly to customers. I certainly don't. . .

S. (curbing impatience)—I'm not saying you're *unfriendly*, Arlene. *Just that it's a good idea to be extra friendly and warm with customers you know. Another thing, try to push our new fall line a bit more if you can. Talk it up. Emphasize our specials in particular. Let customers know how popular they are in the field, and how well they are selling*

E. I do that whenever I can. Some of the other girls never even mention the fall line. They don't. . .

S. Excuse me for interrupting. Let's forget the fall line for the moment, and the way to greet customers. Let's talk about criticism.

E. (frowning) I don't know what you mean.

S. What I mean is very simple. There are two kinds of criticism, negative and positive. Negative criticism is more destructive than useful. It insults people, tries to make them feel guilty, and hurts their feelings. Think about it, Arlene. Did I *accuse* you of anything? Did I imply that you're not doing a good job?

E. (haltingly) No, you didn't.

S. Then I don't think you can rightfully accuse me of being negatively critical, can you?

E. No, I can't.

S. If that's so, why should you be so defensive? All I'm trying to do is help you do your job better. Positive criticism is designed to help people, not hurt them. That's what my suggestions are all about. It's my responsibility as a supervisor. If positive criticism is accepted in the spirit in which it's given, it can only result in improvement. This will help you and in the process help the company. Everyone benefits. Do you understand why I'm telling you all this?

E. I think I do. I've been responding to your suggestions as if you're trying to lay a guilt feeling on me instead of helping me to do my job better. I apologize.

S. (friendly smile) No apology called for. Now let's talk about the advantages of pushing the new fall line and those two specials in particular.

• • • **TALKING POINTS** As Arlene's boss tried to make clear to her, positive, constructive criticism—the kind that helps build and develop people—is a key supervisory tool. The first rule of effective criticism is to administer it in private to minimize possible embarrassment. No worse tactic can be imagined than to scold a person in the presence of co-workers. Insecure employees, and those with a chip on their shoulders, often respond poorly to criticism. In such cases it makes good sense—as Arlene's supervisor realized—to set the stage for effective reception. The way to do this is by hammering home the message that well-intended criticism is beneficial to all parties involved, most of all the employee. This doesn't imply that it's wrong for an employee to counter your criticism with sincere and legitimate arguments. In a democratic society everyone is entitled to a fair hearing. To balance the scales, you owe your people the courtesy of listening to them if they disagree as attentively and respectfully as you would like them to listen to you.

chapter three

. . . .

REINFORCING
LEADERSHIP PRINCIPLES

Supervisors advance up the line to middle management and higher in proportion to the amount of creative thought they put into their jobs. Dr. Paul Parker said it simply enough: "Leaders think. They think because they are leaders. They are leaders because they think." Are you a "born leader?" If so you're the rare exception. Supervisors who believe they are so-called "natural leaders," are in most cases deluding themselves. Leadership isn't inherited. Nor does it happen by accident. It stems from hard work and hard thought on the job. It takes more than just know-how or experience to qualify as a leader. It takes time and special effort as well—time to address and ponder the many challenges and demands of leadership.

DIALOGUE ONE

Frank's operation is highly computerized. Computers are used not only to process work, but for communication and training. This suits Frank fine. It relieves him of that one-on-one chore.

Talking It Out

Manager - Frank, the word's been bruited about that your department is so automated, it's dehumanized. I've been hearing complaints you don't provide enough personal face-to-face contact. I'm curious about your reaction to such comments.

Supervisor - I don't know what to say, John. I regard the computer as a powerful management tool.

M. No argument there. But like any other tool, its value depends on how it is used. Let me give you an analogy. A friend of mine who's a marine biologist has a 12-year-old son who displayed a keen interest in his profession. So he bought a software program that taught him all about marine life and spent a lot of time with his son going over the material. Know what happened?

S. No.

M. The kid's interest dropped off faster than leaves in an October windstorm. Know why?

S. No.

M. Because he never took the kid to a real-life aquarium.

S. (thoughtful) Yeah, I see what you're getting at.

M. It works the same way on the job. The human factor is as important as any other factor in supervising people. The word from the grapevine, for example, is that after running through performance interviews, you use computer printouts to grade your employees and give them the results of your appraisals. Is that so?

S. Well, yeah. It saves me a lot of time, and allows people to spend more time at their work stations.

M. Okay, but that's only one side of the coin. The other side is that it turns employee appraisals—which should be a highly personal procedure—into a routine mechanical procedure, like an extension of the computer.

S. I never looked at it that way.

M. Maybe it's time you did. The same thing applies to training. Personal contact with the instructor is a vital part of the training experience. As one expert puts it, "Interactive videos and remote broadcasts are no substitute for studying under a fired-up teacher who's there in person." In this electronic age it's all too easy to get

carried away with the computer's remarkable capabilities and go overboard. I'd be the last one to dispute that without the computer you couldn't run a plant or office today. But I could say the same thing about the good old human factor. It's as critical an element of good leadership as knowledge, organization, or planning.

• • • **TALKING POINTS**   Experience proves that the computer is a viable substitute for an adding machine or calculator in producing a payroll. It can't be beat for digesting and cranking out large quantities of data. And as a storage facility, it knows no equal. But when it comes to interacting with people on a day-to-day basis, it's no substitute for real life. Virtual reality tends to add up to virtual bull when the human element is missing. As for the supervisor who disregards this truth, so-called "virtual" leadership amounts to virtually no leadership at all.

DIALOGUE TWO

Pete's a conscientious Assistant Supervisor with one serious flaw. His practice of favoritism antagonizes some of his people.

Talking It Out

Supervisor - Let me ask you a question. I've been going over the department's personnel records. What made you select Gary for the Harrison project?

Assistant Supervisor- I figured he would do a good job.

S. Better than George, Mary, or Ann? Any one of them has a better work record than Gary.

A. (uncomfortable) I don't know. Maybe I didn't check the records closely enough.

S. The Harrison project is kind of a plum around here, isn't it?

A. Yeah, I guess so.

S. There's no need to guess, Pete. It's an assignment most employees would welcome and everyone knows it. Could your special relationship with Gary have anything to do with his getting the job?

A. What do you mean, special relationship?

S. I think we both know what I'm talking about. You go out to lunch with him, don't you? You're on the same bowling team.

A. Yeah, him and a couple of other guys. What's wrong with that?

S. I won't get into that at the moment. The point is Gary's a special buddy of yours. Correct me if I'm wrong.

A. (tightlipped) I don't know what you're getting at.

S. I think you do, Pete. But to make sure, I'll cite another example. Charlie Griffin.

A. What about Charlie?

S. This about Charlie. When he asked for a vacation day off next week you gave it to him. But when George Kane asked for a vacation day, you turned him down. Why would you say okay to Charlie and tell George no dice?

A. I didn't want two guys out the same week. It would make the department short handed.

S. That argument might stand up except for one thing: George came to you first. You gave Charlie the go-ahead after turning George down.

A. (lowers his eyes)

S. Pete, I don't want to beat this to death. But we both know what I'm talking about. You're my assistant. You have the smarts and you know your job. If you play your cards right, some day when I get a promotion you may take over the department. But keep one thing in mind: A good supervisor is more than a boss; he's a leader. True leaders treat their people fairly. They don't practice favoritism. Hopefully, that will give you something to think about if you want my recommendation for succession when the time comes.

• • • **TALKING POINTS** Playing favorites is a sure-fire way to undermine departmental morale. It also negates a fundamental principle of leadership: to operate fairly and ethically and give everyone an even break. The practice of favoritism is sometimes as blunt and obvious as in the case outlined above. Other times it's subtle and insidious. Employees get preferred treatment, or are denied a fair shake, because of their race, religion, nationality, age, sex, or political beliefs. If it coincides with the supervisor's preferences they're admitted to the "old boy's club." Otherwise, they're excluded. Whatever the reason, where favoritism exists, leadership falls by the wayside and productivity suffers.

DIALOGUE THREE

Marge is a marginal employee, but her supervisor senses potential if she can be persuaded to set goals for herself.

Talking It Out

Supervisor - (merit increase review time) Tell me the truth, Marge. You're smart, you understand the work, and you have the required experience. Do you think this is the best work you can do?

Employee - (reluctantly) I suppose not.

S. What do you think it would take to improve your performance and qualify you for a merit increase next time around?

E. I guess I'd have to work harder.

S. That's certainly part of the answer if you feel you're not working hard enough now. But I think there's more to it than that. I think you have to *want* to do better. People succeed because they're motivated to succeed. Do you think you're motivated? Would you like to earn more money and advance on the job?

E. Sure. Who wouldn't?

S. No one I know. But some people seem to feel merit increases and advancement ought to come as a matter of course. One reason, I think, is that they lack direction.

E. What do you mean?

S. They tend to flounder because they don't set goals for themselves. Like earning that merit increase, for example, or getting picked for an assignment they really want, or advancing a step up the ladder.

E. That sounds easier said than done.

S. **Not really. Setting a goal is easy. The tough part is seeing it through. I've found it's a good idea to put your goal down in writing: "I resolve to earn a merit increase on such and such date," for example. That's step one. Step two is keeping the goal in mind and monitoring your progress periodically to make sure you're on target. That's all there is to it.**

E. *(thoughtfully) I never looked at it that way.*

S. **It can't help but work if you're determined to make it work. It's a funny thing about setting goals and achieving them. Each one that you set and fulfill makes setting and achieving the next goal easier. You get to experience the pride and joy of accomplishment. That's what motivation is all about.**

• • • **TALKING POINTS**   No leader ever became a leader without having first set and fulfilled goals for him- or herself. Setting realistic goals is as important to leadership as a lug wrench is to removing the wheel of a car. One goal leads to another the way a snowball rolling down the hill gathers snow. A true leader, like Marge's supervisor, recognizes this vital attribute of leadership and does her best to pound the message home to her people.

DIALOGUE FOUR

Nothing undermines departmental morale like an employee who displays disrespect for the organization and its management. Luther Forrester fills this bill.

Talking It Out

Supervisor - (referring to a copy of The Wall Street Journal) You don't read the Journal do you, Luther.

Employee - No, I don't.

S. **(folding the newspaper) Well, there's an interesting article here about the company. Did you know we won the Worthington contract last week?**

E. *Yeah, I heard.*

S. (admiringly) Yes sir, we beat out the whole field of competitors to get the award. This article tells how we did it, the brilliant strategies involved. It mentions Mr. Calvin and Mrs. Berne in particular.

E. *(puzzled expression: why is the boss telling him this?)*

S. We've been getting some great P.R. lately. You probably heard we were cited by the Personnel Association for our outstanding training programs.

E. *I think I might have heard something.*

S. Same thing for Sales. Did you know that Ben Fried leads the entire industry in domestic sales?

E. *No. I didn't hear that.*

S. Well, it's a fact. Luther, don't you think we're lucky to be working for a great outfit like this with such terrific people running it?

E. *(uncomfortable) Yeah, I guess we are.*

S. Then why in the world would you be spouting off to people that the company is second-rate, and that it's being run by a bunch of dunderheads? I'm quoting your exact words.

E. *(eyes lowered) I guess I didn't really mean that.*

S. That makes it all the worse. If you can't speak well of an operation and its people, you should keep your lips buttoned up. After all, you're part of this organization, an important part. When you underrate it, you're underrating yourself. If you don't respect the organization that employs you, you shouldn't be working there. And you won't be if your bad-mouthing persists.

• • • **TALKING POINTS** Employees who show disrespect for an operation and its leadership automatically undermine departmental goals as well as their own self-respect. Pride in performance accompanies pride in association with the people one works with and for. If a person expresses the opinion that his or her employer or supervisor is second rate, what does choosing to be employed there say about that person? People who are willing to settle for second-rate imply they themselves are second-rate. True leaders recognize this reality of business life. They are alert to the negative influences of subordinates who sound off with morale-busting innuendo and gossip, and put a strong and firm end to it.

DIALOGUE FIVE

A supervisor who wants to advance himself must understands the importance of a good succession program. Jim needed to have this key principle of leadership impressed upon him.

Talking It Out

Manager - Jim, I got a call from Mr. Becker this morning. He tried to get clarification on the status of the new building program and no one seemed to know what he was talking about.

Supervisor - I know. I was out of the office checking out a piece of equipment that we may make a bid on.

M. Wasn't there anyone on hand to cover for you?

S. Ordinarily, there would be. But that building program's complicated. No one else understands it.

M. What about Bill Graham?

S. Bill's a good man. But he's limited. He doesn't have the experience.

M. Same thing for Jo Ann?

S. Well yes, more or less.

M. I see. Tell me something, Jim. How many jobs fall into the same category as the building project?

S. What do you mean?

M. Jobs that are so complicated that only you can handle them?

S. I don't know. Maybe five or six.

M. Let me ask you another question. How long have you been employed here as head of the Special Projects Department?

S. (figuring) About five years.

M. That's quite a while. Do you ever think that one of these days a promotion might came through?

S. I sure do. In fact, now that you mention it, I was going to talk to you about that. I think I'm long overdue.

M. So do I. But if one comes through would you be ready for it?

S. Sure. I don't see why not.

M. **Okay, let me put it another way: Would your *department* be ready for it?**

S. Sure. I'd have to train someone to take over. We have several good people. Bill Graham, for example, or Jo Ann.

M. **How long would that take? Don't get me wrong, Jim, I don't want to get your hopes up. I have nothing in mind at the moment. But you never know. I'm just curious.**

S. (thoughtful) I don't know. Maybe three or four months. I'd have to first figure out the best person to recommend for the job. Then there's a lot of stuff. . .

M. **Excuse me for interrupting. But your answer doesn't sound realistic to me. You've been around long enough to know that it doesn't work that way. In most cases, when a promotion comes through, a replacement for the vacancy is needed in a hurry, sometimes within two or three weeks. If you were the person selected, who would take over your operation to ensure good continuity of the projects and work orders in force?**

S. Well. . .

M. **It should give you something to think about. A supervisor with progress and advancement in mind takes the time and effort to prepare for it. If you'll pardon a bit of wordplay, success goes hand in hand with successful succession. Like I said, I'm not making any promises. But as things stand now, if an opportunity for advancement came through, you'd probably be bypassed, not because you're not qualified, but because you wouldn't be prepared to step into it. If you want my advice, I would think about selecting a potential successor or two, and start grooming them. Unless you prefer to think of yourself as indispensable to the Special Projects Department?**

S. No way! Not at all.

• • • **TALKING POINTS** As Jim's supervisor points out, success goes hand in hand with successful succession. That's a good leadership axiom to hang over your desk. It's been said that no employee is indispensable and that's true. But the *perception* of indispensability can do as much damage to a supervisory career as thumbing one's nose at the boss. No executive could afford to replace a supervisor if that would cause the department to flounder and undermine profit objectives. The best favor you could do for your-self as a supervisor is to review your operation's list of responsibilities and tasks, and make sure every one of them is covered in your absence. Then pinpoint a couple of promising alter egos and start grooming them for suc-cession when the time comes. Keep in mind that if you feel a project is too complicated to be understood or handled by anyone but you, your opera-tion will be incapable of being supervised by anyone but you.

DIALOGUE SIX

Alice is a supervisor who has a good creative potential, but doesn't have the time to put it to use.

Talking It Out

Manager - (sees Alice at a computer terminal) Pardon my curiosity, Alice, but what are you working on?

Supervisor - The Accounts Receivable postings are heavy today. I'm helping the girls get caught up.

M. I see. Is anyone working on the Job Planning in the meantime?

S. No. I'm the only knows how to do that.

M. Perhaps that's the problem.

S. (beginning to see the light) Oh.

M. I don't want to be a pest, Alice, but the Planning Sheets are a week behind. I called you about them twice already. Not to mention the Attendance Analysis Report.

S. (frowns) I know. I keep intending to get to them. But every time I get ready to start something else comes up. I never seem to have the time.

M. Did it ever occur to you that you may not *have* the time because you don't *make* the time?

S. What do you mean?

M. Let me put it this way. The other day when I passed through your department you were checking off invoices at your desk. That's routine clerical work. In fact, half the time I pass by you seem to be pitching in on one task or another.

S. I know. I try to keep my people from falling behind.

M. I can't fault your intentions, Alice, but I see two things wrong with that approach. One is that if your employees know you're on hand to pitch in whenever they fall behind, they may not work as hard as they would if keeping up was their own responsibility. Second, and most important, you're paid to supervise, not function as an additional rank-and-file employee. You heard the old axiom about the workload expanding to the amount of workers available to do it. If you become part of that availability you'll never have enough time for the creative and important leadership work that results in improved procedures and cost-cutting innovations.

S. (nods thoughtfully) Yeah. I can see what you mean.

M. I'm not saying it isn't a problem when the work piles up and in-baskets overflow. But there are other solutions than just pitching in as a rank-and-filer yourself. One is to assign other employees to fill in when you can. Another is overtime, which isn't always avoidable. And when a real peak occurs you may have no choice but to hire more people on a full-time or temporary basis. In effect, Alice, when you pitch in yourself no one is actually acting as supervisor.

S. I never looked at it that way.

M. It's something to think about. May I make another suggestion?

S. Sure.

M. It's simply this. Alice, how many reports does your department prepare each week?

S. Eighteen or so.

M. How many of them do you do yourself?

S. Seven or eight.

M. Why?

S. Why do I do them myself?

M. Yes.

S. Well, a couple of them are confidential.

M. No argument there. What about the others, like the Weekly European Sales Comparisons, for example?

S. *That report is pretty complicated. It takes me less time to do it myself than it would to break someone in.*

M. Is it so complicated that Mary or Joe wouldn't be able to understand it?

S. *(thoughtfully) Well, no. But it would take a while for them to get the hang of it. Meantime I would have to spend a lot of time turning it over, and it would take them twice as long to complete.*

M. The report is repetitive week after week isn't it? And that applies to those other reports as well. Am I right?

S. *Yes.*

M. So that once Mary, Joe, or whoever mastered the report they'd be able to do it on their own. That would free up your time for the Job Planning sheets, Attendance Analysis, and some of the other creative work you always seem too busy to get around to. (smiling) Doesn't that make sense?

S. *Yes, it does.*

M. Good. Why don't you give it some thought?

• • • **TALKING POINTS** Perhaps the most common and serious mistake that keeps potentially good supervisors from becoming true leaders is the old pitch-in predilection or syndrome. Twin leadership responsibilities often trip head-over-heels over each other. One is the scheduling requirement that focuses on getting the work out in time. The other is the work improvement requirement that zeros in on finding better and faster ways to reduce costs, boost efficiency, and increase productivity. In reflecting on these responsibilities it's a good idea for every supervisor to keep the critical Wage Differential Factor in mind. This is easy to do. Simply ask yourself: Does it make sense for supervisors who earn $10 or $15 per hour to spend their time doing the work of line or staff employees who earn $7 or $8 per hour?

chapter four

. . . .

Overcoming
Resistance to Change

Industrialist Charles Kettering once said, "The world hates change, yet it is the only thing that has brought progress." Employees resist change for any number of reasons, most of which involve anxiety of one kind or another. People tend to settle for the status quo. They know what they have now and prefer to live with that than take a chance on what the future might bring. They worry that change may jeopardize their security, or threaten their status. Or that they will be unable to understand and cope with a new procedure. Or that the change will result in more work, increased responsibility, or longer hours. Often people don't need a reason at all to resist. They do so instinctively. Your first task as a supervisor is to find out *why* the change in question is resisted, then take steps to eliminate or minimize the resistance.

Dialogue One

Employees in Shipping resist a proposed new system because they don't understand it.

Talking It Out

Manager - Jeff, I hear through the grapevine that there's a lot of opposition to the new billing system in the Shipping Department.

Supervisor - I know. It's hard to figure. Actually, the new setup should benefit everyone.

M. How?

S. Well, for one thing, it will help the stock pullers because the invoices will come through in item-number order according to the way the products are stacked in the bins.

M. What else?

S. They'll come through faster. That means fewer delays in filling orders. Less complaints from customers. It'll help free-up the phone lines.

M. The new system should also cut down the number of short shipments and back orders. Isn't that so?

S. Definitely. That's one of its biggest advantages.

M. Can you think of anyone in your operation who might be hurt in any way as a result of the new system?

S. (frowning) Nothing that comes to mind.

M. Then what's everyone beefing about?

S. Beats me. Maybe because of increased automation. People are instinctively suspicious when a system is computerized.

M. Tell me something, Jeff. You and I are well aware of all the benefits we discussed. But do your people know about them? Do they understand how the new set-up will work as far as their jobs are concerned? Did you take the time to sit down, give them the facts, encourage their questions, and invite them to express their anxieties and reservations?

S. Well, maybe not as much as I should have. I've been so busy. . .

M. There it is again, that old too-busy bugaboo. Maybe that's the problem, Jeff. Let's face it. Change can be hard to accept, harder for some than others. But human nature is still human nature. People want what's best for them. If the benefits outweigh the disadvantages, it's human nature to favor a change. But you have to have the facts. My guess is that resistance will start to dissolve once you make the benefits clear to your people.

• • • **TALKING POINTS** Change in the workplace wouldn't make sense if the pros didn't outweigh the cons. Ideally, when a new system or procedure is installed every person in the department should benefit from it. In the real world, that isn't always the case. In some situations employees are laid off or transferred. Reassigned tasks may not necessarily be to the liking of one worker or another. Or an employee may perceive that her status has been reduced. But the best way to eliminate, or at least reduce resistance is to heighten understanding. Level with people. Explain *why* the change is needed, how it will benefit the company and department and in so doing enhance job security as well. If their work will be altered, explain how. Present change in its best possible light, stressing the pros while justifying the cons if you can.

DIALOGUE TWO

Arthur, 63, resists change because he doesn't want to "rock the boat" before retirement.

Talking It Out

Supervisor - What's the problem, Arthur? You've been acting disgruntled ever since the tolerances were changed and the new gauges introduced.

Employee - I'm not disgruntled.

S. Maybe that's too strong a word. Let's put it this way: You're not exactly thrilled about the new system.

E. Well, maybe. I figure there's nothing wrong with the old system.

S. Except that too many rejects were passing through.

E. We've been running it that way for years. No one complained about my work.

S. That's because you always did a good job. But we have to take advantage of new technology. We have to keep up with our competitors. Most of them use the new gauges. If we don't we could lose a productivity edge that will hurt us in the marketplace. The new gauges are more efficient; studies show they cut rejects.

E. I still don't like them.

S. Why not?

E. They're hard to read; the numbers are too small. With the old gauges my reject rate was one of the lowest in the department. I'm afraid the new gauges will boost my rate.

S. (nodding) You have cataracts, don't you?

E. (reluctantly) Well, yeah.

S. Why don't you take care of them? It's no big deal. And you're covered by Medicare.

E. I know. I've been putting it off.

S. Tell me the truth. Is that the only reason you don't like the new system, because the gauges are hard to read?

E. Yeah, I guess so. I plan to retire next year. I'm afraid that if I pass too many rejects it could jeopardize my pension.

S. There's no way that could happen. I can assure you of that. Tell you what. You're a good man. I'd prefer to keep you at your present job as an inspector. I'd like to see you go for that cataract operation. But if you choose not to, I'll find another job for you until you retire.

E. I guess I'll arrange for that operation. I'll have to do it sooner or later in any case.

• • • **TALKING POINTS** It's natural for senior employees with retirement on their minds to feel comfortable with the status quo. It's natural too for a significant change, proposed or introduced, to disrupt that feeling of security. As a supervisor your main goals are clear: 1) To keep the senior's comfort zone intact; 2) To help the senior adjust as effectively as possible to the changed system or procedure; 3) To maintain the senior's productivity at the highest level.

DIALOGUE THREE

Ellen clings tenaciously to the status quo because of feelings of insecurity.

Talking It Out

Supervisor - Ellen, I'd like to get your thoughts about the new claims-processing system. Do you have any suggestions?

Employee - (ill at ease) No, not really.

S. You're not happy with it, are you? It won't hurt you in any way if you tell me just how you feel. What bothers you about the new system?

E. I don't know. It seems terribly complicated. The old system was simple and easy to understand.

S. I can appreciate the way you feel. I've often felt the same way myself. It's a natural feeling when something new is introduced. How long have you been working here, Ellen?

E. About six years.

S. That's what I figured. I want you to play a memory game with me. The old system—the one you feel is simple and easy—has been in operation three years or so. Do you recall when it was first introduced?

E. (thoughtful) Oh sure, it was in the summer, before the fall season.

S. Right. I remember it vividly too because I was responsible for making the transition between the old system and the new one. But from what I can recall, implementing that system seemed complicated and confusing at the time. Don't you agree?

E. (smiles, more relaxed) Yes, now that you mention it. It was a hard period to get through.

S. How well I know. But let's face it, that's always the case when something new is initiated. It's not easy for people to shift gears from what they're familiar with to something that's different and strange. But as experience proves, a new system becomes easier and easier with each passing day as familiarity increases. Not only that, it becomes more pleasant too as you start cashing in on the advantages that were the reason for the change in the first place. If you can reenact in your mind how that happened three years ago, I think it might help you today. Remember the work backlogs that were reduced along with the pressures they produced?

E. Yes, now that I think of it.

S. Let me ask you something else. I touched on this earlier, but I want to make sure you got it straight. How do you think the new system will affect your job?

E. Well . . . I'm not sure.

S. That's what I thought. I've been checking it out. Actually, there are 46 steps in the job procedure manual. But only six of them affect

you, and out of those six steps there are only three changes, none of them really complicated. They may be unfamiliar for a while, but nothing that a smart woman like you won't be able to master.

E. *(smiles brightly) Oh, thank you.*

S. One final question, Ellen. Do you think the new system will jeopardize your status or security in any way? Tell me the truth.

E. *Well, I don't know. I have to admit I was a little worried. . .*

S. You can put those worries to rest. (smiles reassuringly) You're a valuable employee, Ellen, and that's the way you'll remain. More valuable in fact because you'll be increasing your knowledge. The only effect the new system will have on your job is to make it easier and more enjoyable once you become familiar with it—just as it did the last time. Constructive change doesn't jeopardize anything. It improves working conditions and makes the job more productive, which was the purpose behind the change in the first place.

• • • **TALKING POINTS**   People who feel insecure are by nature status-quo advocates. In most cases, the threats posed by change to their well-being are nonexistent or overstated, caused not by the innovation but by an inherent fear of change itself. As experience proves, there is nothing like hard information and reasoned thinking to set an insecure employee's apprehensions to rest. The good news is that an intelligent person confronted with a well-thought-out mix of reassurance and evidence can be readily converted from a worrier to a believer.

DIALOGUE FOUR

Charlie has nothing against the proposed new stock control system; it's the system's proponent that bugs him.

Talking It Out

Supervisor - Hey Charlie, one big happy family, right?

Employee - What do you mean by that?

S. Teamwork. Cooperation. All for one, one for all. You believe in that concept, don't you? Everyone in the department working together for the good of the company and each other?

E. *(frowning) Sure.*

S. That's what I thought. Let me ask you another question. When the receiving platform was backed up with crates and cartons all the time, that made it tough on everybody, didn't it?

E. *Yeah, it was a mess.*

S. And when a particular item was needed for a rush order and couldn't be found, that got everyone nervous and upset. Am I right?

E. *(growing uneasy) Sure.*

S. And wouldn't you agree that it's a good thing that customer complaints have dropped almost 30% since the congestion was eliminated, not to mention the fact that the Receiving Department is a lot less hectic and pressured?

E. *(unenthusiastically) Yeah, sure.*

S. Then maybe you can explain to me in rational terms why you've been bad-mouthing the new double-tier stocking system that makes life in the department so much easier for everyone?

E. *(reluctantly) I got nothing against the new system.*

S. That's good to hear, Charlie. In that case I'd be curious to hear why you're knocking a system you have nothing against.

E. *I, uh. . .*

S. I, uh, bull. Let's stop playing games. The word gets around. I believe you when you say you have nothing against the system. We both know that what bugs you isn't the system. It's George Keller who dreamed up the system, the guy who designed and helped set it up. Tell me I'm wrong, Charlie.

E. *(lowers his eyes)*

S. (tone softens) Look, I don't fault you for not getting along with George. It happens. Personalities clash. Not everyone hits it off with everyone else. Ideally, I'd like to see you and George shake hands and become friends. But if you can't see your way clear to do that, there's one thing I want to get straight. Your relationship

off the job is none of my business. If you want to be adversaries that's up to you. But your relationship *on* the job is very much my business, especially as it affects the work and influences productivity. The double-tier system is good for the company, the department, and every employee that works here. That's been proved by experience. The fact that it happens to be George's brainstorm doesn't make it any less beneficial. In opposing it you hurt yourself more than George, and if your career is important to you I'd advise you to hop on board and join the rest of the crew with full cooperation and support. Have I made myself clear?

E. Yeah, sure.

• • • **TALKING POINTS** In persuading employees to go along with change, or at least to be less resistant, most often psychological factors play a major role. But where resistance is clearly targeted, not at the change itself but at its proponent, firmer and harsher measures may be called for. This is often best accomplished by getting two points across: 1) The beneficial aspects of the innovation should be spelled out and made clear; 2) The individual's duty and responsibility to his department, company, and fellow employees should be made equally clear, along with the supervisor's refusal to tolerate a disruptive attitude of noncooperation.

DIALOGUE FIVE

Billing Department Supervisor Arlene is afraid the new order-processing system will result in a staff reduction and reduced status for her.

Talking It Out

Manager - Did you set up that meeting with your people to familiarize them with the new system and encourage their ideas and comments?

Supervisor - No, I didn't get around to it yet.

M. This is the second time I asked you to do it.

S. I know. I've been too busy to breathe. I'll get to it as soon as I can.

M. That's not good enough, Arlene. I've explained the meeting's importance. A system is no better than the people who operate it. If we expect our employees to give their wholehearted cooperation and support, we owe it to them to make sure they understand the changes being made. We also owe it to them to respond to their comments and suggestions, as well as any gripes or apprehensions they might have. Does that make sense to you?

S. I suppose so.

M. Then please tell me why you've been dragging your feet on this from the beginning?

S. (hesitating) To be honest, I guess it's because I'm not really sold on the new system myself.

M. In spite of the Systems Department's cost-benefits analysis that proves so conclusively how much we stand to gain from the changes? We've been over this before. You know the problems and bottlenecks we've been having—the short shipments and back orders. Let's face it, the old system has outgrown its usefulness.

S. (morose) Maybe so, but the new system won't help morale any.

M. What makes you say that?

S. Well, according to the cost-benefits report, 10 to 15% of the work force will be laid off.

M. Not necessarily laid off. Most will be transferred to other operations. We both know that we have to cut costs. The department is overstaffed. We have to remain productive to remain competitive. Can you think of a better way to do that?

S. (reluctantly) I guess not.

M. Is the anticipated staff reduction your only objection to the new system?

S. That and its effect on morale.

M. Not to mention the effect you think it might have on your own status. You're afraid that if the department is smaller it will reduce your importance as well. Am I right?

S. I suppose the thought did occur to me.

M. I thought so. You couldn't be more mistaken. The truth is you stand to gain from the new system as much as anyone I could name. I can speak for top management when I say that career growth isn't tied to an operation's size; it's measured by results and productivity. That your department's payroll is larger than that of competitors' of comparable sales volume works against rather than for you. Another plus from your point of view is that the new system will provide an opportunity for you to become familiar with the newest technology in the field which will upgrade both your knowledge and value to the company.

S. I never looked at it that way.

M. It's the only way *to* look at it. Take my advice, Arlene. Hop aboard and get with it. It's the biggest favor you could do for yourself. Get that meeting set up.

S. I will.

• • • **TALKING POINTS**   It is a commonly held misconception that supervisory status, importance, and career growth depend more than anything on an operation's size. This factor shrinks in importance beside a supervisor's contribution to productivity and profits. Another critical factor affecting status is knowledge: business know-how, technological knowledge, savvy gained through experience, human relations understanding, planning and control expertise. Constructive change may cut payroll in some cases. But it also improves productivity and a supervisor's opportunity to upgrade knowledge and experience. That more than offsets any loss that may occur. This is an important message to instill in your employees.

DIALOGUE SIX

Ben resists change because he's afraid the new system will be too hard for him to master.

Talking It Out

Supervisor - Ben, let's talk about this new sprinkler equipment that's being installed. Your job will be to check the units, compare gauge pressures against standards in various locations, and monitor and

repair the equipment when necessary. Ed tells me you put in a request to assign those duties to someone else. Why?

Employee - That stuff is very sophisticated. I never did anything like it. The master system is computer-controlled, and it's outside my range of experience. I think it will be too technical for me to handle.

S. Okay, let me ask you a question. You're a Service Equipment Mechanic Grade A, right?

E. Yes.

S. How long have you held this classification?

E. Two years. Before that I was Grade B for a year-and-a-half.

S. And prior to that a General Mechanic for how long?

E. Two years.

S. That's pretty good progress. The record shows you received four promotions in less than six years. How do you think that came about?

E. What do you mean?

S. Do you think you got that recognition because you're a nice guy? Or because you're good looking?

E. (grins) Are you kidding? I worked hard for it. I think I did a good job.

S. I can't argue with that. Then tell me this: When you were promoted to Service Equipment Mechanic Grade B were you able to read prints and diagrams?

E. A little, but not very well.

S. Now you're an expert at it. How did that happen?

E. I learned. I took a couple of courses, plus on-the-job experience.

S. When you were promoted to Grade A what did you know about maintaining and repairing process refrigeration systems?

E. Absolutely nothing.

S. Bingo! You went to school. Then you learned on the job. If you were asked to recondition a refrigeration system tomorrow, would you be shaken up by the system?

E. Of course not. It's part of my job.

S. That's exactly my point, Ben. It's part of your job because you *made* it part of your job. You did what was necessary to understand and master the job.

E. (nods)

S. Okay, then what gives you the notion that mastering the new sprinkler system will be any different from mastering the blueprints, refrigeration units, hot-water systems or anything else you handle on a day-to-day basis?

E. I don't know. I just thought. . .

S. Ben, take my word for it. Your record shows you've done well on every test you ever took. Your IQ shows you're intelligent. Your promotions and raises were all achieved because you earned them, step by step, by mastering every kind of equipment and skill that was required of you. Your qualifications were evaluated carefully before the company decided to assign the sprinkler equipment to you. I'm confident you can handle it. In the unlikely event you have a problem with it it won't be the end of the world. I'll assign it to someone else. Ben, you tackled everything that came your way since you came here. Don't stop now. For a guy like you, that sprinkler system should be a piece of cake. Take a crack at it.

• • • **TALKING POINTS** Lack of self-confidence is a major cause of resistance to change. A smart supervisor carefully evaluates an employee's qualifications before assigning a new project or task. Once convinced that the person can handle the job, the challenge is to imbue the delegatee with the confidence needed for success. This can be accomplished through the use of evidence as illustrated, and also by bolstering shaky self-confidence with an expression of *your* confidence that he or she has what it takes.

chapter five

· · · · · · · · · · · · · · · · · ·

DEALING WITH
TIME ABUSE

Time utilization studies indicate it is the rule rather than the exception in this nation's plants and offices to find most employees working 20% to 40% below normal standards for the job. A disturbing number perform at 50% below capacity, according to one consultant who defines capacity as "effectiveness that is comfortably achievable without undue effort or time." Work control experts rank the identification and reduction of time abuse high on the list of supervisory responsibilities. Once identified, the quicker corrective action is taken, the faster the damaging effect on productivity will be eliminated.

DIALOGUE ONE

Jim Helfer's productivity suffers an estimated 10% loss attributable to his habit of stretching lunch and rest periods.

Talking It Out

Supervisor - (blank sheet of yellow-lined paper on his desk) Sit down. I want your help working up some calculations that trouble me.

Employee - (warily) Okay.

S. Jim, what's your hourly rate?

E. Eight dollars.

S. (enters figure on pad) Correct me if I'm wrong. Your lunch hour is 12:00 to 1:00.

E. That's right.

S. (enters time on pad) That's five days a week, and you get two daily rest periods of 15 minutes each. Are you with me so far?

E. (nods)

S. Okay, I think you know what I'm getting at. We talked about this before. The figure I'm trying to arrive at is the amount of off time you are paid for on the average.

E. Off time?

S. I'm talking about wages you are paid when you're *off* the job, time when you're supposed to be working. An appropriate alternate term might be stretch time. Like when you stretch your one-hour lunch period to an hour-and-a-half, or add 10 or 15 minutes to your break periods.

E. I don't do that; you can check the times I punch in and punch out.

S. That's the first thing I checked. I also checked the *actual* time you stop working, like ten minutes *before* the lunch buzzer sounds, and the times you *actually* return to your work station, like twenty *after* one—despite punching in and out on time.

E. (employee has no answer to this)

S. Jim, to tell you the truth, I hate having to check up on people like this, but you give me no choice. It's my responsibility as a supervisor. Direct labor costs can make or break an operation. It's my job to make sure the company gets a fair day's work for its wages. That's why I decided to monitor your comings and goings over the past five days. Here are the figures I came up with.

S. (shows Jim a pad with the figures) Now, let's see what we have here. My surveillance indicates that you've been stretching your lunch periods a total of about 2 1/2 hours and your break periods a total of 1 1/2 hours over a 5-day work week. That's a grand total of 4 hours. At $8 an hour that amounts to $32 per week. And this applies only to off time, or stretch time, if you prefer. I didn't

include lost time on the job itself, in the john, at the water cooler, or on nonproductive chitchat. Would you like me to bill you for the stretch time? Or should I deduct it from your pay?

E. *(discomfort level rising)*

S. **(softer tone) Okay, I'll get off your back. Jim, I regard you as a basically honest person and I know you don't think of that $32 worth of stretch time as stealing. But the practical result is no different than if you stuck your hand in the till. Look at the problem from management's point of view. If we multiplied Jim Helfer by 13 or 14 hundred employees, how long do you think we could stay in business having to pay all those people 10% or more of their wages for unworked time? We would have to raise prices an equivalent 10% to make up for it. Do you think our customers would stand for that? I'll give it to you straight, Jim. You can have a good future here if you choose to. Or you can jeopardize your career and everyone else's as well. It's up to you. If you give the company a fair shake for your wages, you'll get a fair shake in return. I don't think I have to spell out the alternative.**

• • • **TALKING POINTS** Let's not pull any punches so far as extended lunch and break periods are involved. We concede it's unpleasant to check up on employees and call them to account for time abuse. As any supervisor would agree, clamping down on subordinates is no fun. Often the temptation is to just let things slide. That's the easy way out. It's also the costly way out, and the boomerang effect is inevitable. It's a matter of facing up to the problem courageously, or having it backfire. Another fact to keep in mind is that when you turn a blind eye to time stretchers, you inevitably encourage more of the same from their compatriots.

DIALOGUE TWO

Where's Alice? She never seems to be where she's supposed to be.

Talking It Out

Supervisor - Alice, do you think the standards in this office are fair?

Employee - Sure, I guess so. Why?

S. Because if they're not I'd like to know about it. If you think you are being driven too hard or put under too much pressure, I'd like to get the specifics and look into the matter.

E. I have no complaints.

S. (smiles) Unfortunately, I can't say the same. (Pulls out the Monthly Productivity Comparison Reports for the past 12 months.)

E. (unhappy glance at the sheets; she begins to get the message)

S. If you want, I can review your performance in detail over the past few months, but I don't think that should be necessary. It's pretty obvious your work has been falling below accepted standards. The record speaks for itself.

E. (concedes the point)

S. Your claims-processing productivity has been going downhill steadily. A few months ago it was better than average. Now it hovers just above barely acceptable. I'd like an explanation.

E. I, I'm not sure.

S. I'm disappointed to have to inform you that I won't be able to put you in for a merit increase this coming quarter. I wonder if you've given any thought to the reason why. I began to notice that your production was declining two or three months ago. I held off making an issue of it because you've always been an outstanding employee, and I hoped the lapse was only temporary. Unfortunately, it's been going down even further. I might add that coincidentally, so has Marge's since she was transferred to your section three months ago. I don't think we have to guess at the reason why.

E. (glum silence)

S. Marge is your best friend, isn't she? At least in this company?

E. (brightens) Yes, she's a great person.

S. I know she is. So are you. And I can appreciate that when two great people are good friends, the temptation is strong to communicate, to discuss your mutual interests and plans. In fact, such conversations are probably more interesting than those boring claims you have to process.

E. (nodding) I know what you're going to say. It's the claims that pay the bills, and I'm being paid to process them, not gab with Marge.

S. (smiling) **I couldn't have said it better myself. You've been doing too much of that lately, not to mention gabbing on the telephone and at the water cooler. I'm sorry about this quarter, Alice. I hope that next time around I'll be able to recommend you for that merit increase. Thanks for your understanding. When you return to your desk, please send Marge in to see me.**

• • • **TALKING POINTS**   The two major ways to nip time drainage in the bud due to chitchat and wanderlust are: 1) Supervisory observation; 2) Close adherence to fair performance standards. More often than not, where employees fail to meet established standards the cause tracks down to supervisory permissiveness with regard to unauthorized visitations in person or by phone. A reasonable and equitable balance must be drawn. On the one hand, we don't advocate a rigidly severe atmosphere in the workplace. Friendly exchanges should be encouraged. Firmly *dis*couraged should be a work environment that goes overboard in the other direction. Finally, another good way to discourage productivity-busting wanderlust is the use of job variety. Periodic change tends to reduce the boredom which impels employees to leave their work stations in search of relief or more interesting pursuits.

DIALOGUE THREE

Herman, a conscientious statistical department employee, abuses time by conserving it. The "shortcuts" he takes can be counterproductive in terms of both cost and time.

Talking It Out

Supervisor - Herman, I just got a call from Ann Pease in Accounting. She says this report can't be right. She advises you to look it over before she passes it along to Mr. Fielding.

Employee - What does she say is wrong with it?

S. **She doesn't know. But she says there's no way the commissions for last quarter could be higher than the commissions for the current quarter. Check it out and let me know what you find.**

E. (two hours later) Ann is right. I made an error in the report.

S. It's hard for me to understand how that's possible. An internal check is built into the procedure at different steps along the way. Each subtotal is supposed to check out to the Master Control Sheet before you can proceed with the report. Let's review that procedure.

E. (produces procedure)

S. Let's follow this step by step down the line to the first subtotal. (scanning report) This one checks out okay. Let's continue. Ah, here's the culprit. This subtotal doesn't balance out against the control figure. How could you have gone on and completed the report with a control figure out of balance?

E. (nervously moistens his lips)

S. You didn't check it, did you?

E. (lowers his eyes) The report was late. I figured it would save some time if I skipped a couple of steps. The subtotals almost always check out against the master controls.

S. Almost always isn't good enough. That's why the control checks were built into the procedure. You were playing Russian Roulette. You ought to send Ann Pease a bouquet of flowers or something. I hate to think what would have happened if Mr. Fielding got that report. He relies on those figures to prepare the quarterly quotas.

E. I'm sorry.

S. You'll have to rerun the report. What are we talking about: a day's extra work, not to mention the delay? Mr. Fielding will be madder than a dog with its bone taken away. But you lucked out this time. I hope it teaches you a lesson: No more shortcuts. Unauthorized shortcuts add up to more time in the end.

E. Thanks. It won't happen again.

• • • **TALKING POINTS** Written procedures are drawn up for a purpose: They are employee guidelines to the tested-and-tried way to complete a project or task. This doesn't imply that a procedure, written or not, is inviolable. But the safest and most sensible way to run an operation is to insist that established procedures be followed to the letter with no shortcuts or improvisation acceptable. On the one hand, subordinates should be encouraged to challenge the procedures they are given and suggest improvements where they seem feasible. If that means eliminating or adding steps, fine. But proposed changes should be investigated and *officially* incorporated in the procedure where warranted. It should be made clear to employees that *unofficially* omitting steps to save time or for any other reason is strictly prohibited.

DIALOGUE FOUR

Joe operates under the assumption that he is "beating the company" when he goofs off on the job.

Talking It Out

Supervisor - Joe, how long have you been in the maintenance department?

Employee - Two years.

S. Do you like your job?

E. It's okay.

S. I'm overwhelmed by your enthusiasm, Joe. How would you feel if you were fired?

E. I have a family to support; I need this job.

S. You have a strange way of showing it. When was the last time you received a merit increase?

E. I never got one.

S. Do you have any idea why?

E. (reluctantly) To tell the truth, I always thought you had a grudge against me.

S. You may be right, Joe. But if I have a grudge, it's not against you personally, but against the way you do your job. I've been checking your personnel record. A couple of months ago you were caught asleep in the storage room when you were supposed to be working. Last week you sneaked out to the local pub for a couple of beers. Today you were missing from your work station for

almost an hour. Do you think that's the way to become popular with your boss and get ahead on the job?

E. I'll try to do better.

S. That's what you said last time. I'm giving you a 3-day suspension. This is your last chance, Joe. One more infraction and you get your walking papers. Like I said, it's nothing personal. You can wipe the slate clean if you put your mind to the task, even get yourself the overdue merit increase. Or you can continue 'beating the company' and beat yourself out of a job in the process. It's up to you.

• • • **TALKING POINTS**   Time theft is the most prevalent kind of corporate larceny. No matter how diligently you screen and interview job applicants, a percentage of sour apples is bound to filter through. "Losers" like Joe can be found in every office, warehouse, and plant. For whatever reason—laziness, lack of ambition, perceived or actual mistreatment—they feel that by goofing off they outsmart the boss or company. Permitting them to get away with it inevitably encourages more of the same from other workers. The ideal supervisory response is to pinpoint the cause of the poor attitude and take steps to reform the time thief. Failing this, the only viable solution is to lay down the law with a 3-strikes-and-you're-out ultimatum.

DIALOGUE FIVE

Billing department's Mary suffers from feelings of insecurity. As a result, she makes sure the invoices she prepares are correct by triple-checking their accuracy.

Talking It Out

Supervisor - Mary, take a load off your feet. This is your first quarterly performance review session. Right?

Employee - (stiffly) Yes sir.

S. (smiling) There's nothing to be nervous about. The reason for these meetings isn't to punish or crucify anyone. It's to talk about the work, air problems and grievances, and hopefully make the

job more pleasant and productive for everyone. You've been here how long?

E. *About four months.*

S. **Do you like it here?**

E. *Very much. It's a good company, and I like the people I work with.*

S. **That's great. I'm glad to hear it. We like you too. How do you feel about the job you're doing? Are you satisfied with it?**

E. *I don't know. That's for you to say, isn't it?*

S. **Well, not entirely. A major goal of these review sessions is to get feedback from you. But since you raised the point, I'll tell you both sides of the coin from supervision's viewpoint. The plus side is that you're one of the most efficient people in the department. I can't recall a single invoicing error since the day you started here. The minus side is that your productivity, the amount of work you turn out, is too low. Do you have any idea why?**

E. *(anxiously) No sir. I'm not sure.*

S. **Well, I have a hunch and I'd like to get your reaction. I have a feeling that those two sides of the coin are tied together. I've been observing you work and I can see you're conscientious, which I appreciate. You stay at your machine, and you seem to work as fast as the other billers. So I see no reason why you shouldn't be producing as much or more, unless—and that's where my hunch comes into play. Mary, how many times do you check your work before clearing it through?**

E. *Twice, then one more time for good measure to make one-hundred percent sure that it's right.*

S. **(nods thoughtfully) One-hundred percent. That's an interesting figure. It's practically a synonym for perfection. Tell me something: How often on that third check do you find an error?**

E. *Very rarely. But it's happened.*

S. **That may be our answer, Mary. There's such a thing as excessive care. Perfection's a beautiful word, but you have to weigh what it costs to achieve it against the cost of being a reasonable degree short of it. My guess is that your productivity would shoot up if you did just two careful checks and eliminated the third check.**

That would make you one of the department's most efficient *and* productive employees. And if a rare error slipped through on occasion it wouldn't be the end of the world. Give it a try, okay?

E. Sure. Thanks for the advice.

• • • **TALKING POINTS** Insecure people worry about their work and tend to be excessively careful in performing it. They are so preoccupied with avoiding mistakes and the criticism it might engender they lose sight of the quantitative aspect of productivity. Your task as a supervisor is to measure the high cost of near-perfect accuracy against its value. If Mary were a bit less careful so that a rare error slipped through, what would be the cost of the mistake? Supervisory guidance is sometimes needed to determine when shooting for perfection constitutes conscientious efficiency and when it simply becomes time abuse.

DIALOGUE SIX

Production Department Carpenter Frank keeps his nose pretty much to the proverbial grindstone, but like Mary, takes too long to complete his assignments.

Talking It Out

Supervisor - Frank, I've been going over the job sheets for the past six months since you've been in the department and the bad news is that your productivity is below standard.

Employee - (worried) I know. But I don't goof off. I try to do a conscientious job.

S. I know you do.

E. I haven't had any complaints about the quality of my work.

S. The problem isn't quality, it's quantity. It takes you too long to complete your assignments. Since you're a relatively new employee, I was hoping that once you got your wings flapping you'd become more productive. But that hasn't seemed to have happened. Do you have any idea why?

E. I work as fast as I can.

S. That's what puzzles me. I've been watching you and I'm impressed by the effort you put into the job. But in checking over these job sheets what I don't understand is this: On some jobs you performed right up to standard. Like #1426, #1430, and #1528. On others, like these two over here, you're well below standard. In short, you aren't consistent.

E. (studies sheets) Maybe it's because those jobs—#1426, #1430, and #1528—are the ones I'm familiar with. I can almost build those jigs from memory. On the others I had to follow complicated line drawings. It takes me longer to figure out the drawings than to do the actual work.

S. (frowning) Weren't you enrolled in the company's Blueprint and Drawing course?

E. No. I was supposed to be, but when the work started piling up I couldn't be spared, so I was never signed up for the course.

S. Bingo! I'm afraid that's the answer. I owe you an apology, Frank. It must have slipped my mind that you never took that course. I'll see to it that you're signed up for the next available date. Something tells me your productivity will shoot up once you get that training under your belt.

• • • **TALKING POINTS**   The employee who takes 3 hours to complete a 2-hour assignment flushes an hour of precious time down the drain. Common reasons for time abuse of this kind are: 1) Failure to perform the assignment continuously; 2) Lack of required experience; 3) Lack of training needed to qualify the employee; 4) Lack of natural technical or intellectual ability. In some cases no amount of training or experience will qualify the individual, however conscientious. The prescription for low productivity due to unacceptable volume of work output is clear: 1) determine the cause; 2) correct the problem posthaste, and transfer the abuser to where he or she will be more productive. Or 3) If all else fails, fire the time abuser.

chapter six

● ● ● ● ● ● ● ● ● ● ● ● ● ● ● ●

DELEGATING MORE EFFECTIVELY

Do you want to know the major key to supervisory success, and from there on-and-upward to executive success? Conversely, would you be interested to know the chief cause behind most supervisory failure? The answer in both cases is the same. *Delegation!* Innumerable surveys by educational institutions, business publications, and management consultants agree: Invariably "ability to delegate effectively" ranks among the top success attributes cited in polls. Similarly, "failure to delegate effectively" rates high as a career wheel-spinning cause at supervisory and management levels. Whether you view delegation as an art, a science, or a combination of both, the biggest career favor you could do for yourself is to pinpoint your level of delegating effectiveness, and in face-to-face dialogues, deal with whatever problems and roadblocks may exist.

DIALOGUE ONE

Bill's productivity as a technologist in the Plant Engineering department would be higher if he were better matched to the job.

Talking It Out

Supervisor - Ed, I can't understand it. You're one of the smartest, best-trained, and most experienced professionals in the department. I had you pegged as a natural for the lab refurbishing project. But it looks like I figured it wrong.

Employee - I'm doing the best I can.

S. The productivity figures don't indicate that. Your personnel record shows you could do a lot better if you set your mind to it. What's the problem?

E. (ill at ease) No problem. I'll try to boost my productivity.

S. That's what you said last time. Is the work too difficult? Is the new stuff hard to understand? Are the computer printouts too complicated? I want to know. Ed, I didn't get you here to rake you over the coals. I'm trying to make life easier for both of us. Tell me, what's bugging you?

E. (reluctantly) Nothing's bugging me exactly. But the truth is I feel like a school kid again, all this new training and the books I'm supposed to crack.

S. So that's it. I assigned you the project because you're one of the best guys in the department. I thought you would welcome the challenge.

E. I guess I would have—10 years ago.

S. I see. How old are you, Bill?

E. Sixty-one.

S. That's not so old. You still have four good years on the job; you can still earn merit increases and bonuses.

E. (shrugs) Not really. To be honest, I don't have the zest for it anymore. I'm planning to opt for early retirement at sixty-two.

S. You never told me that, Ed.

E. I know. I was going to get around to it one of these days.

S. Hmmm, that puts a whole different light on things. I wish I knew about that before assigning the lab project. In any case, I'm glad we straightened it out. I'll get someone else for the project and assign you to something else.

E. Thanks, I'd appreciate it. I've always done a conscientious job. But I don't I have the drive any longer to start all over again if you know what I mean.

S. I know just what you mean. Thanks for leveling with me.

• • • **TALKING POINTS** At times you may have no choice but to delegate a job to someone whether it's wanted or not. But the employee who welcomes added responsibility as a career steppingstone or for the increased status it brings inevitably performs best. People who are mismatched to the work are most likely to do a second-rate job. Whether the assigned employee is mismatched due to inadequate training, lack of experience or technical ability, poor attitude, or like Ed, lack of ambition due to pending retirement, it's your task as a supervisor to pinpoint the reason and make the proper adjustment.

DIALOGUE TWO

This supervisor doesn't delegate work because she's afraid to relinquish authority.

Talking It Out

Manager - You asked for this meeting, Marilyn. What can I do for you?

Supervisor - Can I speak frankly, Mr. Baer?

M. The only way to approach a problem.

S. Well, I think it's unfair that I was bypassed for that promotion to Assistant Manager. I have the training, experience, and length of service. And I think I'm at least as well-qualified as Gloria Davidson who got the appointment.

M. You probably are.

S. (surprised) Then why. . .

M. The 'why' is simple, Marilyn. I've spoken to you about this in the past. For argument's sake suppose I had selected you for the job instead of Gloria. Who would take over your operation?

S. *(hesitating) Why Shirley Marcus. She would be perfectly capable of taking over the section.*

M. **I suspect you are right. But assuming she is smart and capable enough to run the Weekly Price Estimate, or the Daily Capitalization Breakdown and those other reports you handle yourself, is she *ready* to take them over? Tomorrow? Next week?**

S. *I, well, sure . . . I'd have to turn them over and make sure. . .*

M. **Which would take weeks or months. I couldn't afford to wait for that to happen. The opportunity would be gone by that time. Tell me something. If Shirley can handle these assignments, why do you do them yourself? How come you never bothered to delegate them to her, and to others as well?**

S. *I, uh. . .*

M. **I don't think you have a good answer for that. I'll be perfectly frank. In considering that promotion I had two people in mind: you and Gloria. You both head up your sections and do a good job. From the standpoint of length of service and experience you probably have a slight edge. But from the standpoint of accessibility and availability Gloria has you beat by a mile. When she steps into the new job I have every confidence her section will continue to operate as smoothly and efficiently as ever. Unfortunately, I can't say the same about your operation. You never bothered to groom a successor by means of delegation the way Shirley did.**

S. *But. . .*

M. **Marilyn, you still didn't answer my question: You're an intelligent woman. It makes so much good sense to delegate. Why didn't you do it?**

S. *I, uh. . .*

M. **I suspect you'd rather not answer that question. If you did a bit of soul-searching you might not like the answer you come up with. I've seen it happen before. Someone once referred to it as the "Clinging-Vine Syndrome." I suspect you hang on to those projects because you're afraid that if you relinquish them, it might make Shirley Marcus look too good to management and somehow threaten your job. It's an interesting question. You don't have to**

give me your answer; it's more important that you level with yourself.

S. (lowers her eyes)

M. You see, Marilyn, the way this company—and most good companies work—the more you strengthen subordinates by qualifying them to take over increased responsibility, the stronger *you* become as well. If you keep that reality of business life in mind, next time an opportunity comes along you just may step into it.

• • • **TALKING POINTS**   Line and staff employees aren't the only ones who feel insecure. This kind of self-defeating anxiety sometimes applies to supervisors, managers, and executives as well. In rare, *extremely* rare operations the feeling is justified. Cases could be cited where a supervisor was replaced by a lower-paid subordinate to save the wage differential. It's a blockheaded way to run a business, and if that shoe fits your company, you'd be smart to seek greener pastures. In the overwhelming majority of cases, effective delegation boosts not only subordinates' careers but your own fortunes as well. This fact of business life should be made clear to anyone who's in charge of three or more people.

DIALOGUE THREE

Young lab employee Phil balks at increased responsibility because he is afraid he's not qualified for the assignment.

Talking It Out

Supervisor - (shaking hands) Congratulations, Phil. Opportunity strikes. I'm putting you in charge of the Compounding Analysis.

Employee - (worried response) I don't know, Ben, I never did anything like that before.

S. (grinning) Neither did Columbus or the Wright Brothers. There's always a first time. Without a first time no progress would be made in the world.

E. Yeah, but there's a lot riding on that Compounding Analysis. A number of people in the lab are better qualified than I am.

S. Phil, if I didn't think you were qualified, would I have selected you for such an important responsibility? Would I cut my own throat? It's precisely because I have confidence in your ability that I picked you.

E. Yeah, but. . .

S. Let me ask you a question: Didn't you earn your BS degree at Columbia?

E. Well, yes.

S. Did you get top performance ratings the past three quarters running and a merit increase last time around?

E. I. . .

S. And sign up for our advanced training course and come through with flying colors?

E. Yes, but. . .

S. Buts don't count. I'll grant you, taking over the Compounding Analysis will be a challenge. But you've proven throughout your career that you're up to it. On top of that you'll get all the help and guidance you need as long as you need it. Plus, performance controls will be in force to double check the results. As you said, there's a lot riding on this job. I'm not taking any chances on its being fouled up. So you have nothing to worry about.

E. In that case. . .

S. Phil, look at it as a career steppingstone. The more opportunity you accept, the greater your chance for advancement.

E. (nodding) Yeah, that makes sense.

S. It sure does. Phil, between the two of us, since the people who count in this company have confidence in you, all you need now is a little confidence in yourself.

• • • **TALKING POINTS** People like Phil who resist delegated responsibility because they are afraid they can't handle it need a transfusion of self-confidence to bolster their egos. Overcoming such anxiety is usually a simple 3-step procedure: 1) Infuse the delegatee with a healthy shot of *your* personal confidence; 2) Present a rational view of the assignment or project and demonstrate that fear of failure is unwarranted; 3) Hammer home the message that increased responsibility and authority constitute the shortest route to career success.

Dialogue Four

Doris resists delegation because of the extra workload it will entail.

Talking It Out

Supervisor - Have a seat. I want to go over that Army Export report with you.

Employee - Gee, Mr. Carter, I wish you'd give it to someone else. I'm up to my neck already.

S. The last thing I want to do, Doris, is give you an unreasonable workload. That's why I checked your schedule before assigning the project. Let's break down your workday section by section.

(This takes 20 minutes. Spelling out each major time commitment, Doris's boss demonstrates how she has more than enough time to complete the delegated task.)

S. Do you agree with these figures?

E. Yeah, I guess so.

S. Doris, between the two of us, the main reason I selected you for the Army Export Report is because you're one of the few people in the department with the experience and brains to master it.

E. (no comment, but obviously pleased by the flattery)

S. I won't mention names, but I was approached by two other employees who want the assignment because of the status and importance attached. I turned them down because I felt they couldn't handle it as well as you.

E. It's not really that hard.

S. **That's exactly why I want you for the job. That attitude. You're the best one for the job, and we both know it. There's another thing you might keep in mind too. I'm not in a position to make any commitments at the moment, but this project could serve as a steppingstone to better things in the future. It will certainly look good in your personnel folder.**

E. Okay! I'll do my best, Mr. Carter.

• • • **TALKING POINTS**   With delegated tasks in mind, there are two kinds of qualified people: 1) Ambitious employees who welcome the career-boosting opportunity to take on new challenges and opportunities; 2) Status-quo people who, however bright, are satisfied with the way things are and resist anything that will add to their workload. It's the status quoticians like Doris who often need some well-chosen persuasion, a taste of tempting incentive, and an ego shot-in-the-arm to get them to come around willingly.

DIALOGUE FIVE

Data Processing Department Supervisor Al Keeler is a dedicated do-it-yourselfer whose workday never seems to be over.

Talking It Out

Manager - Al, I left the plant at 8:00 P.M. last night. You looked like you were still going strong. What time did you get out of here?

Supervisor - (looking tired) 9:30 or so.

M. What about the night before?

S. Same time. The work's been piling up something fierce. I'm beginning to forget what my kids look like.

M. That's no way to run a shop—or a home. What's the problem?

S. Like I said, the work keeps piling up.

M. Are you shorthanded? Do you need more help?

S. I don't think so. It's just that things keep cropping up. I feel like a traffic cop at Times Square. Everyone seems to need my help all the time.

M. With what? Give me a for instance.

S. *I don't know. A million and one things. Jeff wasn't sure how to run the Attendance Report; I had to spend a couple of hours straightening him out. Janine had a jam on the laser printer; I had to get it cleared out for her. Stuff like that puts me behind on all the special reports and programs I have to work up myself.*

M. (thoughtfully) Do me a favor, Al. To the best of your recollection I want you to prepare a detailed list of everything you worked on over the past three days.

S. *(frowning) Everything?*

M. As much as you can remember. Stuff you handled yourself, and things you worked on when people came to you for help. List and number the items.

(Al presents a list containing 28 items to his boss the following day.)

S. *That's most of the major things. I might have left off a few items.*

M. That's okay. Let's sit down and go over the list together.

(They review the list item by item; manager checks off 8 items.)

M. Al, do these 8 items have any special significance to you?

S. *They're all confidential reports. My-eyes-only stuff. I'm the only one authorized to handle them.*

M. Right. That leaves 20 items without that restriction. In short *anyone* who's qualified could take over that stuff. So let me ask you a dumb question: How come you do it all yourself?

S. *Well, on some of those jobs I'm the only one qualified. On others, if I didn't do it myself it would take a year. On others. . .*

M. Okay, hold on. Let's take that laser printer. Are you the only one qualified to clear up a jam? Or that Grayson report? Is it so difficult someone else can't be trained to take it over? I could go down the list item by item, but I think you get the point.

S. *(sighs) Yeah, I guess I'm not delegating enough.*

M. Enough! You're not delegating, period. The workload's not jamming you up and making you work 12- and 13- hour days. You're

jamming yourself up. In a tough, busy operation like this, if you don't delegate, you're dead. It's counterproductive for the job and counterproductive for the family. It's no way to run a ship, or a home. Let's get on the dime, Al, and start spreading that stuff around. It'll be good for the department, great for your people, and best of all for you.

• • • **TALKING POINTS** Symptoms of supervisors who run themselves ragged because of their failure to delegate are common: Hectic operation, important tasks behind schedule, supervisory irritation and fatigue, wall-to-wall confusion, general inefficiency, inordinately long working hours. Some supervisors have the mistaken notion that they earn career Brownie points when they cut their lunch periods short and work 12-hour days. Supervisors, whether in charge of three workers or fifty, should be encouraged to qualify their people for as many tasks as they can, then delegate, delegate, delegate. Supervisory success isn't achieved by working hard, long, or fast. Clichéd or not, it's by working *smart!* And smart means delegation.

DIALOGUE SIX

The problem with Peggy's system of delegation is that she delegates responsibility along with the work.

Talking It Out

Manager - Peggy, I just got a call from Mr. Cochran. He's fit to be tied. Whatever happened to the Returns Analysis this month?

Supervisor - I don't know. I turned it over to Murray Cadman two weeks ago.

M. Mr. Cochran says the figures are all wrong, and the percentages don't balance out. Didn't you review the report before handing it in?

S. I assumed it was okay. That was on Friday. It was my busiest day.

M. (shaking his head) That's an important report. Key decisions are made based on those figures.

S. *I know. But Murray's a dependable employee. He was supposed to check the controls. I spent more than an hour going over the procedure with him. I was sure he had it all right.*

M. **Murray may be a good man. But that doesn't relieve you of responsibility for the results he produces. Peg, I'm sure you know the expression: "The buck stops here." If you're the guy in charge, "here" means at your desk. Murray may be accountable to you, but final accountability rests with the skipper in charge of the ship.**

S. *(downcast) I realize now I should have checked out that report.*

M. **Let me ask you something else. What makes you assume Murray is qualified if this is the first time he worked up that report?**

S. *Well, he's a smart guy. He seemed to understand the procedure when I explained it to him. At least he didn't have any questions.*

M. **That's not necessarily significant. From what I know of Murray he's not an outgoing person. Reticent people are often reluctant to ask questions when a job is turned over for fear of appearing dumb. They figure they'll work it out when the time comes, or ask someone for help. This shoe may fit Murray. Other times, when a new job is explained, the person may understand it at the time, or think they understand it, but when it comes time to do it they become confused.**

S. *(glum)*

M. **(brighter tone) No sweat, Peg. You're delegating work which is to your credit. But there are fundamentals of delegation just as there are of every supervisory function. You can delegate as much as you want, but you can't delegate your own responsibility for the final result. And when delegating a job you can't kiss it goodbye. You have to follow up to make sure it is going all right. And while it's true that the delegatee should get a certain amount of authority to go along with the work, it must be within carefully defined limits. The most important thing to keep in mind is that as Harry Truman so aptly put it: "The buck stops here." Remember that and you won't go wrong.**

• • • **TALKING POINTS** Effective delegation is what successful management is all about. But a careful path must be trod to make sure the quality of work isn't diminished along with the supervisory workload. If care isn't taken responsibility tends to get delegated along with the work. When this occurs, quality automatically suffers because no one in an operation has so great a stake in results as the person in charge. Responsibility tends to get abdicated for a number of reasons: 1) Supervisors have been known to delegate tasks they don't like, then wash their hands of them; 2) Sometimes the culprit is that old bugaboo—too busy to follow up; 3) Other times the supervisor may forget where "the buck" really stops.

chapter seven
....

MULTIPLYING PRODUCTIVITY

The key to productivity is *people*—the way they work, the tools they use, the way they *feel* about their work. The mechanical factors of work can be evaluated in terms of amount of time taken to do the job, and items or pieces produced. The mental processes involved are harder to assess but no less important. For example, John may have the "productivity edge" on Bill in terms of ability, training, and experience. But if Bill *feels* more positive about his job than John, he will out-produce him every day of the week despite his lower potential. Your challenge as a supervisor is to determine the cause of productivity sag—poor work habits and methods, inadequate training or experience, or poor work attitude—and remedy the situation by means of one-on-one confrontation.

DIALOGUE ONE

Joan's productivity as a Biller in the Credit Department is unacceptable as a result of her chronic indifference.

Talking It Out

(Joan's supervisor discusses the worker's problem with her assistant prior to talking it out with Joan.)

Supervisor - Barbara, you've seen the latest performance report. Joan's at the bottom of the list again. What do you think we should do about it?

Assistant - It's hard to say. When she was stuffing invoices in envelopes her productivity was consistently above average. Since she was moved up to Biller it's as if she's two different people.

S. I know. That's what makes it problematical. If she weren't a 2-year veteran with a fairly good record I would simply lay down the law: Shape up, or ship out. But for some reason I don't think that would work in Joan's case, at least so far as boosting her productivity is concerned.

A. I agree.

S. (shaking her head) I thought I did her a favor to upgrade her to Biller. But it doesn't seem to have worked that way.

A. (sympathetically) No, since her promotion to Biller she spends half her time gabbing when she's supposed to be working. That not only reduces her own productivity but her neighbor's as well. Maybe it's time for a heart-to-heart talk.

S. Exactly what I had in mind.

(Summons Joan to her office.)

Supervisor - (performance report on her desk) You've seen these figures, Joan. What do you make of them?

Employee - (shrugs) I don't know. I guess they're not very good.

S. That's an understatement if ever I heard one. To be blunt, your production is unacceptable. I'd like to hear your side of the story—what steps we can take to improve your performance. Unless you don't care about your job. . .

E. (alarmed) I need the job.

S. All right, that's a starting point. Joan, you know as well as I that as a supervisor I can't turn a blind eye to substandard performance.

E. (nods reluctantly)

S. When you were hired you were assigned to stuffing envelopes. How long did you spend at that job?

E. About a year-and-a-half.

S. During most of that time your productivity was better than average. That's interesting because most employees dislike stuffing envelopes. They find it boring and tedious. You were good at it. I upgraded you to Biller as a reward for your good performance.

E. I don't mind stuffing envelopes. I like it better than billing.

S. Oh? Why is that?

E. Well, for one thing, in Billing there's too much pressure having to keep up with the volume. For another, it makes me feel like a robot.

S. How so?

E. Stuffing envelopes, you don't have to concentrate so hard on what you're doing. You can chat with your neighbor and work just as fast. I'm a naturally fast person so my production is good. I don't know—that's just a friendlier, more social job.

S. The increased status isn't important to you?

E. (shrugs) A job is a job.

S. (nods) Very well, Joan, if that's how you feel about it. I'm glad we had this discussion. I'll put you back stuffing envelopes.

• • • **TALKING POINTS**   Like a great many employees, Joan's employment is motivated solely by the economic need to help support herself and her family. The job and the work itself have little significance to her. As she puts it herself: "A job is a job." On the other hand, the sociability aspect is important to her. It reduces boredom and helps the time pass more quickly. Most clerical and factory tasks require concentration to ensure efficiency and productivity. But in some, like stuffing envelopes or working on an assembly line, productivity isn't hampered by conversation. In such cases, controlled "gabbing" is good for morale, and for performance as well.

DIALOGUE TWO

George, a Purchasing Department Supervisor, is hard working, conscientious, and ambitious. But he doesn't organize his work efficiently.

Talking It Out

Manager - George, do you have time for a story?

Supervisor - Sure.

M. It was a Saturday and this guy named Macdougal was scheduled to take off on vacation the next day with his family. But when he started his car he heard a motor sound he didn't like. A good mechanic, he knew what the problem was and figured it would take about an hour to fix it. He went to the garage for tools but on the way noticed a book he had to return to the library. So he hopped into the car and drove there. On his way home from the library he passed a nursery and reminded himself that he needed a bag of fertilizer. When he returned home he got out the spreader and distributed the fertilizer. Then he remembered that the Yankees were playing the Red Sox and tuned in to the game. During the seventh-inning stretch he reminded himself he needed film for his camera and hopped down to the drug store. After dinner Macdougal's wife asked, "Did you finish fixing the car, Mac?" Macdougal slapped his forehead. "Finished! I didn't even get started." End of story.

S. (frowning)

M. (grins) You're probably wondering what that story has to do with your department's unsatisfactory productivity?

S. (light dawning) Uh oh, I knew you had an ulterior motive in mind. Me and Macdougal, we're both lousy planners and organizers.

M. Pretty close. Okay, George, let's see what we can do about it. First, let me have a look at your list of priorities.

S. I, uh, er. . .

M. You don't have one, do you?

S. No, I don't. The thing is I've been too busy. . .

M. (closes eyes wearily) Those famous words again. Productivity buster number one: "I'm too busy." That's pretty much what I guessed based on some of the stuff around here that's been scheduled and not started, and other stuff that's half-finished, and urgent reports that are overdue. I can't think of anything that kills productivity faster than a lack of organization and planning, or a failure to set and keep resetting priorities. George, do you want me to call you Macdougal?

S. Hell, no.

M. Okay, I'll agree not to, if you get that planning show on the road.

• • • **TALKING POINTS** A harsh fact of business life is that supervisors who are too busy to plan and organize their work are too busy to function productively. Ironically, nine times out of ten, the reason they are too busy is because of their failure to plan. The simplest way to keep productively on top of the job on a day-to-day basis is to prepare a running things-to-do checklist in proper order of importance, and at the start of each day, review the list and make adjustments as changing conditions require.

DIALOGUE THREE

Production Department productivity suffers because Mel, a Department Head, fails to set goal priorities.

Talking It Out

Manager - Mel, how long has it been since Barney Golden opted for early retirement and you took over the department?

Supervisor - Six months, give or take a week or two.

M. Are you satisfied with the way things are going?

S. No. I'm working all kinds of hours in an effort to boost productivity, but no matter how hard I work it doesn't seem to be happening.

M. I like your answer. But if experience taught me anything it's that long hours aren't the answer to poor productivity, and neither is working harder. To coin an old cliché, working *smarter* may be

more on target. Let's put our heads together and see if we can track down the problem.

S. *I know what the problem is—or problems: Production is down, rejects are up, and attendance is worse than ever. But I can't figure out why. I guess I'm no Barney Golden.*

M. **Don't sell yourself short. You're a good supervisor, but you may be off on a wrong track. For one thing, you define lower production, increased rejects, and poor attendance as problems. They aren't problems; they're *consequences* of problems. Problems are what cause the consequences.**

S. *I'm not sure I follow you.*

M. **Then let's take it a step further. Before improving results you have to decide *what* results you need to improve. To do that you must set meaningful goals for yourself. Then you have to make plans to meet the goals that you set. That's Part One. We'll get to Part Two in a minute. Did you set any goals with improved production, less rejects, and better attendance in mind?**

S. *(frowning) Yes I did, for all three. I resolved to improve all of them.*

M. **Those are your goals: To improve production, reduce rejects, and get better attendance?**

S. *Well, yes.*

M. **(thoughtfully) I think that might be the crux of the difficulty. Mel, a resolution to simply *improve* production or anything else isn't a goal, it's a statement and as such is meaningless. A real goal is measurable. It narrows down the objective to a specific time frame or quantity. For example: Improve attendance 10%, decrease rejects 12%, and boost production by 28 pieces—all by such-and-such date. Do you see what I mean?**

S. *Yes, I think I do.*

M. **Good, then that's what we have to focus on. Take attendance as an example. Part One: Pick a realistic figure as a goal; define in specific terms the number of absences six months ago when you took over the department. Let's say they were 10% less. Ten percent is a realistic goal to shoot for. You achieved it once, you can achieve it again. Next, analyze the attendance sheets. Again, specifically. Who is responsible for that 10% increase in absence? Names,** faces. **Discuss the problem with the people responsible. Get them involved in that 10% improvement goal. Make it worth their while to work with you, against their best interests to refuse to cooperate. Are you with me?**

S. *I sure am.*

M. **Good. Hold on, that's not the end of it. Part Two is just as important. After working out a program with your people to accomplish that 10% goal, the next step is to set a deadline. By when can we realistically expect to achieve what we're shooting for? Three months, six months? Whatever. You have to work it out. Is that all there is to it? Not quite. The final step is to monitor progress at periodic intervals along the way. If progress is being made, compliment the individual; if it's not being made, find out why. If need be, crack the whip. If you do this, before long you'll see the situation turning around. You will then be ready for the last lap of the relay: To set new goals with bettering Barney's results in mind. That's the way to become a hero in this business. Goal setting is a neverending proposition.**

• • • **TALKING POINTS**   Supervisory management and goal management are synonymous. A supervisor is judged first of all by results. Results are the byproduct of meaningful goals that are defined, stated, set, and monitored. Ideally, your boss has goals tied into the goals of his or her superior. Your goals are tied to the goals of your boss. Your subordinates' goals should work hand in hand with your goals. A superior manager, outstanding supervisor, up-and-coming line or staff person, is the employee whose individual goals most effectively tie into the goals of his or her supervisor, and thus automatically into the goals of the company. That's what productivity is all about.

DIALOGUE FOUR

It's the busy season. Shipping Department Supervisor Joe Fenning thinks the only way to keep up with the workload is more overtime.

Talking It Out

Manager - Joe, take a look at these payroll figures. They're up 40% over the past month. Mr. Browning wants to know why.

Supervisor - Does he realize how many more orders we've been processing?

M. I'm sure he does. In fact, I checked out the figures for the same period last year. We put through 10% more orders than now and the payroll was 10% lower. How do you account for that?

S. (frowning) It has to be overtime.

M. That's the same conclusion I reached. Let's break this down, okay. The two most common ways to deal with an increased workload are: One, hire more people, and two, assign more overtime. Can you think of a third?

S. (frowning) Increase productivity?

M. Bingo! Let's talk about that. Let's see, you hired ten additional people since the rush began. And the amount of overtime is going through the ceiling. Let's see if we can find out why we're taking such a productivity bust this year over last.

S. I don't know. It's been so hectic around here I haven't had time. . .

M. To operate efficiently? Forgive me for finishing the sentence for you. Hectic is one thing; orderly and well organized quite another. Let's consider your two responsibilities. One is to get the work out. The other is to keep costs down, productivity up. The easy mindless way to push work out the door is to hire more bodies or assign more and more overtime. The *right* way, the cost-effective way, is to plan and manage the operation so you keep overtime at a minimum.

S. (silent, glum)

M. (brighter demeanor) Cheer up, Joe, we can lick this together. Let's work out a procedure for doing it. Use this pad to make notes. First, monitor the production of your pickers, packers, and drivers. I'm sure you'll find some of them aren't meeting quantity standards. In fact, some may be deliberately holding back in an effort to generate more overtime. Cracking down on the miscreants will solve part but not all of the problem. On top of that, I want a report on my desk by Friday with a cost comparison between hiring more temps for the busy season as opposed to assigning more overtime. As I said, the easiest course when work piles up is to assign overtime to handle the extra load. It's also easy in the rush of things to forget that it's the most expensive course. Overtime costs the company time-and-a-half during the week and double-time on weekends. Joe, I want you to make cutting that overtime burden your first priority. Mr. Browning's a big guy. I want to get him off my back.

• • • **TALKING POINTS**   No question about it. Getting the work out is a responsibility you can't put on a shelf. But how efficiently and economically you get it out is what marks you as a smart manager instead of a run-of-the-mill hack supervisor. The hack's vision is limited to what comes in and goes out the door. The smart manager's vision encompasses not only merchandise—product, services, and so on—but the whole profit ball of wax with cost-effectiveness and productivity performance in mind. An executive we know labels this "The 30% Factor" after a high performing department head replaced his ineffective predecessor. (The new supervisor's productivity was 30% higher.)

DIALOGUE FIVE

Frieda confuses cutting procedural steps with cutting costs and improving productivity.

Talking It Out

Supervisor - Frieda, the record shows that you're one of the general office's most intelligent and reliable employees. But lately an increasing number of errors have been called to my attention. I think we should talk about it. Do you have any ideas?

Employee - (concerned) Not really. I try to do a good job.

S. I know you do, and I admire you for it. That's why I can't help wondering about these increased errors, especially on the Late Payments Report and the Monthly Comparisons. Actually, the pro-

cedures for these reports have been set up to eliminate any possibility of error. I know you were only assigned these reports a few months ago. Is there anything that needs clarification?

E. *I don't think so. The procedures are pretty straightforward.*

S. **That's what I thought. Let's take a look at last month's Late Payments Report. You seem to have gotten columns two and three confused.**

E. *Yes, I know.*

S. **Good. Let's review the procedure step by step. Do you have a copy handy?**

E. *(produces procedure)*

S. **Now, starting with Step 11, the instructions are to enter the control figure at the end of Column 2 and carry it forward. . .**

E. *(looking worried) I didn't do that.*

S. **(puzzled) Why not? It says so right here at Step 11.**

E. *I must have overlooked that. I skipped Steps 11 and 12 because I thought it would save some time and get the job done faster.*

S. **I see. Are you in the habit of skipping steps when you follow procedures?**

E. *(reluctantly) Once in a while, if I think it will save time.*

S. **Well, I'm glad we're having this discussion. I think we pinpointed the problem. These procedures have been carefully thought out by systems experts. Every step is there for a purpose. That doesn't mean you shouldn't question a step if you feel it's not needed or should be changed in some way. But skipping a step, or changing a procedure on your own without checking it out first with a supervisor can only cause problems, boost inefficiency, and in most cases lose more time than you save. Frieda, I appreciate your good intentions, but I want you to promise me you will never shortcut a procedure again without getting permission to do so.**

E. *(contrite) I promise.*

• • • **TALKING POINTS** A written procedure is to a plant or office employee what a blueprint is to an architect. Skipping or changing a step is like omitting a construction item or substituting the wrong kind of material.

Employees usually shortcut procedures for one of two reasons: 1) They are behind in their work and feel this will help them catch up; 2) They don't understand the reason for the step in question, and figure that since they are the ones who do the actual grunt work, they know more than the "masterminds" removed from the job who dreamed up the procedure. One supervisory key to productivity is to review procedures periodically and reassess them in light of changing conditions. Another is to *encourage* employees to challenge procedural steps and suggest changes they feel are warranted. But in that case it is important to get the message across that unsanctioned omissions or changes are strictly *verboten*.

chapter eight

. . . .

DEALING WITH PROBLEM EMPLOYEES

Mary suddenly becomes irritable and hard to get along with. Frank is belligerent and threatens co-workers. Jack is overambitious and doesn't care what he does to get ahead. Alice's attendance is getting progressively worse. George has a drinking problem that is getting out of hand. No matter how carefully you screen and hire your people, some problem employees are bound to slip through. To complicate supervisory life even more, there is no telling when today's stable, well-adjusted person will turn into a problem of one kind or other. As if you already didn't have enough responsibilities, here's another one to add to your list: How to deal with problem employees.

DIALOGUE ONE

Vincent, a packer in the Shipping Department, seems to have changed overnight from a friendly, easygoing guy to an angry, hostile person.

Talking It Out

Supervisor - What's the problem, Vince?

Employee - Nothing, why?

S. Let me put it this way. I'm not the only one to notice a change in you. A couple of people have remarked about it.

E. I do my job. Get off my back.

S. I never said you didn't do your job. But whatever became of the cheerful, friendly, popular guy I used to know?

E. (shrugs) I'm still the same guy.

S. I suppose. Same nose, same face, same paunch. But I don't remember the last time I saw you crack a smile. What's wrong? Problems at home?

E. No. Nothing's wrong at home.

S. Bev's okay?

E. She's okay.

S. What about you? Any problem with your health?

E. My health is fine.

S. Any complaints about the work?

E. No, I got no complaints.

S. Okay Vince, I'll stop bugging you. If you don't want to talk about it it's up to you. But if you decide to change your mind. . .

E. (hesitating) Well, if you put it that way. It's not the work exactly. It's the guy you put me next to. Since you transferred Jerry Shea from Soft Goods to Imports I hate coming in in the morning. I can't stand Shea and I guess he feels the same way about me. We keep needling each other. It makes the job very unpleasant. A couple of times we almost came to blows.

S. Thanks for leveling with me. I had no idea. I didn't think you were bosom buddies, but I never thought you were mortal enemies. I wish you had talked to me sooner. It's an easy problem to solve especially if Shea feels the same way. How would you feel about working in Soft Goods?

E. A lot better than working next to that guy. Thanks a lot.

• • • **TALKING POINTS**   A sensitive, caring supervisor is alert to employee symptoms of discontent or unrest. A sudden adverse change in a person's attitude, behavior, or performance is usually a sure sign that something could do with adjusting. Assuming the problem isn't of a nature sufficiently serious or disturbing to require medical or other professional attention, a little persistent probing may be in order. Sudden changes could be due to any number of causes ranging from health or family problems, to festering on-the-job resentments and co-worker disagreements. Or perhaps the employee might have had a bad day or bad week and the whole thing will simply blow over.

Dialogue Two

Al won't admit it, even to himself, but he drinks too much.

Talking It Out

(Production Supervisor Bill Daley had been observing Al, a welder in his department, for weeks now. His performance had been declining steadily. Bill had brought the problem to Al's attention a couple of times and received the welder's promise to improve. Just the opposite happened. Bill suspected the reason, but wisely, instead of pursuing it further with Al, decided to consult the company doctor.)

Supervisor - Doc, I'm sorry to report we may have an alcoholic on our hands.

Doctor - What's his name?

S. Al Griff. He's a welder.

D. (making notes) That's no job for a heavy drinker. What makes you think he's an alcoholic?

S. I've been watching him. He usually spends his lunch hour at the bar down the block. More often than not he comes back smelling like a brewery.

D. That's certainly an indication. What about his performance on the job?

S. No accidents yet. But his work is getting more and more sloppy, and his productivity has been declining steadily.

D. His attendance?

S. Irregular. He's been missing too many days, and comes back late from lunch too often. A couple of times he didn't come back at all.

D. What kind of excuses does he give for missing work?

S. Far-fetched. They keep getting stranger and stranger, more and more unrealistic.

D. Does Al have his own drinking cronies? Or would you say he's more of a loner?

S. He used to spend his lunch hour with three or four other guys. But lately he seems to prefer to drink by himself.

D. (nodding) That follows the usual pattern. What physical symptoms have you noticed?

S. Flushed face, reddish eyes. He's never actually drunk on the job, but at times he's a little unsteady.

D. Have you discussed this with him?

S. Only in terms of his declining performance. As far as the alcoholism is concerned, I figured it would be better to leave that to the experts.

D. Smart decision. Please send him to my office tomorrow morning at 10:00.

S. What if he refuses to come?

D. Give me a call. I'll work it out with Personnel.

• • • **TALKING POINTS**   As a supervisor who suspects an employee of alcoholism, at what point do you intercede? And how? First and most important, keep in mind that the day when the problem drinker was regarded as a moral inferior has long since past. The challenge is to take whatever action might be necessary for rehabilitation and restoration to health. On top of that your concern must involve your responsibility to run an efficient and productive operation. When is a drinker a problem drinker? That's a matter of degree relating to behavior, appearance, and performance, and not your decision to make. But sustaining acceptable performance is your decision to make. Perhaps the most important thing to remember as a supervisor is that after identifying a possible problem drinker, once you have reported your suspicion to a qualified professional, your responsibility ends.

DIALOGUE THREE

Plant Engineering Department Project Supervisor Frank will take any action he feels necessary to get ahead.

Talking It Out

Manager - Frank, that pollution control proposal was an impressive piece of work. I want to congratulate you.

Supervisor - Thanks. I burned a lot of midnight oil before I finally got the report to come out the way I wanted it.

M. You must have. I was surprised to see that your name was the only one that appeared on the report. It seemed like a project for more than one man.

S. (a bit uneasy) Well, I did get a little help here and there.

M. Just a little?

S. (shrugs)

M. (nods thoughtfully) What did you think of the meeting on the lab restructuring plan this afternoon?

S. I thought it went very well. I thought you did a great job of running it.

M. Thank you. I see you seemed to go along with all my suggestions.

S. Yes sir, definitely. I think you have the right approach all the way down the line.

M. Do you really *feel* that way, or are you saying it because you think it's what I want to hear?

S. (flushes) What do you mean?

M. I'm going to level with you and tell you what I mean. Frank, I know how anxious you are to get ahead in this company, but I think you're going about it in the wrong way. Yessing the boss to death, which you seem to have been doing a lot of, is the one way not to get ahead. For example, at the meeting this afternoon, even though Len disagreed with some of my major points, I had far more respect for his opinion than yours because I felt it was honest. Even though I disagreed with him, there was sound judgment behind his argument, and he had the guts to express what he felt. It was not only gutsy, but helpful. It doesn't take brains or imagination to be an echo. Coming up with original thinking and fighting for what you believe in counts for much more.

S. (crestfallen) I . . .

M. I'll tell you something else, Frank. I talked with a few of the engineers and other project leaders about that pollution control proposal of yours. From the feedback I got it was pretty obvious you

got more than a little help from subordinates and associates in preparing that report—enough help in fact for their contributions to have been credited. Is the message getting through, Frank?

S. *(eyes lowered) Yes sir, it is.*

M. **Good. I hope you'll give it some thought. It's all very well to be ambitious and work hard for advancement. But it's the rare individual who gets ahead on the backs of his associates or by kowtowing to the boss. You have a good head on your shoulders. If you keep that in mind you might make it yet.**

• • • **TALKING POINTS**   Ambition is an essential attribute of success if it is ethically and judiciously applied. It is important to keep in mind that one needs the cooperation and support of colleagues and subordinates to get ahead in the marketplace. If you give others the credit they deserve for their contributions, that consideration will revert back to you when you need it. It is also useful to keep in mind that when a subordinate's good work is recognized by management that recognition automatically reflects back to you.

DIALOGUE FOUR

Charlotte's attendance record—absence and lateness—has been going from bad to worse.

Talking It Out

Supervisor - I've been checking your personnel folder. This is your sixth year with the company and the fourth department you've worked in. Your first transfer from Accounts Receivable to Credit was a promotion as a reward for your good record. You did an outstanding job in Credit and were moved to Statistics when your job was eliminated. In Statistics your performance declined. You requested and were granted a transfer to this department, Sales, where your performance continued to slide, your attendance most notably. Have you any comment to make?

Employee - I'll try to do better.

S. (smiles) Where have I heard that song before? Charlotte, I've been reviewing your attendance record and one thing in particular arouses my curiosity. When you were assigned to Accounts Receivable your attendance record was better than average. In Credit it was outstanding; in more than a year you didn't miss a single day and were late only once. In Statistics your attendance fell sharply. And here in Sales—well the record speaks for itself: unacceptable. What bugs me, Charlotte, is why such a decline following your move from Credit to Sales? Can you enlighten me?

E. *(thoughtful but unresponsive)*

S. There must be a reason. Your record proves you are capable of superior performance and outstanding attendance. When an employee excels in one department and performs poorly in another, a number of possible causes come to mind: Lack of ability, which I can rule out right away. Perhaps a problem with supervision or co-workers? If that's the cause I wish you'd level with me.

E. *Oh no, I like the people I work with, and I think you're a fair supervisor.*

S. Thank you. What about the work itself?

E. *(hesitates) It's okay, I guess.*

S. You guess. (glimpsing a light in the tunnel) You did exceptionally well in Credit.

E. *I really liked my job there. The work was interesting.*

S. What about the work in Statistics?

E. *(wrinkles her nose) I hated it.*

S. And Sales? Tell me the truth.

E. *(face flushes, hesitates)*

S. You're not crazy about it?

E. *It's boring. I punch figures into a computer keyboard all day. It drives me nuts. It's even worse than the stuff I did in Statistics.*

S. (nods thoughtfully) I see here you have a pretty high IQ. Suppose if, instead of posting those figures, I assigned you to working on the daily printouts and drawing the averages? How would you feel about that?

E. (face brightens) I think I would like that. I would like it very much.

S. All right, we'll make the switch as an experiment. I'm guessing that the main cause of your excessive absence and lateness was your negative feelings about your job. If you do well with the printouts and it normalizes your attendance we'll both be satisfied. If your poor attendance continues I'll have no choice but to let you go. Agreed?

E. Yes sir.

• • • **TALKING POINTS**   Poor attendance may be attributable to any number of causes from ill health and poor attitude to job friction or boredom. It has been said that boredom slays more of existence than war. Indirectly, it is a major cause of poor attendance as well as other performance problems. As usual, Step One is to track down the problem if possible. Step Two is to make an effort to solve it. Failing this, the final step is progressive documentation and punishment, followed if need be by the ultimate discipline, dismissal. Where uncorrectable, poor attendance cannot be tolerated. If the underlying cause is boredom, adding job interest—by a work switch, or job variety where feasible—can be the happiest solution.

DIALOGUE FIVE

Behind his back, and sometimes to his face, they call him "Yak Yak" because he doesn't know when to shut up.

Talking It Out

Supervisor - (exasperated) I don't know how many times I talked to you about your chronic ailment, the chatterbox syndrome. I'm going to give it to you bluntly. I've reached the end of my patience.

Employee - (glum) Yeah, I guess I talk to much.

S. That's the understatement of the year. Workers are given lunch and break periods during which they can take it easy, relax, and chat to their heart's content. Those are the times you can relate anecdotes, exchange jokes, tell the story of your life for all I care.

But during work hours excessive gabbing disrupts processing, delays shipments, produces errors, and kills productivity.

E. *(nods agreement) I know.*

S. **I know you know. That's why I've just about had it with you. Ted, I've come up with three possible solutions to your problem: I can tape your mouth with sealing tape; I can issue ear plugs to all employees; I can fire you. The first two aren't practical. The third choice is up to you. This is your last warning, pal.**

• • • **TALKING POINTS** Chatterboxes—however harmless their intentions to be friendly, interesting, or funny—usually wind up being bores. Off the job people can choose to tolerate or not tolerate such behavior. On the job excessive gabbing, face to face or on the telephone, is prohibitively expensive. It interrupts work, distracts people from their thoughts, and wastes valuable time. It is the death of productivity because it administers a double-kill shot to both the gabber and willing or unwilling listener. From a supervisory viewpoint it simply cannot be tolerated.

DIALOGUE SIX

The trouble with Gus is that he rubs co-workers the wrong way.

Talking It Out

Supervisor - Gus, I've been getting too many complaints about you.

Employee - Why, there's nothing wrong with my work!

S. **I didn't say there was. The problem isn't the work you produce. It's the way you produce it, the way you interact with people.**

E. *(grumpy expression) What's wrong with the way I interact? Tell me who's beefing and what they're beefing about. . .*

S. **More than one person is beefing. I'll give it to you straight. Some of your co-workers feel you're too argumentative. And from what I've observed I have to agree. You constantly seem to be bickering, ready to pick a fight at the slightest provocation.**

E. (conceding) Yeah, I guess I get irritated too easily, but some of those guys get my goat.

S. Why is that? Because you're so much smarter than them? Because the only right way is your way?

E. No, I don't know why it is. I guess I've always been short-tempered.

S. That's too bad because it hurts you more than anyone else. You're a bright guy, Gus, and I'm sure you want to get ahead. But it's hard to get anywhere as a grouchy solo player. In business, the name of the success game is teamwork, cooperation. If you work with other people, they'll work with you. If you argue and fight with them, you make enemies instead of friends. That applies all the way up and down the line. The more people you have rooting for you, the better chance you will have. Think about that, okay?

• • • **TALKING POINTS** A supervisor must handle all kinds of people and motivate them to perform at their best and work harmoniously with the rest of the staff. This goes for the misfits as well as well-adjusted employees. One general classification of misfit is the irritable grouch whose behavior may range from merely unpleasant to threatening and overtly hostile. How to handle the irritable grouch depends on the degree of his abusiveness. On the low end of the scale, a friendly well-meaning chat is all that may be needed to create awareness of the problem and its self-defeating consequences. Where behavior is at the physically threatening extreme, stronger action may be called for and should not be delayed.

chapter nine

· ·

KEEPING COSTS UNDER CONTROL

The key to cost control is people control. The key to people control is on the one hand, motivation, on the other, the establishment of fair and realistic performance standards. Cost control will not work unless employees *actively want it to work*—ideally, if it is in their best interest to make it work. Even if employees are well intentioned, for effective cost control to prevail: 1) A monitoring and measurement system must be in force to quickly flag cost abuses and deviations; 2) Sustained cost and profit awareness is needed to keep employees on track in all areas of cost management.

DIALOGUE ONE

Gert, a conscientious well-qualified Accounts Payable Department employee, abuses the company's personal telephone privilege.

Talking It Out

Supervisor - Gert, we owe each other an apology. I owe you one because I checked up on you in a rather sneaky way: I monitored the

past five days of your telephone conversations. You owe me and the company an apology because you have been taking unfair advantage of the telephone privilege.

Employee - Part of my job is to be in telephone contact with suppliers and other departments.

S. Is it also part of your job to be in telephone contact with your friends outside the company, and other pals in the company with whom you conduct personal conversations and gossip?

E. (face red) I don't do much of that.

S. Let's level with each other. As I said, I checked up on you. I have a list of the nonbusiness calls you made. If you take a look at the record, you can see for yourself.

E. (no answer for this)

S. I'll give you the benefit of the doubt, Gert. I'll assume you don't realize how much time you waste on the telephone and how much you needlessly tie up the switchboard. Personal use of the telephone is a privilege management could just as easily restrict as allow. We all have an obligation not to abuse it. I don't like having to monitor calls, but I think you can understand that as a supervisor it's my responsibility to keep costs in line and clamp down on practices that undermine productivity.

E. (eyes lowered) I guess I get carried away sometimes and lose sight of how much time I spend on the phone.

S. Understandably. It's easy to do. You'll probably be surprised to learn that you spent almost four hours last week on personal chitchat and gossip. That's about ten percent of your total work week.

E. I had no idea it was that much. I'm sorry. I'll be more careful in the future.

S. Apology accepted. Thank you for being so cooperative.

• • • **TALKING POINTS** What business today could operate without a telephone? What supervisor today operates without an acute case of telephone *agita* incurred by abuse of the telephone privilege? Controlling telephone use is as essential to controlling departmental costs as a supervisor's presence is to controlling continuous work flow. This can be easy or difficult depending on the individual involved. When an employee doesn't have free business access to the telephone, excessive or unauthorized use is simple to control. Most problematical is the situation where the job necessitates talking with customers or others on a fairly regular basis. In such circumstances more intrusive monitoring may be called for. Like it or not, it is a matter of fulfilling your supervisory responsibility.

Dialogue Two

Sales department thumb twiddler Fred disappears from his desk when his assignments are complete.

Talking It Out

Supervisor - Fred, I've been looking for you. How's that report for Mr. Simmons coming along?

Employee - I finished it forty minutes ago. Betty is double-checking the controls.

S. Where have you been all this time?

E. Er, uh, I had to go to the men's room.

S. For forty minutes or more?

E. Well, I finished the report and had no other assignments.

S. That's what I want to talk to you about. Let me ask you something. Do you get paid on a piece-work basis, so much for each report? Or are you paid on an hourly basis? Or, to put it another way: Do you expect to be paid for those forty minutes in the "men's room?"

E. (frowning) I don't know what you mean.

S. I suspect that you do. Around here employees are paid for the work we do, not our physical presence on the premises. This isn't a philanthropic institution. You get two relief breaks each day. That's all the nonworking, or relaxation, time the company can afford. In the future, when you complete a job and have none others scheduled, I want you to report to me at once for another assignment. No self-imposed break period in between. Understood?

E. Yeah, sure.

• • • **TALKING POINTS** Idle time is the bane of every supervisor's existence. In this case the supervisor was as much to blame for the costly productivity-eroding work gap as the employee. He was correct in laying down the law to Fred about reporting for another assignment. But if he had been really on the ball he would have seen to it *in advance* that Fred had enough work to keep him busy. If another assignment wasn't available, the supervisor should have been prepared with a list of fill-in tasks—filing, posting, training, whatever—to avoid the nonproductive gap that existed.

DIALOGUE THREE

Confronted with rising costs, Office Services Supervisor Bill Fallon calls Charlie to account for his abusive use of the office copying machine.

Talking It Out

Supervisor - How would you feel, Charlie, if I presented you with a bill for $54.32?

Employee - Huh? What for?

S. Time, materials, maintenance.

E. For what?

S. For this. (hands Charlie some crumpled sheets of paper.) These cartoons and gags didn't come out so good, so you made them over again, right? I found a lot of this stuff, some of it on the porno side, along with other personal printed materials in the waste bin by the copier machine. Some of them had your name on it. Are you going to tell me you haven't been running this junk and distributing it all over the office?

E. (shifts nervously) I'm not the only one.

S. I didn't say you were, but you're a prime offender. That machine isn't a toy, and the copier alcove isn't a game room.

E. (moistens lips, no response)

S. I've spoken to you about this before and I'm not going to do it again. The copier is an important communications tool. It costs money to keep supplied and maintained. It costs money when

someone who needs it for work has to wait because it's tied up on frivolous nonsense like this. It's especially costly in terms of lost time spent on personal stuff when you're supposed to be working. Do you think it's fair to make the company pick up the tab for this unauthorized waste? Consider yourself as having been put on notice, Charlie: Personal use of the copier won't be tolerated. This applies to you and to anyone else in the department who thinks the machine is a toy. You can take this as fair warning. And to make sure, I put it in writing. (hands Charlie an official warning notice)

• • • **TALKING POINTS**   Copier abuse in some offices has been found costly enough to warrant the installation of special controls as a preventive measure. In some companies, copier use is restricted to a single individual. In others, employees are required to sign in and out when they use the machine. Where special controls aren't used, it is the cost-conscious supervisor's responsibility to get the message across to his or her people that as Bill Fallon made clear, personal use of the office copier won't be tolerated.

DIALOGUE FOUR

Data Processing's Carol is guilty of a supervisor's worst offense. She assigns low-level tasks to high-salaried personnel.

Talking It Out

Manager - Carol, was that Alex Carlton I saw working on the keypunch machine when I passed through your department this morning?

Supervisor - Yes. We were behind schedule on the EOM Sales Recap. I asked Alex to pitch in for awhile.

M. How long is a while?

S.   Four or five hours or so.

M. Is this something you do often?

S.   Only when we're in a bind.

M. Did you call on Alex because you had no other assignments for him?

S. No. Alex had his own work. But the Sales Recap was top priority.

M. Did it occur to you that as a programmer Alex gets more than twice the hourly rate of a key puncher?

S. I know, but I had to get that report out. We were a day behind schedule.

M. I can't argue with your motivation. But using a high-salaried employee for low-level tasks is a supervisory no-no. It may get you out of a temporary bind. But it usually lands you right smack in another: an economic bind.

S. Alex was the most accessible person. What else was I supposed to do?

M. Good question. Let's talk about that. One thing you could have done was borrow one or two people from the word processing pool. Their wage level is fairly close to the key punchers'. Also, their skills are more compatible. A typist's output would be greater than Alex's. Plus, a typist wouldn't resent a key-punching assignment; someone like Alex probably would.

S. (nodding) I guess that makes sense.

M. Another thing you could do is take advantage of slack periods to train some lower-level people to pitch in on key punching and other tasks. You could create skill pools of your own to be tapped as needed. Job diversification is a good idea in any case. It makes the work more interesting for people to change tasks from time to time. It provides the flexibility you need to match wage levels more economically when a switch is necessary. Most importantly, it makes your operation cost-effective.

• • • **TALKING POINTS**   You wouldn't use a two-ton truck to deliver small packages if you had a pickup at hand. It can be a temptation at times when you're in a hurry to get a job done by turning it over to the handiest, or most accessible employee without considering the wage cost involved. Even more self-defeating than picking a high-salaried person to pitch in as illustrated above, is the mindless practice of some supervisors to pitch in themselves. Just as Alex was paid for his programming know-how, you as a supervisor are paid a higher wage for your planning, organizing, leadership, and cost-improvement expertise. Low-level utilization in place of these crit-ical skills is cost-*in*effective.

DIALOGUE FIVE

Productivity in Carl's department has fallen to an unacceptable level as a result of excessive materials waste. The supervisor discusses this problem with various members of his crew.

Talking It Out

Supervisor - The amount of waste around here is getting out of hand. Any comments?

Employees - (no response)

S   Okay, let's confront the problem head on. Joe, I'll start with you as an example. Your last job called for running a batch of 384s on the automatic screw machine. Right?

E. Yeah.

S.   According to your work slip you used 72-inch steel stock for the run when you could have used 66-inch stock. Using the 72-inch stock, the scrap output totaled 58 inches. Had you used the 66-inch stock it would have been 34 inches. That's 24 inches of unnecessary waste. Do you agree?

E. Yeah, I should have used the 66-inch stock.

S.   I could cite other examples. Ellen, I noticed that in doing the arith-metic for the job tickets you use the tickets themselves, then rewrite them on other tickets. Those forms cost six cents each. Scratch paper provided for that purpose costs less than a fraction of a cent. More unnecessary waste. Is the message getting through?

E. (nodding) I'll use the scratch pads from now on.

S.   Good, that will help. Bill, I checked a few of those drill bits you discarded because you were too lazy to sharpen them. More waste. I could go on, but I think the point has been made. (looks

around, nodding heads) **Okay, I'd like to talk now about another aspect of this waste situation. After all, you don't have to pay for this stuff out of your own pocket. Why do you think the waste should concern you as well as me? Any ideas? Joe?**

E. Well, I guess it's been drilled into us often enough: Waste erodes profits. When the company makes a profit we all benefit from it.

S. Right on. The more profitable a company, the more competitive it can be. That ensures our job security, yours and mine. On a more personal level, it comes down to a question of dollars and cents. I don't think there's anyone here who would object to a raise or promotion. Well, productivity, of which waste control is an important part, figures prominently in your performance evaluation when bonus and salary review time roll around. Hopefully that will give you something to think about.

• • • **TALKING POINTS** It's easy to disregard materials waste when the direct cost doesn't come out of your own pocket. Most employees give little if any thought to the cost of the items they use day to day. An important part of your supervisory responsibility is to make them aware of the cost and to sustain that awareness. An employee's conscientiousness in this regard should be part of his or her performance evaluation. The more effectively you can convince people of their personal stake in materials handling and use, the more successful your effort will be.

DIALOGUE SIX

Jack is careless and thoughtless in his use of tools and equipment.

Talking It Out

Supervisor - Jack, that's a great electric saw you have at home in your basement.

Employee - I know. It cost me plenty.

S. How do you think it would operate if you didn't moor it down solidly to the base because you didn't bother to use the right size bolts?

E. *It would probably cause a lot of chatter. It could mess up both the saw and the work.*

S. **You wouldn't be happy about that, would you?**

E. *You gotta be kidding.*

S. **I'm not. That electric saw's your pride and joy, right? You couldn't be more careful in the way you handle it. But this morning I saw you use a pipe wrench to remove a spindle on an Acme machine because you didn't want to bother requisitioning a spanner wrench. And the other day you used a hammer to make an adjustment because it was handier than the special tool provided.**

E. *(lowers his eyes)*

S. **Because you don't personally own a tool or piece of equipment doesn't make you any less responsible for it. It's a matter of dollars and cents. That spindle you abused costs $89.29 to replace. The price tag is fifty dollars or more to reshape that forming tool you adjusted improperly.**

E. *I guess I didn't think about that.*

S. **That's the problem, Jack. We forget to think. You owe it to yourself as well as the company to treat the tools and equipment you use as if they were your own. Mistreating company property is self-destructive. It not only boosts costs, but puts a bad mark on your record as well.**

• • • **TALKING POINTS**   A good way to get employees to take care of company assets is to convince them that it's in their personal best interest to do so and self-defeating to be abusive. It helps to make employees aware of the high cost of tools and equipment these days and to sustain that awareness. If a worker knows that a machine costs $23,000 or that a special wrench costs $78, he will automatically have respect for these items. Finally, it goes without saying that employees should never be permitted to use tools or equipment unless they have been properly trained to do so.

chapter ten

· · · · · · · · · · · · · · · ·

ENCOURAGING INITIATIVE

It was with a great deal of thought that a half century or more ago IBM placed plaques and placards in its home and customers' offices with the word THINK on them. Left alone, most people give little thought to the day-to-day tasks they perform. The status quo was good enough yesterday, it will be good enough today, and tomorrow is too far away to think about. The trick, if quality performance is your goal, is to come up with strategies and incentives that get people to question and challenge their jobs and suggest ways to improve them. As creatures of habit, we are accustomed to repetition in the things we do from when we get up in the morning to when we turn in at night. The smart supervisor encourages subordinates by means of inspiration and incentives to create new, different, and better ways to do their job.

DIALOGUE ONE

Bored by her job, Arlene, an intelligent, well-qualified employee, has started scanning the want ads.

Talking It Out

Supervisor - I hear via the grapevine that you're thinking of making a change. What's the problem? Is it the money? The work? Has someone been mistreating you?

Employee - (ill at ease) No, nothing like that.

S. What then? I've always had a high regard for you. You're a valuable member of the department. You're intelligent, know your job, get along well with co-workers. I would hate to lose you. Let's talk about it. Maybe we can work something out.

E. I don't know what to say. It's nothing I can put into words, nothing specific.

S. Then it must be something general. Do you feel you don't have enough opportunity for advancement?

E. (hesitates) I don't know; that may be part of it.

S. (smiles) I wish I was a better detective. Give me a hint.

E. Well, one thing that bugs me is I do the same thing day after day. But I guess that's the nature of the job.

S. That always a problem, but it's not insurmountable. All jobs have an element of repetition, some more, some less. Some people thrive on dull routine; others hate it. That it drives you up a wall is a testimonial to your intelligence and imagination. If you had your druthers, what would you rather be doing?

E. I'm not sure. I'd want the work to be more challenging and interesting, not the same darned thing all the time.

S. Okay, let's think about that. When you complete your part of that daily report, what do you do with it?

E. I just do the preliminary phase. After that, it goes to Peggy for Phase Two. She completes the processing and checks the final figures to make sure they balance.

S. How would you feel if, instead of passing what you do to Peggy all the time, you alternated with her. Sometimes you would do Phase One, sometimes Phase Two. Same thing for Peggy.

E. (face brightens) That would be great. I'd like it much better. So would Peggy.

S. (smiles) See? I told you the problem wasn't insurmountable. Let's give it a try and talk again.

• • • **TALKING POINTS** Boredom defeats initiative. It's impossible to eliminate repetition entirely from routine work, and most jobs are routine. But there are many ways to spark job interest and thereby encourage initiative. One, as illustrated by Arlene's situation, is division of labor on a daily job or project basis. Another is to simply switch tasks periodically. Change—any kind of change—is often a welcome reliever of boredom. The more mindless a task, the greater the monotony factor and also, the easier to make switches. Plus, the more switches put into effect, the more diversified and flexible the work group becomes. This becomes especially useful when employees are out sick or on vacation. As an added caution, however, keep this disclaimer in mind: Some people prefer mindless routine. Reasons vary. One person may be so lacking in self-confidence, the less challenging the job, the greater the feeling of security. Others are qualified for simple tasks but struggle with work where decisions are needed or problems encountered. Finally, in some mindless tasks performance isn't hampered by conversational interaction, which can be beneficial to the work itself.

DIALOGUE TWO

In asking for a higher-level job, customer-service employee Jeff takes the status quo for granted.

Talking It Out

Employee - I've been in this department six months longer than Ed Horlick as a Grade Two compounder. It's not fair bypassing me and advancing Ed to Grade One, especially since I have seniority.

Supervisor - Did you ever ask yourself why you were bypassed?

E. Sure, and I didn't come up with a reasonable answer.

S. Maybe that's because you didn't take into account all the key factors involved when a promotion decision is made.

E. Like what? I thought seniority was supposed to mean something around here.

S. It means a great deal. But it's only one factor.

E. I know that. Experience also counts. So do education and training. I have the same training as Ed, and even more experience.

S. You're overlooking the most important factor of all.

E. What's that?

S. Performance.

E. There's nothing wrong with my performance.

S. I didn't say there was. But there's nothing outstanding about it either. That's where Ed has the edge. If your performance was as good as Ed's you would have gotten that promotion because of the other factors, or even if it was almost **as good. My responsibility as a supervisor is to select the person best qualified for the job. Jeff, even though your performance is satisfactory, Ed's was so far superior it was no contest.**

E. Superior, how?

S. Well, apart from a slight edge in attendance and productivity, what was most notable is his participation in the company's suggestion program. Ed's come up with seven suggestions in the past eight months. Four were accepted. One of them is saving the company $180,000 a year; another cut processing $42,000. How many ideas did you come up with?

E. (reluctantly) None.

S. I hope that answers your question. Try to see the situation objectively. In my place, who would you pick for the job?

E. Yeah, I see your point. I guess it's a matter of luck. Opportunities to come up with suggestions never seem to come my way.

S. That's where you're mistaken. Luck is rarely a factor. Opportunities don't just happen; it takes initiative to make them happen.

E. How?

S. No one said it was easy, but you had the same chance as Ed. You were both exposed to the same problems and challenges. A better way to do a task is usually there if you look for it. The trick is to keep your eyes open and question every part of every job. Is there a better way to do this or that? A faster way? A less costly material? A more efficient tool? Ed questioned these things and came up with some answers. You took them for granted. That's why Ed got the promotion.

E. (frowning skeptically) Maybe I don't have enough imagination.

S. Wrong again. We all have imagination. But too many of us permit it to rust instead of cultivating it. It's like your car's engine. If it lies idle, it rusts out. Take my word for it, Jeff, if Ed can do it, so can you. Try it some time. You may be surprised by the outcome, and I'm here to help if you need me. Who knows? If you do, next time a promotion list is posted, your name may be on it.

E. I'll give it a try. Thanks for the tip.

• • • **TALKING POINTS**   THERE'S ALWAYS A BETTER WAY is a great credo to live by and a good message to get across to your people. The easy and most common job approach is to follow the leader. If it was good enough for grandpa it's good enough for me. If everyone adopted that philosophy the word initiative wouldn't be in the dictionary and progress would never be made. The trick for a supervisor is to: 1) Hammer this credo home to his or her people; 2) Show them how they can profit and grow by adhering to it.

DIALOGUE THREE

Fran is justifiably restless. She deserves a raise, but a wage freeze prevents you from giving it to her.

Talking It Out

Supervisor - How's it going, Fran? Correct me if I'm wrong, but you're looking kind of disgruntled these days.

Employee - (shrugs) I didn't think it showed. To tell the truth, I feel I'm beating my head against a stone wall in this company. My ratings have been consistently high, but where does it get me?

S. That's a fair question. The problem is, things are tight around here, and you're earning top money in your job classification.

E. With that information and a quarter I can make a local telephone call.

S. I know. I've been trying to get your wage level unfrozen.

E. You said that last time. How long am I supposed to hang around in the hope that one of these years you may succeed?

S. **Good point. I can appreciate your frustration. You're one of my best people and I admire your initiative. I would hate to see you leave.**

E. *Thanks for the compliment, but my bank doesn't accept compliments in lieu of cash.*

S. **(smiles) There must be something we can do. Remember that idea you told me about a couple of months ago?**

E. *The one to eliminate purchase orders on requisitions under $100?*

S. **Right. I thought it had merit and asked you to give it more thought and write it up as a formal suggestion. But you never got back to me.**

E. *(shrugs) I figured, what's the use? You don't get the recognition you deserve around here.*

S. **I sympathize with the sentiment. But do me a favor just this once. Expand on that idea and get it down on paper. I don't care how rough it is. I'll work with you to refine the idea and hand it in to the Suggestion Committee.**

E. *(looks skeptical)*

S. **You have nothing to lose. I think it stands a good chance of acceptance in which case you'll win a suggestion award. And if it's accepted I want to use it as a lever to sell management on unfreezing that wage level, creating a new classification for you, or getting you transferred to a better-paying job in another department. I can't give you any guarantees, Fran, but I think it's worth making the effort. Will you go along with me on this?**

E. *Okay, and thanks for trying to help.*

• • • **TALKING POINTS** One way to hang on to outstanding people is by cashing in on their initiative. Gaining management recognition by means of money-saving, money-making, and time-saving ideas is the quickest and surest way to jump-start a career. Whatever your level, the key to recognition and growth lies in calling yourself to management's attention. A smart executive knows that creative and aggressive employees are too valuable to turn off or lose. Pounding this fact home to your people is: 1) A good way to spark initiative and keep it fueled; 2) A good way to get your own wheels spinning as well.

DIALOGUE FOUR

Production Department's Harry has a lively imagination but doesn't take advantage of his creative potential.

Talking It Out

Supervisor - Harry, you've been in this department almost three years. This morning, out of curiosity, I did a rough estimate of how much money your idea to spray paint the cabinet display panels after final assembly instead of before is saving the company. It's an impressive amount. That idea was a gem.

Employee - Thanks.

S. As I recall you won a nice award for that brainstorm. But for Pete's sake, that was two years ago! Since then not a single idea. Has the old well dried up? You certainly proved you have the potential.

E. I don't know. That spray painting brainstorm was a stroke of luck. It just came to me.

S. That's hard to believe. Ideas don't 'just come' as a rule without a lot of thought and effort directed at a particular problem or need.

E. What am I supposed to do? Sit down with a pad and pencil and meditate?

S. That would be a step in the right direction. But what helps most is finding a mental hook to hang your thoughts on.

E. That's easy to say. But isn't that what the professional systems geniuses are paid to do?

S. Sure, but from one standpoint a guy like you has an edge over the pros. You're on the line working with the procedures and tools and materials day in and day out. You're continuously exposed to every aspect and facet of the job. No one understands the problems and needs better than the guy with the hands-on experience. You have the detailed, step-by-step knowledge. When mistakes, delays, or problems occur, you're the one who has to deal with them. No one's better qualified than you to track down the problem and sometimes the solution as well. Like you demonstrated with that spray painting suggestion.

E. Maybe so, but I'm not a scientist, or engineer; I don't even have a college degree.

S. Harry, you have a degree in on-the-job expertise which is sometimes more useful than a college degree, even if there's no piece of paper to prove it. That spray painting idea won you a nice piece of change and helped you get a promotion. The trick is to focus on problems and come up with alternate ways to do the job, however wild they may seem. Then come to me with your brainstorm and we'll refine it together. You did it once; you can do it again.

E. Okay, let me give it some thought.

S. That's all it takes, buddy.

• • • **TALKING POINTS**   It takes more than creative ability to come up with ideas. A mix of motivation and self-confidence is also needed. Harry's rationale is common in the workplace: If the systems pros can't solve the problem, how can I be expected to? The message to bring home to your people, as Harry's boss put it, is that the detailed insights provided by on-the-job, day-to-day, step-by-step exposure to the work and its requirements, give line employees a unique advantage no book learning can match. It's a reality of business life that should be made clear on an ongoing basis.

DIALOGUE FIVE

Gary is a good supervisor. But his department rarely participates in the company's suggestion program.

Talking It Out

Manager - Gary, have you seen the latest Suggestion Program Summary?

Supervisor - (glum) Yeah.

M. Your operation's down near the bottom again. Let's talk about that. Maybe we can find out why.

S. I've been racking my brain. If the crew doesn't come up with ideas, I don't know how I can make them.

M. You can't *make* them. But you may be able to provide a trigger or two to stimulate the process.

S. Trigger? What do you mean?

M. Another word might be reminder. When was the last time you gave your people a pep talk about the suggestion program?

S. I guess a long time ago.

M. Maybe that's the problem. People rarely come up with ideas automatically or on the spur of the moment. It can happen, but more often people need to be reminded that a suggestion program exists, and that participation can be satisfying and rewarding. Someone once said that ideas are the starting points of all fortunes. Also, a good idea is the most effective career booster I know. If you get this message across periodically you may be surprised by the results it can produce.

• • • **TALKING POINTS** Most people take their jobs for granted. Unless prodded, today will be no different from yesterday, and tomorrow will be no different from today. Everyone directly or indirectly involved cashes in on the good idea: the company's stockholders, management, customers, you as a supervisor, and the creator most of all. Employees rarely think in these terms. They need reminders from you.

DIALOGUE SIX

Accounts Payable Department Supervisor Sally is a conscientious hard worker. But she's spinning her career wheels because she's satisfied with the status quo.

Talking It Out

Manager - Sally, let's take a look at the semiannual Departmental Performance Review. It covers 14 departments and rates each one individually. Your operation's rating is just barely satisfactory. Are you satisfied with the rating?

Supervisor - No. Of course I'd like it to be better.

M. So would I. That's a start. Out of the 14 departments covered, 4 are rated outstanding, 6 good, 3 satisfactory, and one unsatisfactory. That puts Accounts Payable at the bottom third of the pile. It could be worse. But it's certainly nothing to crow about. Any comments?

S. I don't know. I certainly work hard enough. Lately I've been putting in a lot of extra hours.

M. I know. Too many extra hours. That's one of the reasons I summoned you. A supervisor shouldn't have to put in a whole lot of overtime to do a good job.

S. (unhappy, doesn't comment)

M. Suppose we take a closer look at the report and take Mae's credit department as an example. One thing that boosted Credit's rating was its increased suggestion program participation. Another was attendance improvement. A third was faster transaction processing. When I asked Mae to what she attributed the increase, she had a one-word reply that might be of special interest to you: Delegation.

S. Delegation.

M. That's right. Correct me if I'm wrong, but from what I've observed of your operation, you've simply been too busy to do much delegating. Am I mistaken?

S. (thoughtful) No, I guess that's true.

M. Sally, it's a fact of management life that if you're too busy to delegate, it means you're too busy to provide a cushion of time for yourself. Supervisors should provide for themselves a certain amount of quiet, preferably uninterrupted time each week to contemplate various aspects of the job: attendance, productivity, motivating employees, and departmental problems and logjams in particular. I have a suggestion. Sit down at your desk for a few minutes to list as many tasks as you can that you have been doing yourself and could possibly delegate. Alongside each task enter the employee best qualified to take it over. Then work up a program to act on it, setting deadlines for each task on the list. The more work you delegate, the more time you provide for creative initiatives, the more qualified and productive your people will be, and the less time pressures you will put on yourself.

• • • **TALKING POINTS**   You wouldn't have been given supervisory responsibility for a department or work group if you weren't capable of developing creative initiatives. But that old bugaboo "too busy" can cripple initiative faster than the sun can melt ice. It is worth repeating that supervisors who are too busy to provide creative time for themselves are too busy to function productively. Nine times out of ten, the solution to this dilemma is delegation.

chapter eleven

• • • • • • • • • • • • • • • • • • • •

BOOSTING MORALE

When you're forced to do something, you do it because you have no other choice: it's your job to do it, or else. When you're *asked* to do something, you do it as a favor or because it would be selfish, or foolish to refuse. Say someone asked you to bring back a container of coffee when you go out to lunch, for example. When you're *motivated* to do something, you do it because you want to do it and get the benefit involved—for instance, taking on an extra workload, or signing up for a training course because it will help your career. Clearly, employees function most effectively when motivated, whether self-motivated, supervisor-motivated, or a combination of both. No less clearly, the more effective the motivation, the higher the employee morale.

DIALOGUE ONE

Shelly in Statistics fulfills routine assignments in a lackadaisical manner. Since she sees no chance for advancement, she sees no sense in exerting extra effort.

(Department Head Joe Farrow discusses Shelly's morale with Alice, her group leader.)

Talking It Out

Supervisor - Alice, correct me if I'm wrong, but from what I've observed, Shelly's morale leaves much to be desired.

Group Leader - I can't argue with that.

S.   What's the problem?

G.L. I'm not sure. On the one hand, she needs the job, on the other she acts as if she doesn't care if she loses it.

S.   Any idea why?

G.L. Nothing specific. Her performance is no better than her attitude, in the gray area between satisfactory and marginal. Nothing flagrant enough to jeopardize her job, but that's the best I can say for her.

S.   People like that we can live without.

G.L. I agree.

S.   Tell me something: Does she act that way consistently?

G.L. No, that's the funny thing. She's a smart woman. Every so often she comes up with an idea, or performance, that surprises me.

S.   That's interesting. Can you narrow it down, pinpoint circumstances to explain her occasional resurrection?

G.L. Nothing I can think of offhand.

S.   Let me make a suggestion. Check back over her record for the past six months or so. Try to pinpoint assignments where her performance was better than usual, and see if you can find a common denominator.

(Alice reviews assignments and the dialogue with Farrow is resumed.)

G.L. Her overall performance hovers around average or lower. But she seems to do much better when assigned to sales analysis or special reports for Mr. King.

S.   Hmmm. Those are more complicated and challenging assignments, aren't they?

G.L. I guess you could say so.

S. **Would you also say there's more status attached?**

G.L. Definitely. Those jobs are the plums.

S. **That should tell us something. It might be a good guess to say that Shelly takes more pride in those assignments than her usual work.**

G.L. You may have a point there.

S. **Does she get special recognition for that work? Compliments? Pats on the back?**

G.L. From Mr. King, perhaps.

S. **What about you?**

G.L. I don't remember. I'm so busy all the time. Probably not.

S. **It's something to keep in mind, Alice. Among effective motivational tools, taking pride ranks close to the top. One way to fuel pride is with assignments people are delighted to accept. Another way is with occasional pats on the back when deserved. Give it a try. You may be surprised by the difference it makes.**

• • • **TALKING POINTS** If a dollar value could be attributed to motivational tools, compliments would exact a high price. A variety of ways exist to spark and stimulate pride: 1) Being part of an outstanding work group; 2) As a member of a company that stands out from its competitors; 3) Doing a tough, demanding job well; 4) Working with exceptional teammates; 5) Being held in high-esteem by a supervisor you respect; 6) Recognition for work well done. Consider them all.

DIALOGUE TWO

Herb's morale leaves much to be desired because he's mismatched with his work group.

Talking It Out

Supervisor - How long have you been in the Specialty Products Department, Herb?

Employee - A little over six months.

S. Before that you were in Receiving for a year. Your performance and attitude ratings were much better there. What happened?

E. What do you mean? Nothing happened.

S. That's hard to believe. When a person's performance and morale decline there's usually a reason to explain it. Am I right to assume you were happier in Receiving than in Special Products despite your having been transferred here at higher pay as a reward for your good work?

E. (clearly uncomfortable) Yeah, I suppose so.

S. What's the problem? Is the work harder, or less pleasant?

E. The work's okay.

S. Is the problem your co-workers?

E. (hesitates) I got no complaints.

S. (sniffing a breakthrough) Are you sure? The reading I get is that something's bothering you. Let's have it, Herb.

E. (reluctantly) I don't want to sound like I think everyone's out of step but me. . .

S. But?

E. Well. . . I just don't seem able to get along with Jerry Shea and some of those other guys in the group. We seem to clash. I'm not saying it's their fault.

S. (nods thoughtfully) That happens. People working together aren't always compatible. Thanks for leveling with me. I'll think about it and get back to you later.

(Supervisor discusses the interview with Herb's group leader, Bill.)

Supervisor - Bill, what's your reading on the situation? What do you think of Herb's remark about not getting along?

Group Leader - It doesn't surprise me.

S. Why is that?

G.L. A couple of things. For one, there's a pretty strong clique in the group. Shea and his pals are rough, hard-drinking guys. Herb's soft-spoken and keeps to himself. Also, he's the oldest guy in the group. My feeling is that Shea and company might be prejudiced on that account.

S. (nodding) How does Herb rate as a worker?

G.L. Above average, but he doesn't measure up to his potential.

S. In a more compatible group, do you think he might do better?

G.L. I can't guarantee it, but it wouldn't surprise me.

S. Okay. I think it might be time to do a little shifting around. Let's give it a try.

• • • **TALKING POINTS** Off the job a person is free to accept or reject friends and associates at will. On the job it's another story. It's not uncommon for employees to be teamed up with people who, for one reason or other, are incompatible. The teammates one works with can have a strong influence in shaping attitude, morale, and performance. Employees resent having to work alongside individuals with whom they don't get along. The worst cases of incompatibility involve prejudice due to age, gender, religion, race, and ethnicity. It makes good supervisory sense to evaluate team members in terms of their similarities and dissimilarities, likes and dislikes. A useful rule of thumb is that if people are unlikely to click off the job, they would probably have difficulty working harmoniously toward common goals on the job.

DIALOGUE THREE

Jane Wilson, an ambitious and disgruntled secretary, feels she is inadequately compensated.

Talking It Out

Employee - Mr. Gordon, I think I'm long overdue for an increase.

Supervisor - I wish I could put you in for one. But at the moment most employees, including myself, are limited by constraints of the wage structure and table of organization.

E. A friend of mine with a job similar to mine is employed by one of our competitors and earns 30 percent more than I do. I don't think that's fair.

S. Every situation is different. Also, there's more than one kind of compensation.

E. Maybe so, but I'll take the cash.

S. (smiles) **All right, let's consider this from a purely financial stand-point. We both know you're ambitious. I have no insight into your friend's job or company, but I know this company's policy is to promote from within. Since you're one of the most valuable peo-ple in the department that means you have already chalked up a good number of career Brownie points with the future in mind—Brownie points you would lose if you made a fresh start else-where.**

E. (thoughtful, but no comment)

S. Also, I can think of no company with a better training program than ours. You're smart enough to know that's money in the bank.

E. That's true. I didn't think of that.

S. Another thing you may not have thought of is that secretaries in this company enjoy a unique status. You are less regimented than most other employees, more flexible with regard to such things as working hours, lunch periods, and so on. In fact, I could compose a list of special privileges you enjoy.

E. Still. . .

S. Let me finish. I don't like to blow my own horn, but getting back to dollars and cents, I don't have to tell you that your immediate superior is a key factor when it comes to career progress and growth. I think you have to agree that the personal time and effort I devote to your training and development are second to none in the field.

E. (enthusiastic) I couldn't agree more with that.

S. Thank you. Jane, my advice is to be patient. Your turn will come if you give it a chance.

• • • **TALKING POINTS** No employee, however bright and knowledgeable, is any better than his or her morale. There's no question that inadequate compensation is a primary morale buster and an invitation to explore green-er pastures. Talented and experienced employees who feel they are under-compensated can be especially problematical, particularly where a signifi-cant investment in training and grooming is involved. Where a compensa-tion complaint is justified your best bet is to make an upward adjustment if possible. Your next best recourse is honest persuasion. As Gordon made clear to Jane, money isn't the only payoff for work well done. Other forms of compensation range from special training and privilege to choice assignments and a host of status inducers.

DIALOGUE FOUR

Bill's morale problem stems from the perception that his work isn't appreciated.

(Bill's attitude concerns Engineering Manager Gerald Teller who discusses the situation with Project Leader Ted, Bill's direct supervisor.)

Talking It Out

Manager - Ted, what's the problem with Bill? He seems to lack the get-up-and-go and enthusiasm he used to have.

Supervisor - I don't know. Something's bothering him, but I can't figure out what.

M. Does he get along with his associates?

S. Far as I can see. That's never been a problem.

M. Domestic problems?

S. I asked him about that. He assured me everything at home is okay.

M. What about the work itself? Is he satisfied with his assignments?

S. He's made no complaints along that line.

M. And you say he's well-qualified?

S. Absolutely. He's one of the best engineers in my group.

M. Does he know you feel this way?

S. I assume so. I never criticize his work.

M. What about the flip side of the coin? How often do you compliment him?

S. (frowning) I don't know. I'm always so busy I don't have time. . .

M. Maybe that's the problem, Ted. You can't automatically assume an employee knows you think well of him. You have to demonstrate it tangibly with an occasional pat on the back or compliment

before a third party. A need we all share is to know our work and expertise are appreciated. I think it was Mark Twain who once said, "I can go for two months on a good compliment." Give it a try. It could make a big difference.

• • • **TALKING POINTS**   One more time let's attack that old bugaboo, "too busy." There is no accounting for employee perceptions of how you feel about their work. It is an area of people management every supervisor should ponder and explore. If you are too busy to let your good people know how much you value them, you could be creating a morale problem you don't suspect. Recognition is a vital human need. Failing to acknowledge it is an all too common demotivator.

DIALOGUE FIVE

Betty doesn't realize it but her questionable morale could be improved if she were given more opportunities to solve problems and make decisions on the job.

Talking It Out

Manager - Betty, is that report ready yet?

Employee - I hit a snag, Mr. Philips. I can't figure out how to make the returns balance out. Usually George helps me when I get into a bind, but he's at a meeting.

M. What seems to be the problem?

E. I'm not sure. The Column A figures were taken from last month's estimate, but I don't understand how they were arrived at.

M. In that case, I'm not surprised by the difficulty you're having. What don't you understand about the Column A figures?

(Betty and Mr. Philips discuss the report. But instead of solving the problem for her, the manager explains to Betty what she needs to know to come up with the solution herself.)

M. When you run into a snag like this what does George usually do?

E. Oh, he's very helpful. I tell him the problem and he completes the report for me.

M. Don't you find it frustrating, not being able to complete your own work?

E. I guess so. I never thought about it that way.

M. Now that you understand what was confusing you, do you think you can complete the report on your own?

E. I'm not sure. George usually does it.

M. This time, why don't you see if you can complete it yourself.

(A couple of hours later Betty, all smiles, sets the report on Mr. Philips's desk.)

E. (beaming) It's all done. Everything balances.

M. Congratulations! I knew you could do it. It makes you feel much better, doesn't it, when you complete a job on your own?

E. It sure does.

M. Let's try to do more of that in the future. It's more satisfying to complete work yourself, and more interesting too. And as frosting on the cake, it helps you build your self-confidence.

(Later Mr. Philips has a talk with George and urges him, on the one hand to give his people guidance when it's needed, but on the other to encourage them as far as possible to solve their own problems and make their own job decisions.)

• • • **TALKING POINTS** Enhanced problem-solving and decision-making capability increases job interest and satisfaction and automatically boosts morale. Like Betty, most employees don't think in these terms. It's your responsibility as a supervisor to do it for them. Unconsciously, when people complete challenging tasks independently they give themselves a mental pat on the back. And if you supplement that morale builder with a deserved pat of your own it can't help but reinforce the benefit.

DIALOGUE SIX

Charlie probably wouldn't admit it even to himself, but his perceived lack of status contributes to his low morale.

(Marketing Services Supervisor Ben Broome discusses the state of Charlie's morale with Assistant Supervisor Frank Sauter.)

Talking It Out

Assistant Supervisor - I have a feeling Charlie may be flying the coop one of these days.

Supervisor - That would hurt the department, but it doesn't surprise me. His attitude in recent weeks leaves something to be desired. What do you think we can do about it? Charlie's a good man; I'd hate to lose him.

A.S. I couldn't agree more. He's on my back for a raise again, and to be frank, he's overdue for one.

S.   I know. I sympathize with his frustration. But he knows as well as we do that wages are all but frozen around here since we lost the Acme contract. I'll try to squeeze out another five bucks, but that's the best I can do.

A.S. I doubt if that will satisfy him. He's pretty disgruntled.

S.   He's not the only one. When business declines everyone suffers. I've got my hopes pinned on getting the Walden contract and on one or two others coming through. When things pick up I'll probably be able to do better by Charlie, and a few others as well.

A.S. I'm hoping the same thing, but that's six months off at best. Charlie could use a morale shot before that.

S.   Let me think about it. Tell Charlie you talked to me and that I'll get back to him.

(Ben discusses the problem with his boss, Regional Manager of Marketing Arthur Fermery.)

Manager - I can appreciate your concern, Ben. Charlie's a good man. I'd hate to lose him. I suppose we could go for a five dollar raise,

explaining it's the best we can do right now under the circumstances and urge him to be patient.

Supervisor - Patience is hard to come by when a guy's denied the compensation he deserves and already has been patient for a long time.

M. I agree. I have another suggestion with that thought in mind. What's Charlie's job classification?

S. Clerk, First Grade.

M. That's not too impressive. In conjunction with the small increase why not upgrade his classification to Marketing Research Associate and see how that sits with him.

S. (thoughtfully) Like calling a garbage man a sanitation engineer. It might work.

(It wouldn't be fair to say that Charlie was thrilled with this arrangement. But he could hardly conceal his pleasure at the sound of his new job title and opted to be patient—for the foreseeable future at least.)

• • • **TALKING POINTS**   While money is a key motivator, it's no news to anyone that it is not the only one. Status, among other motivators, can also be quite effective. As one consultant puts it: "You can keep an antsy employee off your back for months with an impressive job title." It's no substitute for fair treatment and adequate compensation. But a good title can have a strong influence on how a person is perceived within and outside the organization, and equally important by him- or herself as well. It is human nature to want friends, relatives, neighbors and co-workers to think well of us. Job status derives from a combination of monetary compensation and pecking order rank. Both play major morale-building roles.

chapter twelve
· · · · · · · · · · · · · · · · · ·
DEALING WITH
ATTITUDE PROBLEMS

Entrepreneur Clement Stone wrote: "There is very little difference in people, but that little difference makes a big difference. The little difference is attitude. The big difference is whether it is positive or negative." Invariably, organizations and their subdivisions where employee attitudes are predominantly positive are more successful than those where attitudes are poor or marginal. Invariably, the individual who does most to shape an employee's attitude one way or the other is his or her immediate supervisor.

DIALOGUE ONE

John is a "yes man" who enthusiastically endorses every idea you propose.

Talking It Out

Supervisor - I see from your comments at this morning's meeting that you think my suggestion to relocate the storage bins is a good idea.

Employee - Yes sir. I sure do. I don't see how it can miss.

S. You were equally enthusiastic about my proposal last week to revise the inventory procedure, and the one the week before to eliminate clocking in the transmittal slips. In fact, you seem to be gung-ho for all my ideas.

E. I guess I am. No one comes up with ideas as great as yours.

S. Thanks. What did you think of Frank's argument for keeping the storage bins where they are?

E. He made some good points. But I agree with you they should be moved.

S. Why?

E. Well, uh, for all the reasons you cited.

S. I'll tell you something, John. The storage bins are going to stay put. I feel Frank's points against moving them are too strong to deny.

E. (moistening his lips) Oh.

S. Another thing that occurs to me, John, is that for as long as I can remember, I can't recall a single time that you spoke up against an idea of mine, or came up with an idea of your own although I've always considered you to be a pretty smart fellow.

E. (no comment, becoming uneasy)

S. John, you're also a pretty ambitious fellow, and I agree that currying favor with the boss may be a good way to get ahead. But I'll tell you something else. Unless your boss is a complete ninny, the one way not to curry favor is by being a "yes man." I respect and value outspoken opposition—even if I don't happen to agree with it—a lot more than mindless endorsement. I'm going to give you a tip for the future, John. Speak your mind honestly. Don't be a "yes man." You'll get a lot further much faster if you do.

• • • **TALKING POINTS** Productive improvement and growth derives more from an *exchange* of ideas than it does from bland, or blind acceptance. This applies equally whether the idea man is you and the "yes man" a subordinate, or if the idea man is your boss and the "yes man" is you. Smart supervisors make it clear to their people on a regular basis that they have high regard for honest and open disagreement, and encourage subordinates to speak their minds. The perpetual "yes" is a no-no.

DIALOGUE TWO

Estelle, who acts as if she knows all the answers, irritates co-workers and superiors alike.

Talking It Out

Supervisor - Estelle, where did you get the figures for that Product Stockout Projection report?

Employee - From last year's report. I factored in orders for the past six months.

S. You should have used the midyear report. Last year's figures distort the projection. Relying on your figures, some of Mr. Wolfe's purchase requisitions were thrown off. As a result we could run out of some items, and overload on others.

E. I'm sorry. I guess anyone can make a mistake.

S. That's true. But what bothers me about this one is that Gloria advised you to use the midyear reports. Why did you ignore her advice?

E. I don't know. I didn't think she knew what she was talking about.

S. Without even checking out if she was right or wrong?

E. I'm sorry. I should have checked it out.

S. This kind of thing has happened before: automatically assuming you are right and the next person wrong, then making a decision based on that assumption without checking it out.

E. (lowers eyes, no comment)

S. Estelle, you're a smart and valued employee. But you don't walk on water. It's bad enough for someone to act as if they know it all, but when they make business decisions based on that belief, they jeopardize the company's profit goals, and their own careers as well.

• • • **TALKING POINTS** Employees who act as if they know it all are not only annoying to work with, but detrimental to the operation if they are in a decision-making position. Harmonious interaction is contingent upon members of the team respecting each other's expertise and opinions as well as their own. However unpleasant it may be to bite the bullet, people like Estelle should be put in their place.

Dialogue Three

Maintenance department electrician Vincent acts as if he's being ripped off by the company.

Talking It Out

Supervisor - You're skating on thin ice, Vince. This is the second time this month I had to talk to you about leaving your work station for an excessive length of time. What do you have to say for yourself?

Employee - I had to go to the men's room.

S. That's bull and we both know it, unless you have a kidney or some other health ailment, in which case a doctor's note would be required.

E. (sulky, no comment)

S. I don't have to tell you the policy around here: Three strikes and you're out. Or maybe this job isn't important to you.

E. I have a family to support. I need it.

S. You don't act that way. What's the problem?

E. Okay, if you want it straight. I think I'm being ripped off by the company.

S. Ripped off? How?

E. Well, for one thing, I can't remember the last time I got a raise. For another, when there's overtime work I'm usually bypassed. Guys with less seniority than mine are getting a better deal.

S. Do you have any idea why?

E. (hesitates) The only thing I can figure is you got a grudge against me.

S. I wish I could convince you how wrong you are. I take pride in being objective. The way I run this department, an employee's length of service is important to me. But what counts most is the person's performance and attitude. No one knows better than you

how crummy yours has been in recent months. Shape up, Vince, and I'll put you back on the overtime list. You might even get that raise one of these days.

• • • **TALKING POINTS** What's the best way to handle an employee who thinks he's being ripped off by the company? First, and most important, make every effort to determine *why* the person feels that way. Don't automatically assume there's no valid reason. If the individual has a reasonable beef, do your best to accommodate it and alter his or her attitude. If, like Vince, the attitude is a byproduct of the person's poor performance and behavior, confront the problem realistically and let the employee know where he stands.

DIALOGUE FOUR

Addicted to rumors and gossip, Darlene would be more at home at a back fence than in an office environment.

Talking It Out

Supervisor - Darlene, what's this about Easton Products Co. taking over the company's export division?

Employee - I don't know. What do you mean?

S. I think you know what I mean. The story's been making the rounds, and from what I can gather it seems to have started with you. Half the people I've talked to credit you as the source. Where did you get this information?

E. I, uh, I don't remember. I guess I heard it somewhere.

S. Oh, you did? From a reliable source, I assume.

E. I, uh. . .

S. Darlene, you were in Mr. Crane's office the other day when Mr. Easton paid him a visit, weren't you?

E. (face flushes) Yes, I was.

S. Did you hear Mr. Easton say he was taking over the division?

E. No, but they were discussing the product line.

S. **Did Mr. Crane say anything that led you to believe a takeover was anticipated?**

E. No.

S. **That's what I thought. You simply put two and two together and got six. Then you circulated the rumor based on your wild assumption.**

E. (eyes lowered)

S. **Darlene, do you have any idea how damaging false rumors or gossip can be, especially when some people tend to make important decisions based on them? Would it surprise you to hear that a couple of employees have been shopping around for new jobs because of that rumor?**

E. I'm sorry. I didn't mean anything by it.

S. **I'm sure you didn't. Apology accepted. But next time please think through the possible consequences of what you say before you shoot off your mouth.**

• • • **TALKING POINTS**   Step One when a rumor circulates, and sometimes *before* if you know a rumor is likely to circulate, is to straighten your people out with the truth. In the early days of the computer thousands of employees quit their jobs or sought others because of false rumors that their operation was being automated and they would be thrown out of work. Equally damaging is gossip discrediting people for one reason or another. A good axiom to keep in mind is that the person who gossips *to* you, will probably gossip *about* you. Squelching rumors and gossip along with their perpetrators is a supervisory responsibility.

DIALOGUE FIVE

Production worker Peter has negative thoughts about life in general and himself in particular.

Talking It Out

Supervisor - Pete, I want to talk with you about your lack of cooperation, team spirit, and simple get-up-and-go.

Employee - What do you mean? I do the job I'm assigned to.

S. Maybe so, but there's more to the job than just following orders. There's the question of attitude.

E. What's wrong with my attitude?

S. It's hard to put into words. The impression I get is you simply don't give a darn. You don't show any initiative. You just "show up" if you know what I mean. You don't make suggestions. You don't volunteer for overtime. You haven't signed up for a training program in the two years you've been on the job. You're 26 years old and married with two children but you act like an old man about to retire. I get the feeling you don't like your job or resent being in the production department. Am I right?

E. (shrugs) The job's okay.

S. What kind of answer is that? You scored better than average in the tests you took when you were hired. In fact, you did exceptionally well in the problem-solving questionnaire, the kind of skill needed for computer programming. That's one of the reasons you were chosen over other applicants. Yet you didn't sign up for the company's programming course. Why not?

E. I didn't think I would pass.

S. You'll never know if you don't try. Don't you want to advance? Do you want to keep spinning your wheels?

E. (glum, no comment)

S. Pete, I wouldn't bring this up if I didn't think you had the ability.

E. I don't know. Half the things I try to do don't work out. Maybe I just don't have what it takes.

S. You had what it takes to get the job when you applied. You know, it's a funny thing about having what it takes. A lot of people actually have what it takes, but talk themselves out of it. What it often boils down to is that you're as good as you think you are. If you feel you can't make it, you probably won't. Have you ever heard about the power of positive thinking?

E. Yeah, sure.

S. Then why not try to apply it? Look at it this way. Suppose you signed up for one of those training courses and didn't pass. What would you lose? You'd be no worse off than before you signed up.

E. I guess that's true. I never looked at it that way.

S. Maybe this is a good time to start. I'm not going to twist your arm, but there's another trainee programming course starting next week. If you're interested I'll put your name in for it.

E. Okay, I'll give it a try.

S. Good man, Pete. I think you can make it.

• • • **TALKING POINTS**   The thoughts we have about ourselves affect the way we perform and the quality of our performance. The human brain is programmed much like a computer. We make choices based on our positive and negative inputs. As a supervisor you can latch onto and respond to your own inputs and those of subordinates. One of the most important developmental assists you can give your people is to acquire sensitivity to their negative thoughts and self-doubts and prop them up with assertions of confidence and belief where they seem warranted.

chapter thirteen

• • • • • • • • • • • • • • • • • •

MAKING MORE
EFFECTIVE DECISIONS

Decision-making skills aren't inherent, they must be learned. Decision making is one of the most complex and least understood processes of the human equation. From a career standpoint, the one absolute fact that can be said about it is that, with rare exceptions, the more important and highly compensated the job, the more demanding the decision-making requirement. The best way to learn how to make effective decisions is to face up to them courageously and make them repeatedly. There is no better teacher than experience. The next best way to learn is via the emulation and good counsel of an experienced decision maker. Towards this end smart supervisors can render a valuable service to their people.

DIALOGUE ONE

Plant Engineering Department Project Supervisor Bob Allen has trouble getting his group to make effective decisions.

Talking It Out

Manager - Bob, when am I going to get that report on the roofing job estimate?

Supervisor - I've got Jim Collins working on it. He says it's close to completion.

M. You told me that two days ago. What's the holdup?

S. I don't know. Most of the spade work is done. Jim seems to be having problems deciding which contractor to recommend for the job.

M. Last week a construction report was delayed because one of your guys couldn't decide what kind of materials to use. The week before the bottleneck was waffling on a security-system decision. What's the problem? These are all straightforward decisions based on hard facts.

S. The same question's been bugging me. I don't know what it is. I've got a staff of well-qualified engineers and technicians, but when it comes to decision making they act like sixth graders. Their self-confidence plunges.

M. That's something to think about. When confidence falls there's usually a reason behind it. Let's look at some of the specifics and see what we come up with.

(Bob and his boss review a number of projects that were backlogged due to faulty or delayed decisions and analyze what took place on a step-by-step basis.)

M. Bob, if there's one common denominator to these decisions it's this: The projects were all more or less unfamiliar to the people assigned to them. I can recall a study where psychologists found that when decision makers are familiar with the material involved decisions take less time and are more effective. Not that the material is more difficult, or the principles and conclusions unknown; it's mostly in the way the problems and facts are presented. If the assignment is presented in an unaccustomed way, it tends to produce a loss of confidence which results in decision-making delays and inefficiencies.

S. I guess that makes sense. What would you suggest?

M. Try this. In making nonroutine assignments, slow down a bit when turning them over to your people. Familiarize them if possible with the factors and aspects involved. If you can, refer to previous project reports that are similar and let them review them. Encourage them to repeat their understandings of the decision-making process requirement. Don't use language that intimidates them. It could make a big difference.

• • • TALKING POINTS   Repetition creates familiarity and stimulates self-confidence. It is human nature to fear what is new and different. The more complicated an assignment, the more important it is to inch your way into it slowly and thoughtfully. Invite questions. Ask employees to repeat your explanations and instructions to be sure their understandings coincide with your own.

DIALOGUE TWO

Sales Department Correspondent Frieda tends to make abrupt decisions without getting all the facts.

Talking It Out

Supervisor - Frieda, I just got a call from a customer who's fit to be tied. He says a whole batch of products was spoiled because you didn't tell him to set his sensitivity gauge on medium-soft when instructing him how to use the machine most effectively.

Employee - I assumed he knew that.

S. On what did you base that assumption? Did you read his letter carefully and check the file?

E. I read his letter, but I didn't check the file. My in-basket was starting to pile up. I was trying to save time.

S. More often than not, when you shortcut necessary steps, or neglect to get all the facts in the decision-making process you wind up losing more time than you save. This kind of thing happened before. You should know better by now.

E. I'm sorry. I'll try to be more careful in the future.

S. Apology accepted. In my experience, one of the most important questions to ask yourself before finalizing any decision is: "Am I well-informed on all aspects of the problem?"

E. Thanks. I'll keep that in mind.

• • • **TALKING POINTS** There's a Ford Motor Company story circulating in the field; it states that when company executives interview managerial-level job applicants, they try to observe if the candidates season their food with salt and pepper before tasting it. If they do, the conclusion is that such a person is apt to make decisions before getting all the facts. Whether the anecdote is true or spurious, or the reasoning valid, it's an interesting look at decision-making behavior. So, whether the person involved is yourself or a subordinate, it always makes good supervisory sense to check that significant facts are weighed before *any* decision is made.

DIALOGUE THREE

Faced with a decision to confront a nonproductive employee, Billing Department Supervisor Marge Neely keeps putting it off.

Talking It Out

Manager - Marge, Shipping's backed up again. They claim there are too many billing errors and duplicated back orders coming through.

Supervisor - I know. That problem's been bugging me.

M. Being bugged is the first step. What action are you taking in response? Do you know what, or who is responsible?

S. Well, Bonnie seems to be a major offender. I don't know how many times I talked to her. She keeps making the same mistakes.

M. How long do you intend to put up with it? Don't you think it's time to let her go?

S. I guess so. But I keep putting it off. She's one of my fastest billers, and she's a longtime employee.

M. It's that old beast postponement again. You keep telling yourself you'll do it tomorrow or next week, and when the day arrives you stall for another day or week. Am I right?

S. I'm afraid so. I keep rationalizing, making excuses of one kind or another.

M. Which only compounds the problem. Firing someone, especially a longtime employee, is one of the toughest decisions a supervisor has to make. But as a leader it's your responsibility to run an efficient and productive operation. Sometimes you have no choice but to bite the proverbial bullet. You have to consider the consequences of Bonnie's inefficiency on everyone concerned: Shipping, your own department, the company, and the customers whose orders are being delayed. In some cases it's in the unproductive employee's best interest as well. The person who can't perform well on the job just might be able to perform better at another type of job elsewhere.

S. (nodding) I guess I should have fired Bonnie long ago. I won't delay any longer.

• • • **TALKING POINTS** Hard decisions, in not being faced, create harder decisions that will have to be made. Step One is to ask yourself: What's the bottom line? Who's adversely affected by your inaction and how? Where profit and productivity goals suffer as a result of procrastination, your department's and your personal reputation suffer as well. One of the most common causes of procrastination, or equally harmful at times, half-measures, is that, as in the case cited above, taking action is unpleasant and painful. A good analogy is a toothache where a quick trip to the dentist might save the tooth, and where delay might necessitate extraction.

DIALOGUE FOUR

Fred is a "Do-It-Yourselfer." This has its advantages, but some serious disadvantages as well when decision-making help is required.

Talking It Out

Supervisor - Fred, fortunately I spotted this purchase requisition before it was processed.

Employee - Why, what's wrong with it?

S. Whatever prompted you to specify these Type 14A filters for the new electronic air-cleaning units?

E. I don't know. We've been using them for years.

S. On electronic units?

E. Well, no, but. . .

S. How much do you know about the electronic units and their requirements?

E. I never worked with them before, but since their efficiency was declining I figured it was time for the filters to be changed.

S. Fred, don't you know that in electronic air cleaners air drawn into the unit passes first through a prefilter to remove the large particles? It then enters an ionizer where smaller particles are electrically charged. It's a completely different system from the conventional units you're familiar with.

E. I didn't know that. I assumed the same kind of filters would be used.

S. In making decisions, where you lack knowledge or don't have all the facts, you can't make assumptions. You have to consult someone with more experience or know-how for advice. One of the engineers, for example, or myself.

E. (thoughtful) I realize that now. I figured why bother someone if I didn't have to. I prefer to make decisions myself if I can.

S. That's all to your credit. But that "if I can" proviso is a key question to explore. If you're not one-hundred percent sure of the answer, the sensible and safe course is to seek the help that you need.

• • • **TALKING POINTS**   It is a matter of pride with some people to operate independently, solve a problem, or make a decision on their own. The plus-side of self-dependence is that there is no better way to learn than the do-it-yourself route. In addition, making a hard decision on your own enhances your personal image while it bolsters your self-confidence. But the minus-side merits close attention. When you're not absolutely sure, solo decision making can involve a lot of extra time, as well as adversely affect the result by failing to take important information you don't have into consideration. On top of that, another viewpoint might broaden your outlook and thus enhance the decision. Keep in mind that seeking help or advice in wrestling with decisions or problems is more often a sign of intelligence and concern than a symptom of weakness.

DIALOGUE FIVE

Maintenance Department's Mark Hammond loses a lot of time making decisions that have already been made.

Talking It Out

Supervisor - I don't believe it, Mark! Do you mean to tell me that hoisting jig hasn't been built yet? You've been working on it most of the day. It should have been completed in a couple of hours or less.

Employee - I didn't goof off, I can give you my word.

S. I know you didn't. That's what makes me wonder why it's taking you so long. You're a skilled and experienced carpenter.

E. It's a complicated project. I ran into a couple of snags.

S. What kind of snags?

E. Well, for one thing, I had trouble figuring out what kind of brackets to use on this elbow. For another, I couldn't decide on which side of the support structure this spring should be placed.

S. No wonder it's taking so long. Let me ask you a question. Is this the first time a hoisting jig has been specified in a work order?

E. (frowning) No. Probably not.

S. Okay, now I'll ask you another question. When a jig is completed, what's the first thing you do?

E. Take a Polaroid picture of it and put in the file.

S. Why do you do that?

E. So that the next time around. . . . (light finally dawning) Oh boy, I'm a nut! All I had to do was go to the file and pull out a picture of the jig and I wouldn't have had to rack my brain trying to decide which bracket to use or where to place that spring! It would have saved me at least two or three hours.

S. You've got it, pal. Try to remember that the next time around. Once the barn has been found, finding it all over again wastes a whole lot of time.

• • • **TALKING POINTS** It is a common oversight people make: wrestling with decisions that have already been made. As in this example, a print may already be on file picturing a unit to be assembled or built. Where an assignment for a report is involved, a copy can be accessed displaying exactly what is needed column by column and total by total. Where a decision must be made with regard to a particular infraction, personnel records can be reviewed to ensure the discipline administered is consistent. Accessing prior documentation, or consulting individuals who already made the decision in question, can be of invaluable help from the standpoint of both time saving and accuracy. Make sure *in advance* that your subordinate takes advantage of a prior decision instead of wrestling with it anew. It just makes good supervisory sense.

DIALOGUE SIX

Customer Service Supervisor Anne sometimes has trouble deciding which employee to assign to a project.

(Sales Director Bill Fried informs Anne that Mr. Bostwick, a key customer, seeks advice on which items of the new product line would be best suited for his three stores in the suburbs. Her boss wants Anne to research the subject and work up a report on the line's sales potential as it applies to the customer. An important project, Anne can't make up her mind whether to assign it to Charlotte or Tony. She turns to Mr. Fried for advice.)

Talking It Out

Manager - What's the first name that came to mind when you considered whom to assign?

Supervisor - I can't say. It's almost like tossing a coin. Both Tony and Charlotte seem equally qualified.

M. Perhaps they are. Maybe you should toss a coin.

S. (frowning) I don't know. I think that would bother me for some reason.

M. Hmmm. Let's see if we can come up with the reason. Do your instincts favor one or the other?

S. (thoughtful) Not that I'm aware of.

M. In that case let me make a suggestion. This usually works for me; it might work for you too. Sit down at your desk with a blank sheet of paper and divide it into three columns. In column one at

the left, list all the attributes you can think of that would be needed by someone to do a first-rate job compiling that report. Why don't we do that together right now? (hands Anne a yellow-lined pad)

S. *Okay. (listing words as she speaks) Experience, knowledge of customer needs, analytical mind. . .*

M. (adding to list) Training, intelligence, ambition, writing ability, creativity. . . . Anything else you can think of?

S. *Not at the moment, but I may come up with another item or two. What goes into those other two columns?*

M. Head one up with *Tony,* the other with *Charlotte.* Then, on a scale of 1 to 5 rate your two candidates for each of the attributes listed. The one with the highest score should be the one to select.

(Following her boss's suggestion Anne goes through the exercise and finds that Tony's rating edges Charlotte's by more than 10 percent. With the decision made for her, she assigns the project to Tony.)

• • • **TALKING POINTS** Mr. Fried's charting system is a powerful decision-making tool used by consultants, executives, and supervisors. It is applicable to any and all kinds of decisions, and is especially useful in deciding which of two or more job choices to make. In some cases the plus and minus values are apparent. But where a decision is too close to call, the rating procedure can make the judgment for you and cut wrestling time to a minimum.

chapter fourteen

• • • • • • • • • • • • • • • • • • • •

MAKING MEETINGS PAY OFF

Search your memory. How many times can you recall being inaccessible to your people when urgently needed because you were tied up at a meeting? How often were priority tasks or projects delayed because you and your subordinates, or both, were in conference? How much creative supervisory time tackling problems and dreaming up ideas for improvement was sacrificed because of meetings you and your people attended? It has been estimated that some managers and supervisors spend as much as 70 percent of their time conferring with others. This is not to imply that most meetings are counterproductive. But it does underline the importance of one question before any meeting is called: <u>Is it necessary?</u> And the follow-up question: Is it being conducted efficiently and effectively? Or stated another way, has a worthwhile goal been defined, and is the meeting designed to accomplish this purpose?

DIALOGUE ONE

Customer Claims Supervisor Helen Rich calls too many meetings and ties up her people needlessly.

Talking It Out

Manager - Helen, I've been trying to reach you all morning. Where were you?

Supervisor - I was tied up in a meeting.

M. Another meeting! What was it this time?

S. The claims have been piling up and too many of them are being lost or misplaced. I felt I should get to the bottom of it.

M. A worthwhile objective. Do you think the meeting achieved this purpose?

S. Yes, I think a lot was accomplished.

M. That's great, but from what I can gather the pile-up is bigger than ever and your department even further behind.

S. I know. We're doing our best to catch up.

M. How many people attended the meeting this morning?

S. (calculating) Nine.

M. That's almost the whole department. I'd like to go over the list of participants with you if you don't mind.

(Helen compiles a list that she and her boss review together. The manager inserts check marks after four names on the list.)

M. I'm curious. What do Tom and Jean have to do with claims being lost or misplaced? They're word processors who handle the record-keeping end of the job.

S. That's true. But I figured as members of the department they might have some ideas to contribute.

M. Did they?

S. No, I guess not. They are too far removed from the problem.

M. What about Edgar and Sid? Aren't they pretty much removed as well from the actual clocking in and claims processing functions?

S. Yes, but I didn't want to offend them by leaving them out.

M. Helen, I know how important it is to get that handling problem resolved, but isn't it also important to keep the work flow moving?

S. Yes, I suppose it is.

M. I think you'll agree there's no way you can do this with most of the department tied up in a meeting while their work piles up further. Maybe it's true that the more heads applied to a problem the better. But you have to ask yourself: At what price?

S.   I see your point.

M. Good. Actually, when you boil it down, there are no more than three or four people directly involved in physically handling and processing these claims. Am I right?

S.   Yes, you are.

M. In that case, mightn't it have been just as effective to consult with those individuals one or two at a time rather than set up a big formal meeting to do it?

S.   (thoughtful) Yes, possibly. I'll have to give it some thought.

M. (smiling) That's all I'm asking you to do.

• • • **TALKING POINTS**   Is this meeting necessary? Too often the question is ignored. Except in rare cases meetings shouldn't be called on the spur of the moment. Cost-effectiveness is a critical factor. The reality should not be overlooked that if the hourly wages (and fringe benefits) of say, 8 employees included in a meeting amounts to $80, a three-hour session adds up to a total compensation cost of $240, plus the cost of your supervisory time. That's in addition to the cost of delays in processing customer shipments, invoices, cash receipts, reports, and the like. Keep in mind too, the high cost of inviting people to attend the meeting because they might feel slighted if not included. Also, ponder the likelihood that more work may actually get done faster with fewer participants.

DIALOGUE TWO

Ed snipes at every idea presented and contributes little himself.

Talking It Out

Supervisor - Ed, how do you think the meeting went this morning?

Employee - Okay, I guess. Why?

S. I got the impression you felt it wasn't very productive.

E. I don't know. Some good ideas were presented.

S. I agree. But you seemed to knock most of them down.

E. I only said what I felt.

S. No argument with that. It's what you should do. The trouble is when you were asked what you had against the reserve fund idea, for example, you had little to say in response. Same thing for the other ideas you objected to.

E. (fidgets uneasily)

S. On top of that—correct me if I'm wrong—but I can't recall a single suggestion of your own.

E. I guess nothing came to mind.

S. But plenty came to mind about those other suggestions. Ed, I don't want to beat a dead horse or embarrass you. But I want to make clear that the purpose of this meeting, and of most meetings, is to come up with money and time-saving ideas. There's nothing wrong with opposing an idea if you honestly feel it's not practical, if you have a solid reason to do so, and ideally can come up with an alternative suggestion. But saying an idea won't work because you don't like the suggester, or for some flimsy reason you didn't take the time or effort to think out in depth is another matter entirely. Do you understand what I'm talking about?

E. Yeah. I'll try to keep that in mind for the future.

S. Please do. Keep this in mind too. Your personal image is part of it. People who say no to ideas off the top of their heads create negative images for themselves. Being able to prove *why* an idea won't work can be very helpful. But consider this too. It is at least equally helpful, and beneficial from a personal point of view, to lend your support to an idea that makes sense and suggest ways and means to make it work.

• • • **TALKING POINTS** In an ideal meeting, ideas, however wild, feed and fuel other ideas, thus creating a chain to positive action. The chronic naysayer hampers this process. A cagey manager we know has developed an effective strategy for stopping negative participants in their tracks. In his role of moderator he pins down a suggestion's opponent with a hard and firm challenge: Why specifically do you think the idea won't work? What would you suggest in its place? He refuses to settle for vague or inconclusive responses. On the one hand, he encourages opposition. On the other, he makes clear to his people that if their no votes lack substance, both the meeting and their personal images would be better served if they kept their lips sealed.

DIALOGUE THREE

Joe's effectiveness at meetings suffers from his refusal to listen to the ideas and opinions of others.

(A meeting in progress is continuously bogged down by Joe's interruptions. When the meeting is over, in the privacy of his office, Joe's boss lays down the law.)

Talking It Out

Supervisor - Joe, I have some good news and bad news. The good news is that I appreciated your eagerness to contribute your ideas and opinions at this morning's meeting.

Employee - Thank you.

S. The bad news is that I wasn't thrilled by the way you went about it.

E. What do you mean?

S. Simply this: You're a smart guy with a good imagination, which makes you a useful participant at sessions like the one called this morning.

E. But?

S. You're right, there's a "but." Half the time you're so anxious to talk, you don't give the next person a chance. Like this morning, Ellen had some useful things to say about that rewiring proposal. But you stuck your two cents in before she barely got started. I had to intercede to get you to hold off and give her a chance. In fact, if you'll recall I had to do that three or four times.

E. Yeah, I guess I get carried away.

S. You sure do. Enthusiasm's a definite plus, but sometimes you need to keep it in check. You're an intelligent person, but you're not the only fish in the pond. Nor are you the only one capable of expressing good ideas and opinions. That's why it's so useful to have multidiscipled personnel at meetings designed to develop ideas and initiatives. Different perspectives brought to play in making decisions and solving problems can be valuable. Do me a favor, Joe, and yourself as well. Keep coming up with those ideas. But for Pete's sake, give the next person a chance too. Don't forget that when human beings communicate, listening is every bit as important as talking.

• • • **TALKING POINTS**   A critical and sometimes difficult responsibility of the meeting moderator is to keep one or two people from dominating the proceedings. Participants who are so anxious to get their own ideas across that they're reluctant to listen to others come in a variety of forms. Type One is the obnoxious character who thinks he or she is smarter than everyone else and knows all the answers, so why listen to anyone else? Type Two is the self-serving individual so anxious to sell his or her own ideas, he or she refuses to listen to others opposed to it. Type Three is a person who simply likes to hear him- or herself talk even with little or nothing to say. Type Four is the insecure person who refuses to listen because he or she feels the speaker poses a threat of some kind. The moderator's task isn't an easy one. This individual must determine which type he has to deal with, and take appropriate action to keep the motor-mouth in check.

DIALOGUE FOUR

Reticent Rita is a superior and knowledgeable employee, but her natural shyness makes her reluctant to speak up at meetings.

Talking It Out

Supervisor - Rita, that was a great idea you had to save time in processing rush orders.

Employee - Thank you.

S. **But I found squeezing it out of you harder than it would have been to pull an elephant's tooth.**

E. (blushes)

S. **That's why I called you into my office. You're a valuable member of this department. You're conscientious and hardworking. Equally important, you're bright, pick things up quickly, and have a lively imagination. I can't make specific commitments at this point, but I have interesting plans in mind for you. I think there's a good future for you here in this company. But I'd like to encourage you to be more aggressive, at meetings in particular. When you come up with a good idea like the one you had this morning, you shouldn't hesitate to express it.**

E. (frowning) I guess I'm kind of laid back.

S. **That's an asset at times, and it's preferable to being overly aggressive. But from a career-building standpoint, it's usually the person who's outspoken in a positive way that scores Brownie points by winning management recognition.**

E. Sometimes I hesitate to express an idea because I don't know when or where to stick in my two cents. Then, before I know it the opportunity has passed.

S. **That can be a problem. Let's try this. Meeting agendas are always distributed in advance. It might be a good idea for you to review the agenda beforehand, and come to me prior to the meeting if you have an idea that seems applicable. That way I'll have a chance at the meeting to bring up the subject and take the initiative in helping you share your thoughts.**

E. Thanks. I think that might be helpful.

S. **You're welcome. When someone like you has the potential it's a shame to waste it. A good idea is a springboard to progress and development. It benefits the department, the company, and the creator most of all. One way or other we have to cash in on the pearls.**

• • • **TALKING POINTS** Reticent people need a periodic charge to keep them performing up to their best potential. This applies not only to meetings but to every aspect of an operation. Fortunately for Rita, her supervisor is smart and savvy enough to understand that one way to spark initiative is with the help of well-deserved flattery. Another way is to come up with plans and incentives designed to encourage shy employees to climb out of their shells.

DIALOGUE FIVE

Shipping supervisor Al Morton conducts meetings that are twice as long as they should be.

(Al's boss, Plant Manager George Tandy, sits in on a meeting as an observer and subsequently discusses his findings with Al.)

Talking It Out

Manager - Al, what did you think of the meeting? Are you satisfied with how it went?

Supervisor - More or less.

M. Do you think you accomplished what you wanted to accomplish? Cover everything you intended to cover?

S. Yeah, mostly, except I never got to the stock picking backlog, or the problem with the freight tickets. I guess I'll have to call another meeting for that.

M. Why do you think you didn't get to those two items? They were on the agenda.

S. I don't know. I guess I didn't expect the meeting to run that long.

M. Do you mind if I offer a suggestion?

S. No sir, I'd welcome it.

M. Okay, I'll preface it with a question: How long did you expect the meeting to run?

S. Four or five hours at most. I didn't expect it to run all day.

M. My next question is how long did you *plan* for the meeting to run?

S. *(frowning) I didn't plan any specific time.*

M. Maybe that's why it ran into all that lengthy and expensive over-time. I note from the agenda that you listed seven topics you hoped to cover; you only covered five of them. If you *planned* your coverage I think you might have included all seven in less time.

S. *I don't get it. How could I know how long people would talk, or how many ideas they might come up with?*

M. You don't know. But by controlling the time—allocating a given amount of time for each topic—you can set up your own time frame. An executive I know does this by setting a clock so an alarm will go off when each predetermined phase is completed. Unless you control a meeting it tends to get out of hand. People ramble, or veer off into tangents that aren't germane to the subject. When participants are aware you're working within a strictly disciplined time frame, they adjust their thoughts and contributions accordingly. Try it some time. You may be surprised at the result.

S. *Thank you. I will.*

• • • **TALKING POINTS** The meeting leader or moderator is the most crucial determiner in making a session either efficient or meandering. Some employees view meetings as annoying interruptions because they take them away from their work and make them fall behind. Others welcome the diversion because it relieves the day-to-day routine and drudgery. Any number of factors can cause a meeting to run overtime: 1) Diversion from the subject at hand; 2) Excessively wordy participants; 3) Inability of one or more people to express their thoughts clearly. Effective meeting control can be honed into a fine supervisory art if you work at it. The trick is to keep meetings on target and moving ahead briskly. To achieve this goal one manager we know holds meetings with participants standing up. "It's hard to be long-winded when you're on your feet," she says. One New York advertising account executive schedules meetings as close as possible to quitting time. When people are itchy to get home, he reasons, it tends to speed up the proceedings.

Dialogue Six

"Rambling Rose" hampers meeting effectiveness and waters down her own good ideas because she tends to talk on and on.

Talking It Out

Supervisor - I wanted to tell you, Rose, you expressed some interesting thoughts at that meeting this morning. You made an important contribution. We may be able to put one or two of your ideas into the works.

Employee - That's great, Mr. Price. Thank you.

S. Another thing you deserve to be complimented on is that you came to the meeting well prepared. It's almost as if you had written out in advance what you had planned to say.

E. As a matter of fact, I did. I had it all worked out in advance.

S. I thought so. That's the best way to operate. But if you don't mind I'd like to suggest a way to make your meeting participation even more effective in the future.

E. I don't mind at all. I'd appreciate it.

S. Good. You may recall that I had to interrupt you a number of times because you went off track and were getting too wordy.

E. Yes, I remember that. It sort of threw me off at the time.

S. I apologize for that. I'd like to draw an analogy that might help in the future. Formulating and presenting an idea can be compared to writing a book or article. Experienced authors first work up a rough draft, then review it, simplify what they have to say, and dispose of unneeded thoughts and words. Many authors do this again and again, paring down prose until the final version is a fraction of the size of the original but ever so much sharper, clearer, and more interesting. I remember reading somewhere that Leon Uris's original manuscript of *Exodus* was nearly ten times the size of his final work.

E. (nods) I think I'm beginning to get the point.

S. (smiling) I knew you would. Your presentation at the meeting was great. But you tend to ramble and go off on tangents when you

speak. It's a common failing that not only drags out a meeting and makes people restless, but dulls the impact and bite of the points you are trying to put across. Next time, try a little revision beforehand and see how much more effective you'll be.

• • • **TALKING POINTS**   As a meeting moderator if you do nothing more than keep the "Rambling Roses" in line you will add greatly to the meeting's effectiveness. When it comes to this all too common deterrent, the standard rules of politeness no longer apply. Interrupt when you must. It may take a bit of self-discipline but the faster you clamp down on the compulsive talker and off-track participant by cutting into the monologue, the more exacting the proceedings will be.

chapter fifteen

● ● ● ● ● ● ● ● ● ● ● ● ● ● ●

WINNING
AND KEEPING RESPECT

As a supervisor you can't insist on respect; you have to earn it. Nor can you expect others to respect you if you don't first respect them. Experience indicates that the level of success achieved by an organization or work group is usually directly proportional to the level of respect achieved by its leader. In employee survey after survey consultants' findings indicate that the source of problems and poor performance reported can in most cases be traced to the leader's failure to win the respect of his or her subordinates.

DIALOGUE ONE

Sales Correspondent Joe Curran pooh-poohs the opinions and ideas of his peers.

Talking It Out

Supervisor - Joe, where have you been these past six weeks or so?

Employee - What do you mean? I've been here on the job.

S. **If that's so how come you're still running to the copier machine when duplicate copies of letters or reports have to be made? Alice's idea to run them off on the laser printer makes a lot more sense. It's done faster, it costs less, the machine's right at hand, and you don't tie up the copier. The suggestion was put into effect six weeks ago. Everybody complies with it but you.**

E. *I don't know. Alice is a jerk. Most of her ideas are half-cocked.*

S. **They are? And you in your infinite wisdom are a good judge of that?**

E. *Okay, okay, from now on I'll use the laser printer.*

S. **Thank you. But quite frankly, Joe, your attitude concerns me more than this matter of the duplicate copies. In your opinion is Alice the only jerk in the department, or do others qualify as well?**

E. *(face flushes) Hey, get off my back. I didn't mean that exactly. But that dame irritates me. She's always spouting off one thing or another.*

S. **"One thing or another?" You mean like ideas, or suggestions?**

E. *Yeah, I suppose.*

S. **And you think that's a dumb thing to do?**

E. *(embarrassed) Well, no. I was out of line.*

S. **You sure were. Let me ask you something. How does Alice feel about you?**

E. *I guess she doesn't like me either.*

S. **Do you think maybe she feels *you're* a jerk?**

E. *(unhappily) Could be.*

S. **Joe, I'm going to give you a tip. The only way people can live or work together harmoniously is if they respect one another. That's what this is all about. It's not about the best way to duplicate copies. It's about respect. If you don't respect your co-workers, you can't expect them to respect you. And human nature being what it is, if people don't respect one another, they're not going to like one another. Alice happens to be a smart woman. But that's beside the point. Even if she weren't smart, she would still deserve your respect. And that goes for everyone else in this department as well. Do you understand what I'm talking about?**

E. *(sheepish) Yeah, I think so.*

• • • **TALKING POINTS**   Respect is a two-way street. One doesn't have to agree with or approve of everything one's co-workers say or do to respect them, or their right to express themselves. It makes sound supervisory sense to examine and assess the attitudes of your subordinates with regard to themselves and the people they work with and for. Where an employee shows lack of respect for others, supervision, the organization—or lack of respect for his or her own self—it could be time to set that person straight.

DIALOGUE TWO

Do-It-Yourselfer, General Office Supervisor Ruth Hobson, shows lack of respect for her people.

Talking It Out

Manager - Ruth, how many daily, weekly, and monthly reports is your department required to turn out?

Supervisor - I don't know, a couple of dozen or so. Why?

M. This morning a thought came to me. Checking over your output, I noticed that at least half of those reports are produced by you personally. That's a remarkable accomplishment. It must take hours on end.

S. That's an understatement. I put in two or three hours of overtime almost every day of the week.

M. I can believe that. It makes me wonder how you have time for anything else.

S. What do you mean? Like what?

M. Like reviewing and revising the department's work schedules and programs. Devoting time to coaching and developing your people. Thinking about ways to improve the department's attendance record which leaves something to be desired, or generating better participation in the company's suggestion program. Like planning. Things like that.

S. I keep meaning to get to those things, but quite honestly, you're right. I don't seem to have the time.

M. Let me ask you a question. Why do you feel the need to produce all these reports yourself?

S. *(sighs) Because I want to make sure that they're right.*

M. And you don't think your people are qualified to get them right?

S. *Not the ones I do myself. They're pretty complicated. My staff doesn't have the know-how or experience.*

M. You must think they're pretty incompetent.

S. *(frowning) No, I wouldn't say that. It's just that they don't have the training and these reports are important. Key decisions are based on them. I don't want to take any chances of getting them wrong.*

M. Ruth, I'm going to ask you to think back to ten years ago when you first came to work for the company. At that time would you have been qualified to prepare these reports?

S. *No way. I was green and inexperienced.*

M. And now you're an expert. What happened?

S. *(nodding) I see what you're getting at.*

M. Of course you do. What this all boils down to is a matter of respect—respecting your people enough to have confidence in their ability to learn and gain experience if given the opportunity, just as you responded to that opportunity over the years. If you select employees thoughtfully, train them carefully, and give them a chance to try their wings, there's no reason you won't be able to delegate most of these reports, ease your personal time pressures, and make the department more productive in the process. And in delegating that work you can still maintain control of it by checking the final output to make sure it's done right.

S. *Yeah, I can see that makes sense.*

M. No question about it. Here's another thought to take with you. Showing enough respect for your people to delegate authority and responsibility judiciously is the best way to ensure your own career advancement and growth. It provides a cushion of time to think and work toward the next step on the ladder.

• • • **TALKING POINTS** A skyscraper-high stockpile of magazine articles, booklets, and books has been written on the subject of delegation. But if you think about it you will realize that the sum and substance of delegation boils down to having enough respect for your people to credit them with the intelligence and judgment to tackle a job and do it well given the opportunity and support they require. In short, just as you made your own way based on the respect of your supervisors who demonstrated their respect in your ability to succeed.

DIALOGUE THREE

Lab supervisor Bill Roche overindulges subordinates in an effort to woo them.

(Roche's boss, Lab Manager Harry Stempler, observes Roche's actions and behaviors. Among the things he notices is Bill's habit of joining staff members for lunch too often, socializing with them at the local bar after work. Bill also drives to and from work every day with George Hammer, one of his subordinates. And he tends to give employees too much leeway with regard to departmental and company rules, and sometimes turns a blind eye to the way their tasks are performed.)

Talking It Out

Manager - Bill, I notice that you let Charley change his lunch hour from twelve to one today. How come? That left the lab empty-handed between twelve and one.

Supervisor - Yeah, I know. He said he wanted to meet a buddy of his at twelve.

M. That's a flimsy reason in view of the circumstances. Maybe you're trying too hard to be a nice guy. The lab should have been covered. Also, I was talking with Carol this morning. She's still processing powder samples the old way. I thought you were supposed to show her the new procedure for doing that.

S. I did, but she says it takes her longer to do it the new way.

M. It shouldn't. It should be faster and more efficient. Your job is to make that clear to her, and help her if she can't do it herself.

S. I know. But I figured it was too minor an issue to quibble over. As long as she gets the job done.

M. I'm afraid I don't see eye to eye with you on that but let's leave it for the moment. There's another thing I want to discuss with you. On the one hand, I understand that how a person spends time off the job is his or her own business. On the other hand, many consultants and other management experts recommend that more efficient management usually results when a certain amount of distance is maintained between supervisors and the people they supervise. It's okay to be "one of the boys" up to a point. But when you go beyond that point it can create problems on the job.

S. You mean because I drive to and from work with George Hammer?

M. That and other things like going to lunch with the guys you supervise, and joining them for a beer after work. It makes people harder to supervise when they regard you as one of their buddies instead of the boss. I'm not saying you shouldn't be friendly and let your hair down at times. I'm in favor of kidding around once in a while and not being stiff. But it's been proven that keeping a little distance from your people makes good supervisory sense.

S. Okay, I'll cut out some of that stuff.

M. Fine. I'd like to give you something else to think about. It's this question of respect. Do you think your subordinates respect you?

S. I don't know. Sometimes I wonder about that.

M. I don't want to criticize you unfairly, Bill, but experience proves that managerial control suffers in operations where respect for supervision is lacking. I've often observed that supervisory laxity coupled with a tendency to be buddy-buddy with subordinates is sometimes an unconscious effort to win employees' respect by fraternizing or overindulging them. The only way to gain respect is to earn it, and one way to do that is to demonstrate that you know your stuff, are firm in your opinions and decisions, and base your actions on what's best for the operation, not on whether people might be put out by them. I'm not saying that's a problem in your case, but it might give you something to think about.

• • • **TALKING POINTS** Tough-mindedness combined with fair-mindedness is a sure formula for winning the respect of your people. Toadying is a sure formula for turning people off and losing their respect. The most successful supervisors we know impress subordinates with their competence, open-mindedness, and most importantly, their refusal to compromise when it comes to adherence to high quality and ethical standards.

DIALOGUE FOUR

Production Department employee Stanley Hoctor shows lack of respect for the organization and its leadership.

Talking It Out

Supervisor - Hey Stan, I think maybe I'd better start checking the want ads. I just learned that the company has a lousy product line and is being managed by a bunch of incompetent morons.

Employee - (frowning) I don't get it.

S. You should. You're the guy who's been circulating this information.

E. (no comment, lowers his eyes)

S. My sources tell me you've been blabbing it all over the lunchroom to anyone willing to listen. That's valuable information to anyone working here. How did you get it? Maybe we can arrange to have it published.

E. I guess I've been shooting off my mouth.

S. So I gather. But you're a pretty bright guy. I'd be interested in the source of your information. Why do you feel our products are lousy? And what makes you conclude that our company's chairman and president are morons? I'm curious. You can level with me, Stan. Does that evaluation include me too?

E. (face flushed, no response)

S. (turning tough and firm) Okay, I'll level with *you*. The way I see it Stan, is that if anyone's a moron it's you. I'll tell you why. Anyone who believes they work for a company where the products are lousy and the leadership incompetent would have to be pretty dumb. You could never get ahead in such an organization, and the company itself would be in danger of folding. So I don't get it. If that's what you truly believe, why do you work here?

E. I guess I exaggerated.

S. I fail to see to what purpose. But I can tell you one thing, Stan. If you can't function as a loyal team member and show respect for your organization and the people you work for, you shouldn't be working here, and we don't need you working here. Keep that in mind for the future. Bad-mouthing your company is the quickest way for an employee to find himself in disrepute, and if it continues, out of a job. Do I make myself clear?

E. Yes, you do.

• • • **TALKING POINTS**   No supervisor should sit still for the employee who bad-mouths the department, the organization, or its people. Harmonious teamwork is the key to a pleasant and enjoyable workplace and a productive operation. Where bad-mouthing exists the supervisor should call the worker to account for it, determine the reason for the poor attitude, and take whatever steps necessary to put an end to the disruptive and destructive remarks. Where lack of respect is aired before customers it is particularly damaging and tends to undermine the customer's respect as well. In such cases the bad-mouther should be quickly disciplined and if the discipline doesn't take, fired.

DIALOGUE FIVE

Receiving Department Supervisor Eileen Graff thinks the only right way to do the job is her way.

Talking It Out

Manager - Eileen, some of the information about your department that was disclosed on the consultant's recent employee attitude survey concerns me.

Supervisor - What's that?

M. It involves the section on the questionnaire dealing with employee participation in the company's suggestion program. I'm sure it isn't news to you that Receiving is one of the poorest performers in this regard. Do you have any idea why?

S. Not really. It's been bugging me.

M. Then some of the comments on the questionnaire may provide insights into the answer. As you know, the replies were made anonymously, but one employee said, "I see no point in making suggestions; they're never followed." Another reply states, "What's the use? Eileen thinks there's only one way to do a job—*her* way." Other comments were made in a similar vein. I'd be interested in your reaction. Do you think they might have any validity?

S. (worried) How many answers like that were there?

M. (checking) At least five.

S. (sighs) I don't know. I had no idea so many of my subordinates feel that way.

M. In that case, having this brought to our attention should be helpful. This kind of attitude about a supervisor indicates a possible lack of respect on her part for the opinions of others. You're smart enough to understand that there is more than one way to do almost any task. A smart supervisor tries to remain aware of this and not only listens carefully when ideas for change are submitted, but actively encourages subordinates to make suggestions on an ongoing basis.

• • • **TALKING POINTS**   Enhanced departmental productivity is at its best a team endeavor. Team members perform most effectively when respect for each other's ideas up and down the line has been developed and sustained. The smart supervisor recognizes too that workers on the line are in a unique position because of their detailed day-to-day exposure to and interaction on the job to come up with ideas not readily apparent to higher-ups further removed. This is a reality of life every supervisor would do well to acknowledge and respect.

DIALOGUE SIX

Personnel Department word-processing machine operator Mario rates as a mediocre performer because he lacks self-respect.

(Personnel Supervisor Dorothy Kamen has been conducting semiannual performance evaluations of her department's employees with recommendations for merit raises and advancement in mind. When she gets to Mario, his marginal performance gives her something to think about.)

Talking It Out

Supervisor - Mario, you were selected for Personnel work because of your good educational background, your excellent performance on the tests you were given, and your above average IQ. A high IQ doesn't necessarily indicate you are intelligent, but it does show a potential for intellectual superiority if you take advantage of opportunities to learn and develop. I won't pull any punches. In the ten months you have been here your performance has been disappointing. I expected better from you. It always hurts me to see an employee's potential not being fulfilled. If possible, I'd like to know why.

Employee - (shrugs) I do the best I can.

S. If you believe that I think you're fooling yourself. You haven't taken advantage of the company's voluntary training courses and seminars. You don't seem to show any ambition. (smiles) Are you independently wealthy?

E. (snorts) You gotta be kidding.

S. I suppose I am, but not entirely. Don't you want to make more money and get ahead?

E. Of course. Everyone wants to get ahead.

S. From the way you act you'd never know it. You're 26 years old. I understand you're making plans to get married. Stop me if you feel I'm getting too personal, but is your fiancée employed?

E. Sure, she has a pretty good job.

S. Are you planning to raise a family?

E. Yeah, sure, after a while.

S. When that happens do you think you'll be able to live comfortably on one salary if you don't advance on the job?

E. No, I guess not. We would struggle.

S. You wouldn't be the first, but are you willing to settle for that?

E. (glum) I see your point.

S. I'm glad you do. Mario, I have a theory you may or may not agree with. My feeling when a person fails to take advantage of a God-given potential to succeed is that he or she lacks self-respect. Either that, or lacks respect for the knowledge one needs to succeed. I don't think it will surprise you to know that in view of your performance during these past few months I'm unable to submit your name for a merit increase, and that at this point a mediocre rating is the best I can do for the record. I hope this will give you something to think about and that your next evaluation will be improved substantially. But that is all up to you.

• • • **TALKING POINTS** Employees, especially young employees, need a periodic shot in the intellectual arm to keep them on the right track. The point Dorothy made to Mario about self-respect is a good one to keep in mind. People with inherent ability who are willing to spin their career wheels and settle for the status quo demonstrate, among other personality failings, a lack of respect for themselves.

chapter sixteen

• •

IMPROVING HUMAN RELATIONS

How employees interact with each other and their superiors determines in large measure how they perform and how the department performs. Getting along is what good business is all about. A qualified supervisor learns as much as she can about the job and acquires the special skills needed to perform it effectively. But the best-trained supervisor will be inadequately qualified if, under job pressures, she short-changes her education on the critical elements of human relations—getting along with her people and helping them get along with each other.

DIALOGUE ONE

Shipping platform employee Jerry Shea demonstrates his shameful prejudice in an all too blatant way.

Talking It Out

Supervisor - You'll probably be happy to hear that the dispatcher I wanted to hire turned me down. He didn't give me a reason but I learned via the grapevine that you helped him make his decision.

Employee - What's that supposed to mean? I don't even know the guy. I never said a word to him.

S. Maybe not, but you influenced his decision nonetheless. You helped him decide indirectly. For your information the guy's name is Bernie Goldberg. Does that suggest any thoughts?

E. No, except that he's a Jew-boy.

S. That's right, he's a Jew-boy, and from what my sources tell me, he was tipped off to the prejudice that exists around here toward employees of the Jewish faith, not to mention other minorities. Goldberg's a good man. I was sorry to lose him.

E. You got my sympathy. But it's no big loss as far as I can see. The last thing we need around here is another Jew-boy.

S. That's an unfortunate attitude. What does that make me: a Protestant-boy? What are you, a Catholic-boy? What's Ernie Gonzales, a spic-boy? And is Charley Jones a nigger-boy? Can't you get it through your fat head that we're all human beings with the same problems and needs, struggling to make a buck and stay healthy?

E. Hey, get off my back. I don't care about none of that stuff.

S. Of course you don't. Some of your best friends are Jew-boys, right? Look here, Shea, it's common knowledge that you give employees of the Jewish faith a hard time; you've been riding Harry Rosen for months.

E. Well, between the two of us, I don't like the idea of having to work with guys like Rosen. I'd rather work with my own kind.

S. Your own kind? You mean a work force comprised of bigots?

E. I'm no bigot. I can't help the way I feel. That's the way I was brought up.

S. Don't I know it, and I feel sorry for you. I'm putting you on notice, Shea. I'm gonna watch you like a hawk from now on. All it will take is one incident of religious or racial prejudice related to you and you won't have to work with guys like Harry Rosen any more. You'll be out on the street.

• • • **TALKING POINTS** Just as a physician roots poison out of one's system with antibiotics, a good supervisor roots out poisonous prejudice from the work group with prompt, firm, and decisive action. The precept of equality that stems from the Declaration of Independence and has been a cornerstone of the American way for generations must stand as a credo in the workplace. But too often the venom of deeply ingrained prejudice seeps into the best of organizations. There's a lyric in the show, *South Pacific,* that says, "You have to be *taught* to hate . . .;" With regard to bigots in the work group, the proper and decent supervisory response to the bigot must be, *you* have to be taught that intolerance in this operation *will not* be tolerated.

DIALOGUE TWO

Engineering Supervisor Dan Parker professes to subscribe to equal-opportunity practices—yet sees some employees as more "equal" than others.

Talking It Out

Manager - Dan, my sources tell me some of the people in the department are upset over your promotion of Jack Crane to Project Leader.

Supervisor - I don't know why. Jack's a good man. I've been grooming him for the job.

M. I won't argue that Jack's a good man. But level with me: Is he the *best* man?

S. (nervously) Sure. That's why I picked him.

M. (meets Dan's gaze, the supervisor flinches) The evidence says otherwise. I've been checking the record. Max Shulman's performance has been far superior. Same thing for John Hallman. Both have the seniority edge on Crane.

S. I know. It was a tough decision to make.

M. I can't see why. You have to consider the factors involved in conferring a promotion—performance record, education, background, experience, seniority, leadership qualities, ability to get along with people—and you select the candidate who stacks up the best. Using these criteria, the way it appears, either Max or John has Jack Crane beat by a mile.

S. I didn't see it that way. I felt Jack would do a good job. He's well-liked by the staff.

M. And by you in particular. Correct me if I'm wrong, but isn't Jack a special buddy of yours? The scuttlebutt has it that you and Amy socialize with him and his wife. Am I mistaken?

S. No, but that didn't influence my decision.

M. Come off it, Dan. The evidence denies that contention. I want that promotion retracted and either Max or John selected in Jack's place. I'll give it to you straight, Dan. This promotion disturbs me. I'm keeping a sharp eye on future decisions of this kind and I give you fair warning. Your own career progress hangs in the balance. Equal opportunity means just that. Favoritism has no place around here, and for your information, close personal friendship doesn't rate as a factor in promotion, wage-increase, or job-assignment decisions.

• • • **TALKING POINTS** "Old boy" clubs and privileged cliques play havoc with departmental relations and productivity. Morale problems, poor teamwork, and friction are inevitable when promotions, wage increases, or preferred tasks are based on factors other than job performance. Human nature being what it is, when it comes to equal opportunity, objectivity isn't always easy to come by. We all have preferential leanings toward people based on any number of factors from personal appearance and age to political leanings and gender. But objectivity is a critical ingredient of good and fair leadership. With this goal in mind you will serve both yourself and your organization well by examining every decision you make under a high-powered microscope. Ask yourself: Is it fair? Does it violate equality principles? If you can't answer with a clear conscience review the facts one more time.

DIALOGUE THREE

Production Supervisor Fred Garnet doesn't appear to understand the importance of his function as a role model.

Talking It Out

Manager - Fred, I want to have a chat with you about your department's declining performance.

Supervisor - (glumly) I was expecting this visit.

M. **It's long overdue. This is the third quarter productivity has fallen. You're turning out too many rejects, and attendance is worse than ever. I'd like to get to the bottom of it.**

S. Well, for one thing, I'm not getting the cooperation I should from my people.

M. **That's as good a place as any to start. It could well be the crux of the problem. Do you have any ideas to explain it?**

S. Only that morale in the department leaves something to be desired. I wish I knew why.

M. **There has to be a reason and I have an inkling of what it might be. Fred, I hope your skin's not too thin. I have a hunch the answers we're looking for may be contained in the employee attitude survey conducted last month.**

S. (nervously) I can take it. Shoot.

M. **Basically, I conclude from the survey that your operation may be suffering from human-relations problems, and unless I'm mistaken the main cause may be you.**

S. (bracing himself) What makes you say that?

M. **Simply this. Let's take a look at some of the comments made by your people in response to the survey: "Makes promises he doesn't keep." "Wants us to work hard but takes it easy himself." "Violates rules he expects us to adhere to." "Isn't open-minded when it comes to suggestions." "He's a hard guy to talk to." Want me to go on?**

S. (flabbergasted) God, no! I had no idea they felt that way about me.

M. **Apparently they do. I've been reviewing your record with the company. You've been with us eight years now. Until a year or so ago your evaluations were outstanding. You worked hard, ran a tight productive operation, made some great innovations, and were a well-rated supervisor. Since then your rating, and the department's performance, have gone downhill steadily. The inevitable conclusion is that you're either burned out, or simply resting on your laurels.**

S. If I am I'm not aware of it.

M. Maybe that's the problem. I'll give you an example or two. You've been taking extended lunch hours. You often arrive late in the morning and sometimes take off before the shift ends. And I don't remember the last time you came up with an idea to cut costs or make the department more efficient.

S. *(glum expression, no comment)*

M. Fred, as any star athlete could confirm, yesterday's triumphs have no more impact on a team's success than yesterday's weather. What counts is what you're doing today. To be effective and respected, leaders have to conduct themselves as exemplary role models. That's what subordinates respond to and emulate. It's your current performance that counts. Last month's, or last year's doesn't mean a thing to them. I'd advise you to keep this in mind if you want your group's cooperation and support. I don't think I have to spell out the alternative.

• • • **TALKING POINTS**   Human relationships are shaped by human behavior, especially when they involve men and women in leadership positions. It is human nature for employees to emulate their supervisors. A good leader is responsible for setting standards of attitude and behavior for their team, staff, or crew. It is no news to anyone that as a supervisor you live in a glass house. Subordinates watch and judge every move that you make. When department heads show by their action and attitude that quality performance and ethics are important to them, their people usually respond in kind and morale problems are minimized.

DIALOGUE FOUR

Twenty-one-year-old Evie treats older co-workers as if they are second class citizens who don't deserve her respect.

Talking It Out

Supervisor - Evie, your calculations on these Special Deal orders are wrong. What happened?

Employee - (anxiously) I thought I had them right. I must have gotten them mixed up.

S. Didn't you follow the procedure?

E. Yes, but it's kind of complicated. This was only the second time I did them.

S. If you weren't sure, why didn't you try to get help?

E. I did. I asked Marcie. She thought I was doing them right.

S. Marcie! For Pete's sake, she's only been on the job six months. She has less experience than you. Why didn't you ask Sheila? She's the resident expert on Special Deal orders and just about everything else around here.

E. I don't know. I guess I should have.

S. Is it because Sheila has gray hair and is soon due for retirement? I can't help but notice you give a cold shoulder to people like Sheila, Ben, and other older people in the department. Why is that?

E. I'm not sure. I guess I'm not comfortable with them. We have nothing in common.

S. That's not true, Evie. You may not have much in common socially, but as far as the work is concerned you have a good deal in common. You're all part of the order-processing team. You have a mutual interest in doing a good job and avoiding the problems and embarrassment of mistakes like this. And it is certainly in your best interest to get reliable help when you need it.

E. (frowning) I know, but Sheila acts so cold and unfriendly at times.

S. You're mistaken there too. Sheila's one of the warmest people I know. If she acts cold it's in response to your own reaction. That's simple human nature.

E. I guess you're right.

S. I *know* I'm right. It's foolish for young people to rebuff and avoid senior co-workers. No one is better qualified than they to give you the help and guidance you need to do a better job and earn a good performance rating and the benefits that go with it. Take my advice, Evie. Warm up to Sheila, and see how fast she warms up to you.

• • • **TALKING POINTS** You won't get better advice than that with regard to the treatment and handling of seniors. Actions of younger people toward seniors often run from cool and disrespectful to hostile for a variety of reasons. Some mistakenly equate gray hair with declining intelligence. Others assume that, nearing retirement, older people no longer care about their jobs. And some employees in their 20s unconsciously associate senior co-workers with their parents and put parental conflicts into the mix. As countless studies show, the reality of the marketplace is that as a group, workers in their 60s and 70s perform at least as well if not better than younger workers. Older people are more cautious and thus less accident-prone, more patient and cooperative, and more likely to show up on time every day. Also, given the advantages of medical science and more healthful living, "old" today starts at a more advanced age than it did in the past. Research proves that a growing number of seniors perform productively well into their 70s and beyond. Finally, and perhaps most important, seniors represent a treasure trove of priceless experience that can only be gained by spending many years in the workplace. As short-sighted Evie failed to see, it makes good sense to take advantage of that expertise.

DIALOGUE FIVE

Office Services Supervisor Frank Meritt doesn't respond to the personal needs of his people.

Talking It Out

Manager - Frank, did you receive a copy of this quarter's Employee Turnover Report?

Supervisor - Yeah, I just got it.

M. Then I don't have to tell you your department's turnover continues to be one of the company's worst. Do you attach any significance to that?

S. I don't know. It may be just the way the chips fall; more people thinking they can do better elsewhere, or whatever.

M. I suppose that's always a possibility, but it bugs me for some reason. Experience shows that Office Services is more popular with

people than many other departments. The work is clean and pleasant. When a help-wanted ad is placed, you get a flood of applicants.

S. I know. I don't understand why our turnover is so high.

M. Do you mind if I do a little snooping around on my own to see if I can come up with some answers?

S. No. Is there anything I can do to help?

M. Yes. I made a list of seven of your employees at random. Please send them to my office one at a time.

(Frank's boss interviews the seven workers. Promising anonymity, and assuring them no one will be hurt by their comments, he encourages them to speak their minds regarding conditions in the department. After compiling and analyzing the responses, he summons Frank to his office.)

M. I think you'll be interested to learn what I came up with.

S. (waiting anxiously)

M. On the plus side, your people have great respect for your knowledge and the high performance standards you set. On the minus side, they feel you are too cold and impersonal in your treatment of them.

S. (frowning) I'm not sure I know what you mean.

M. Okay, let's get it right from the horse's mouth. As you know, I promised them anonymity. No names will be disclosed. With this in mind, let me give you a rundown. One of your people said, "All he seems interested in is getting the work out; he doesn't care about us personally." Another one says, "He treats us like robots." Still another, "If I ask for a couple of hours off to take care of personal business, he makes a big deal of it." And here's one that says, "He treats me like an extension of the machine I operate." Finally, "He's so stiff and formal, it makes me ill at ease. I don't enjoy working here."

S. (blows out his cheeks) Wow! That makes me feel like some kind of ogre.

M. You're anything but, Frank. But perceptions are important, especially those of your subordinates. Your conscientiousness and compulsion to get the work out on time and done right is very

much to your credit. But you have to keep in mind that your people are no less human than you are with their special needs and
desires, psychological as well as physical. My suggestion is that
you loosen up a bit. Relax. Try to show a personal interest. Kid
around every once in a while. Make comments like, "How are you
doing?" "Any problems?" Ask how the wife and kids are getting
along. If you show people you care, it may surprise you to find
that you will really start caring.

• • • **TALKING POINTS** Consider your own situation in the workplace.
Isn't one of the most important aspects of the job how you relate to your
boss on a personal basis? Ask yourself: Does he or she really care about me
as a person? Then evaluate the difference your yes or no answer makes from
the standpoint of your attitude in general and level of enthusiasm for the job
in particular. As educator and consultant Leonard J. Smith states the case:
"You don't have to *like* your boss per se. But your perception of how he or
she *feels* about you as a human being makes all the difference. If you think
he's interested only in the work side, your contribution toward getting the
job done right and on time, and couldn't care less about your personal well-
being, your typical response is likely to range from indifference to resentment. All in all, not a pleasant working environment." That should give you
something to think about.

chapter seventeen

· · · · · · · · · · · · · · · · · ·

SOLVING PROBLEMS MORE EFFECTIVELY

Generally speaking, the higher level your job, the tougher and more complex the problems you will be called upon to tackle and solve. Processing problems, productivity problems, people problems. Problems should not give you wrinkles. If you have problems, be thankful. Thomas Blandi knew what he was talking about when he described problems as opportunities for growth. Each problem you meet head on and solve successfully boosts you a notch further up the ladder of success. Keep this in mind next time you are confronted with what looks like a dilemma—the tougher the better. Face up to it squarely with a positive mental attitude. And if a career competitor shies away from the problem you face, consider yourself a step ahead in the game.

DIALOGUE ONE

Alice Kempner in the Returns Department has a problem meeting established deadlines and goals.

Talking It Out

Supervisor - Alice, is that recap report on the Model 540 returns ready yet?

Employee - No, I'm still working on it.

S. What's taking you so long? It was supposed to be done this morning.

E. I know. I've been working as fast as I can.

S. That's what I can't understand. You're not a slow person. It's not the first time you've run this report, and I know you're not stalling. The time standard shows it's a 3-hour job on the average. You've already spent more than four hours.

E. It's nearly done.

S. I'm glad to hear that. But that's almost twice as long as it should have taken you. Do you think the standard is unfair?

E. I don't know. I was wondering about that.

S. All right, let's review the procedure step by step and see if we can come up with an answer. Steps One through Four seem simple enough. No possible problem there. Do you agree?

E. Yes.

S. Step Five instructs you to enter the total returns from all six receiving stations. How do you do that?

E. I call down to each station and get the figures over the phone. Then I total and enter them.

S. No wonder you're taking so long. Don't you know those totals have already been tallied with the grand total entered on the master sheet?

E. Oh, that's right! I forgot about that. That accounts for a lot of lost time. Sometimes when I call people they're not available and have to call me back.

S. (smiles tolerantly) Let's check the rest of these steps. What about Step Nine where the instruction is to balance the regional returns totals? How do you do that?

E. I do the calculations, then I check my figures twice to be sure they're correct.

S. Aha. Another step that can be eliminated. All you need to do is check your total against the one on the master sheet to be sure they both agree.

E. I didn't realize that. No wonder I'm so far behind schedule. I'm sorry.

S. No need for you to be sorry. The delay is more my fault than yours. I should have spent more time with you beforehand to make sure you were doing it right.

• • • **TALKING POINTS** The supervisor's final comment says it all. When problems erupt, the first thing to do is to trace the source of the trouble step by step. This case brings up another important good management practice: *Preventive* medicine is more effective than writing out a prescription after the patient is sick. A large percentage of processing problems occur because procedures aren't understood, aren't followed properly, or haven't been updated. Other problems develop because of procedures being hastily reeled off by word of mouth instead of stated in writing. In most cases verbal instructions are permissible only in the simplest assignments. A clearly stated written procedure has another important advantage as well: Where an error or misunderstanding occurs, it is easier to track down the source of the problem.

DIALOGUE TWO

Showroom Supervisor Don Ziffer puts difficult and unpleasant tasks on the back burner.

Talking It Out

Manager - Don, how come you're still permitting George to greet customers and write up orders?

Supervisor - We're shorthanded. I've been meaning to break in someone else for that job.

M. Meaning to? That's what you said last time. How long a period does "meaning to" cover? It's been more than three weeks since we discussed the problem. I've been getting complaints about

George. For one thing, his personality is unsuited to dealing with customers. For another, he doesn't follow instructions to push premium items in the line. We're losing business as a result.

S. *I'm sorry. I'll substitute someone else as soon as I can, and put George back handling stock.*

M. Please see that you do. Tell me something, Don. Why has it taken you so long to get cracking on this thing?

S. *I don't know. It's a big step down for George. I guess I keep putting off breaking the news to him.*

M. I thought that might be the answer. Thanks for leveling with me. Now let me level with you. I can't tell you how many promising careers have been damaged because men or women who are supposed to be leaders defer priority tasks because they are unpleasant or difficult. Supervisors are judged by their operation's performance and productivity. When they produce, they grow. When they waffle and flounder, they jeopardize not only the operation, but their own jobs as well. Do you understand what I'm talking about?

S. *(nods gravely) Yes sir, I do.*

M. Good. With that thought in mind, my advice is to bring George down before he brings *you* down.

• • • **TALKING POINTS**   Do you have any tough or disagreeable problems facing you? Consider the pros and cons of this approach: 1) It's disturbing to have a problem like this on your mind; 2) The longer you defer facing a problem, the longer it will be there to bug you; 3) Tackling and overcoming a hard problem will not only get it out of the way, but give you a special lift as well; 4) The sooner you solve a difficult problem, the sooner the *consequences* of postponement will be eliminated.

DIALOGUE THREE

Young and inexperienced, warehouse employee Bernice Lane has problem-solving potential but lacks the knowledge and self-confidence she needs to put it to use.

Talking It Out

Supervisor - We had a good meeting this morning regarding the storage backlog problem, but I was disappointed that you didn't participate.

Employee - I wanted to take part, but didn't feel qualified. Most of those people have so much more knowledge and experience than I do. I would have felt like a sixth grader telling the teacher what to do. Also, I don't know how to organize my ideas and present them.

S. Let's talk about that. The meeting's agenda was written up and distributed two days ago. I assume you got a copy.

E. I did.

S. What did you do when you got it?

E. (puzzled) What do you mean? I didn't do anything. What was I supposed to do?

S. The smart thing would have been to give it some thought in advance. The backlog problem was well-defined and clearly stated on the agenda. Since you're a smart woman who is exposed to the problem every day, I'm sure you understand it as well as anyone in the department. Am I right?

E. I guess so. I'm certainly familiar with the hassles and delays caused by the backlog.

S. All right, Step One in solving any problem is to make sure you understand it. So we're okay from that standpoint. From there we proceed to Step Two.

E. What's that?

S. Breaking down the problem into its component parts.

E. I don't have the experience to do that. I'm not sure I understand what that means.

S. Let me clarify. There's no better way to gain experience than by doing something. All it takes is a pad, a pencil, and a little hard thought. You start with major aspects of the problem and you ask yourself questions. What is causing the backlog? Where does the work flow bog down? Is the paperwork compounding the problem? Can anything be eliminated or simplified? Are we getting the cooperation we need from other departments? Should more peo-

ple be assigned, or people with different skills? Is equipment a problem? What about space limitations? Do you get the drift?

E. (nodding thoughtfully) I can see where questions like that could touch off ideas.

S. Exactly. When they do, you jot them down. Before long you're ready for the next step.

E. Which is?

S. To organize your thoughts into some kind of logical order. Typically, when you do this, more ideas spring into your mind. That's the way the creative process works, one idea feeding and fueling another until it all comes together. By then you're ready for the next and final step.

E. I know. Presenting your ideas at the meeting.

S. Right. Or to your supervisor if there's no meeting involved. That's when *your* ideas start other ideas. Some may be discarded, and others refined with new thoughts added, so that what you wind up with is that magic phenomenon called innovation. Something new and different emerges—simpler, smarter, cheaper, or less time consuming. Then presto! Before you know it, the problem is solved and you wind up a heroine.

E. You make it sound easy.

S. It's not. Creating and developing ideas is hard work. And not all ideas that seem good at the outset pass the test of cost-effectiveness and practicality. That's why meetings are called to exchange ideas and filter out the ones that seem best. It's also why *every* idea is worth considering. Often suggestions that seem a bit wild and impractical trigger other ideas that are useful.

E. (takes a deep breath)

S. (smiling) Bernice, you're a perceptive intelligent employee with good creative potential. If you attack problems in the way I described, then organize your thoughts before presenting them, you can make an important contribution to the department, and yourself as well.

E. Thank you, I'll try.

• • • **TALKING POINTS**   Problem solving is the toughest and most challenging aspect of one's job whatever your classification or level. Most people must be motivated to tackle problems creatively—imbued with the self-confidence and conviction that they have something tangible to gain. Typical line workers are usually hampered by the perception that they aren't qualified as problem solvers. After all, that's what supervisors, systems professionals, and other experts are paid to do. It must be pointed out to them that supervisors, systems professionals, and other experts do not have their day-to-day exposure to the detailed aspects of their jobs, which qualifies them in a very unique way.

Dialogue Four

In attempting to solve problems, Assembly Department Supervisor Phil Hempstead loses sight of priorities.

Talking It Out

Manager - Phil, how come you're not working on that report for Mr. Wilson? He's on tenterhooks waiting for it.

Supervisor - I'm planning to get to it as soon as I get this problem with Ellen and Mary out of the way.

M. Oh? What's that all about?

S. I'm not sure myself. They seem to have trouble working together. I'm trying to get to the bottom of it, then decide what to do.

M. And you feel that's more critical than the Wilson report? Mr. Wilson's a Senior Vice President of the company.

S. (frowning) I didn't look at it that way. I figured departmental harmony was important, and it's something I already had started to work on.

M. What do you suppose would happen if you deferred working on that personnel problem until you completed the report for Mr. Wilson?

S. I don't know. Nothing drastic, I guess.

M. That's what I thought. Phil, problem solving is a critical part of every supervisor's job. But in tackling problems it's vital to keep priorities in mind at all times. Ideally, at the start of each working day you should have a things-to-do list at hand and review it from a priorities standpoint. Items with the highest priority should

take precedence over everything else. That includes problems as well as work tasks. Had you done that, you would have realized in reviewing your list that getting out that report had a much higher priority than the personnel problem.

S. *I can see that now.*

M. **One more question. I'm curious. What makes you feel this situation between Ellen and Mary constitutes a problem you have to deal with? When did it first come to your attention?**

S. *Two or three days ago.*

M. **What do you think might happen if you disregarded the problem for the time being at least?**

S. *I don't know. It could get worse. If two people don't get along they shouldn't be working together.*

M. **I agree. But in this case, suppose you ignored the situation for a while and simply monitored it. Since it's of such short duration, isn't it possible the conflict might resolve itself?**

S. *Yes, I guess that's possible.*

M. **I'm not making a judgment one way or the other. But I'd like to make some suggestions with regard to the recommended approach to problem solving. To address and solve problems effectively, there are a few questions you should ask at the outset. First, is it really a problem? If so, is it *your* problem to solve? Is it worth solving? Do you need help or guidance in addressing the problem? What might be the consequences if you don't deal with it? Finally, and most important, how does it rank in the order of problem-solving priority?**

S. *I see what you mean.*

• • • **TALKING POINTS** Some problems are of major significance; others are no more than minor irritations. Some problems are agonizing and painful to solve; others are challenging and fun. But the question of what to do first is always a pivotal one for supervisors to consider. Nothing can be more self-defeating than devoting your efforts to putting out the fire in the barn while the main house burns down. One final point: Some problems are easy to misdiagnose with symptoms of the disease mistaken for the disease itself. Simple solutions are almost always the best. In this age of specialization, some "experts" urge use of techniques that are so complex that the temptation may exist to focus more on the techniques than the problems at hand.

DIALOGUE FIVE

Assistant Customer Service Department Supervisor Gloria Redlich tends to attack problems in a disorganized way, without first obtaining all the facts of the case.

Talking It Out

Supervisor - Gloria, Ruth is up in arms over your decision to recommend a suspension.

Assistant Supervisor - Well, I think she deserves a suspension after that run-in with Fran. A heated argument is one thing, but Ruth actually pushed her. Fran could have fallen and injured herself.

S.   The way I heard it, that's more Fran's version than what actually happened.

A.S. Her story was supported by Selma.

S.   That's no surprise. Selma is Fran's best friend. Did you talk with anyone else?

A.S. Well, no. I figured that since Selma was a witness. . .

S.   That's not good enough. In solving a problem it's important to get all the pertinent facts that you can. That means investigating the situation thoroughly from all angles and aspects. The worst thing you could do in arbitrating a dispute between two people is to make a decision based on one-sided information. Do you know why the dispute between Ruth and Fran originated in the first place?

A.S. Not exactly. Something about whose figures were correct on a report.

S.   That sounds kind of vague. Can you pin it down more accurately?

A.S. No, I don't think so.

S.   That's because you didn't investigate thoroughly. Do you know to what degree Fran might have provoked Ruth to the point

where she actually pushed her? Pushing isn't the ultimate violence. Sufficiently provoked, it might even signify restraint.

A.S. (frowning, distressed)

S.   All of this is purely hypothetical. I don't know what actually happened and from what I can gather, neither do you. That's the
point I'm trying to make. In problem solving or decision making
the biggest mistake one can make is jumping to conclusions pre-
maturely. Only when armed with evidence and facts can you
decide objectively and honestly. Before you conclude who's at
fault in this case and why, I'm afraid you have a long way to go.

• • • **TALKING POINTS**   Psychologist William Ross writes: "We go off half-
cocked, without trying to get at the facts, and therefore often believe things
that are as far from the truth as the ends of the earth." But experienced
problem solvers know all too well that not even the so-called facts are the
be-all and end-all of problem solving. The fact is that not all presumed
"facts" are factual. Important as it is to get evidence in tackling problems, it
is equally important to sift through and weigh the evidence. Remember to
ask: Has the information been checked for accuracy? Is it based on actual
observation and if so, is the observer credible, with no personal stake in the
outcome? Is the information supported by expert testimony? How relevant
is it to the situation at hand? Only when such questions are resolved satis-
factorily can fair and objective decisions be made.

DIALOGUE SIX

Advertising Assistant Sherry Butterfield doesn't seek the help and guidance
she needs in tackling problems.

Talking It Out

**Supervisor - Sherry, what's the holdup on delivery of the new cata-
logs?**

*Employee - The printer is running into all kinds of hang-ups. I have to prac-
tically hold their hands every step of the way. First it's a mix-up on typogra-*

phy. Then it's confusion about layout. When the samples finally came through they were on the wrong stock.

S. (puzzled) I don't understand. ABC's been doing that job for years. Why should they suddenly run into so much trouble?

E. Because Fred Welch resigned, went to work for a competitor, and took his assistant along with him. He was the foreman who handled our stuff.

S. Did you know this before you gave ABC the job?

E. Yes, Fred called me when he quit.

S. Didn't you see this as a potential problem?

E. Yes, but I didn't realize there were so many implications involved. When I talked to the guy who replaced Welch at ABC he said "piece of cake," we had nothing to worry about.

S. What did you expect him to say? So you gave ABC the job without consulting anyone. Don't you think Susan Lustig would have been better qualified to make that decision, or at least give you guidance? After all, she's the one who designs and sets up the catalog.

E. That didn't occur to me. We were behind schedule. I figured the sooner I got the order in, the sooner the catalogs would be done.

S. (shaking his head) Sherry, this isn't the first time you took it into your head to make a decision like this on your own. This department's a team, or that's what it's supposed to be. Solo flyers don't make good team players. Since Fred Welch is the guy who supervised the catalog's production all these years, it should have at least occurred to you that switching the job to his new outfit might be an option to consider, an option Susan might be better qualified than you to evaluate.

E. Yeah, I can see that now.

S. Well, please be sure to see it in the future as well. The one thing we don't need around here are seat-of-the-pants decision makers.

• • • **TALKING POINTS**   What often complicates problem solving is the availability of alternative solutions. With the growing sophistication of computer technology, today's supervisor is faced with an outgrowth of new dilemmas to unravel. Before finalizing a decision it makes good business sense to ask: Is this the best solution? Am I sure it's the best solution? If there is the smallest doubt in your mind, pretend the problem is a serious operation and turn to another "doctor" for a second opinion. Even if your answer is an unqualified yes, with a guru in mind ask yourself: Would he or she agree it's the best solution? Or might he or she have a completely different approach to the problem? It all depends, of course, on the seriousness and/or complexity of the situation at hand. Where the problem requires something more than a simple routine decision, a multidisciplined approach often helps to ensure that all viable options are considered.

chapter eighteen

• • • • • • • • • • • • • • • • • •

IMPROVING CUSTOMER SERVICE

The customer service ideal is to keep customers happy and coming back for more. That in a nutshell is what good business—and successful career growth—are all about. No one has to tell you about competition these days. Tough and growing tougher. No one has to tell you what it costs to woo, develop, and open a new account. Nor does anyone have to tell you how much a company loses when a customer goes sour on a supplier because of service inadequacies and turns to a competitor for fulfillment of needs. Study after study shows that invariably the most profitable companies are those that serve customers best—and the most successful supervisors and managers are the men and women who come up with the most imaginative strategies and techniques to make that happen.

DIALOGUE ONE

Traffic Supervisor Mildred Gates receives a customer complaint that dispatcher Joe Schultz has been rude and offensive.

Talking It Out

Supervisor - Joe, I received a complaint this morning from Mr. Stewart at Carnival Lighting. He's unhappy about the way you responded to his call wanting to know why his order wasn't shipped.

Employee - (edgy) I told him we were a little behind and would get it out as soon as we could.

S. That's not good enough for an important customer like Ed Stewart. He had run out of Type 14B brackets and it was costing him business. He needed more specific information.

E. I explained we were doing the best we could. I couldn't get the guy off the phone.

S. He says you hung up on him.

E. (sullen) Well, okay, maybe I did. But I was busy as hell. I tried to get through to him that if he didn't let me get back to my work it would only delay his order further. He got nasty, so I hung up on him.

S. Just like that?

E. What was I supposed to do?

S. I'll tell you what you were supposed to do. You were supposed to use your head for a change. Your attitude leaves a lot to be desired. Joe, this company may be your employer and mine, but your primary employer is the customer. Without customers there would be no orders to fill, pack, or dispatch. Without customers we would all be out of jobs. Do you understand what I'm saying?

E. (morose) Yeah.

S. Joe, your outlook disturbs me. This isn't the first customer complaint I've had about you, and I'm giving you fair warning that it better be the last. I don't care how busy you are or what your other priorities may be. When a customer calls, satisfying his or her needs becomes your number one priority. A call from a customer is no less important than a call from the President of the company. And a customer's impatience or rudeness is no excuse for your response in kind. Your responsibility as a supervisor is to keep your cool and act polite at all times.

E. I understand, yes.

S. This is doubly important when the customer has a valid complaint. You wouldn't feel kindly disposed to someone who was costing you money. Well, the customer is no less human than you are. It makes good business sense, as well as good human relations sense, to take this reality into consideration. When you are rude to a good customer like Mr. Stewart you hurt yourself more than you hurt him. He can go elsewhere for his needs. It's not that simple for you. I'm telling you for the last time, Joe. If I ever hear that you hung up on a customer again, I'll hang up on you.

• • • **TALKING POINTS**   You can't be too tough on an employee who mistreats a customer, even if the person perceives that mistreatment to be justified. Joe's boss's point was a potent one when she told him that a customer call is as important as one from the head of the company. Her explanation was right on the mark. The customer is the ultimate employer and boss. In an employee's shoes, you might ask: "What am I supposed to do if a customer acts obnoxious and insulting? Am I supposed to keep my mouth shut?" Or, as one woman on the order board asked: "How am I supposed to deal with the customer who uses unacceptable language, or makes sexual advances? Am I expected to take such abuse?" Absolutely not. No person should be expected to sit still for unacceptably abusive behavior. In such cases, says management consultant Leonard J. Smith, "I would advise an employee to keep his or her cool if possible, and switch the call to your supervisor just as soon as you can."

DIALOGUE TWO

Betty Kramer sometimes forgets to follow through on promises she makes to customers.

Talking It Out

Supervisor - Mr. Williams is fit to be tied. You promised to send him a breakdown on new product sales almost a week ago and he never received it.

Employee - Oh no! I was very busy that day. It must have slipped my mind.

S. That's as lame an excuse as I can imagine. Mr. Williams is an important customer. That breakdown will provide a useful guideline for him in placing his next order. Your failure to comply with his request not only costs the company business because of the delay in ordering, but could jeopardize the account as well.

E. I'm sorry. It won't happen again.

S. Apology accepted, but there are a few things I'd like to impress upon you. A promise to a customer is an obligation, or commitment. If you can't follow through at that moment you shouldn't entrust it to memory. The safest course is to write it down in a place where you can't overlook it. Is that clear?

E. Yes, it is.

S. One more thing. A promise to a customer should rate as your highest priority. It shouldn't be made on the spur of the moment unless you're absolutely sure you can keep it. If it turns out you can't follow through, you should call the customer and explain why. Same thing if you find yourself late in fulfilling it. Finally, if you need help to carry it out and can't get to it yourself, ask your supervisor to help you out or make other arrangements. Finally, if you're too busy to follow through on a promise or can't do it for some other reason, don't hesitate to pass the buck to your supervisor. Any questions?

E. No. I think I get the message.

S. Good. Now let's get that breakdown out before you break down Mr. Williams's confidence in this company to serve him.

• • • **TALKING POINTS** Shakespeare defined a promise as "a debt unpaid." Debtors are a sign of poor management. When a salesperson or employee makes a promise to a customer it is not only his or her commitment; it is the company's commitment as well. Prompt fulfillment tells the customer that you care, that the organization is efficient, businesslike, and reliable. Failure to keep a promise, or to keep it on time, conveys just the opposite message.

DIALOGUE THREE

Credit Department Adjuster Eleanor Young loses her temper and argues with a customer.

Talking It Out

Supervisor - I can't believe you did that, Eleanor. Haven't you heard our company's motto that "The customer is always right?"

Employee - Sure, but this guy kept insisting that he ordered the 188s when I know for a fact that he ordered the 183s, and he got really obnoxious about it. Even when I pulled out his original order and proved he was wrong he still wouldn't believe me.

S. So you got into a scuffle with him.

E. Well, I tried to get the message across in as polite a voice as I could manage, and when I did he flared up. He wanted to know if I was calling him a liar. I guess that's when I got mad.

S. I don't believe I'm hearing this. And you said. . .?

E. I said, "No sir—I called him sir—you may believe *you are right, but you're not." That's when he hung up on me and I guess he called you.*

S. How would you describe the tone of your voice at the time?

E. (frowning) I guess it was cool, but polite.

S. With maybe a trace of anger. Did it occur to you at the time that an 8 could be written to look pretty much like a 3?

E. Yes, it did. But that wasn't the case on this order. I double checked. Here, you can see for yourself.

S. (examines order) Okay, I agree. The figure looks more like an 8 than a 3. But, actually, that's beside the point. What is the point is that you made an important customer angry. In proving him wrong, you made him lose face. You may even have lost the account. Would you say it puts you ahead of the game if you win the argument and lose the account?

E. (sulking) I guess not. But the customer was mistaken. What was I supposed to do?

S. **I can tell you what I would have done in your place. For one thing, I wouldn't have argued with him. I would have used a little diplomacy. I certainly wouldn't have come right out and told him he was wrong. I would have tried to reason with him as tactfully as possible. You can tell people they're wrong without making it look like an accusation, or that you're getting the best of them in an argument, or making them feel like an antagonist. And the worst tactic you could use with an angry customer is to meet his anger with your own.**

E. *(contrite) I guess I got a little hot under the collar.*

S. **That's a bad practice in dealing with customers, whatever the situation may be.**

E. *I can see that now.*

S. **Let me ask you something else. In arguing that point, did you consider the issue at stake? How much did the whole thing amount to in dollars and cents?**

E. *The credit he wanted me to approve came to $138.69.*

S. **That's another thing to consider when a disagreement with a customer occurs. How much is involved? Does it make good business sense to argue over a relatively small amount like that and risk alienating a good customer?**

E. *No, I guess not.*

• • • **TALKING POINTS** It is good sales psychology to keep in mind that the customer usually has the upper hand whether you like it or not. In rare instances the seller may be in the unique position of being the only supplier accessible for the particular product or service. But most often the customer has the option to go elsewhere for what he or she needs, and at the slightest provocation, justifiable or not. The question at times arises: How much crow must I eat to avoid losing the customer's good will and jeopardizing the account? Each situation must be assessed on its merit. In rare instances, where a customer is insulting, unacceptably out of line, or obnoxious, behavior may reach a point where a matter of human dignity and self-respect is involved. But even in such cases, employee response in kind isn't justified. If the customer is obnoxious or out of line, why put yourself in the same class as him or her? A far better approach is to transfer the call to a supervisor as politely and quickly as possible. And in all cases, the question should be raised: How much is it worth—or more to the point, how much might it cost—to win the battle at the risk of losing the war?

DIALOGUE FOUR

Customer Service Representative Donna, anxious to please, sometimes guesses in response to a customer's question or request when she's not sure of the answer.

Talking It Out

Supervisor - Donna, did you tell Mr. Kreissman that the Cartwright reels are self-winding and don't have to be reversed by hand when the initial run is complete?

Employee - (nervously) I guess I did. Was I wrong?

S. I'm afraid you were. Where did you get that information?

E. Uh, I don't know. I thought they were probably self-winding.

S. Probably? Then you weren't sure?

E. (hesitates) No, I guess not.

S. Something else you don't know is that Mr. Kreissman is going to return four units because of your misinformation.

E. Oh, I'm sorry.

S. Well, it can't be helped. The milk has already been spilled. But this should teach you a lesson. Never—and I mean never—tell a customer anything unless you are sure of the answer. If the slightest doubt exists, ask someone more knowledgeable and experienced than yourself, or refer the question to an expert. Is that clear?

E. Yes sir, it won't happen again.

S. Good. Donna, it's okay not to know. No one knows the answer to everything. But it is inexcusable when you don't know and pretend you do, or to guess at the answer.

• • • **TALKING POINTS** We are already deep into the so-called information age. In today's marketplace quality of information is as important in the buying decision as the product or service itself: Information about how to assemble or use the product, how to store and preserve it, and in some cases how to display and sell it. Every employee in oral or written contact with the customer should be reminded of this periodically. When a customer requests information it should be supplied as promptly as possible. But promptness at the expense of accuracy is not an acceptable option.

DIALOGUE FIVE

The employees in Frank Holland's department need to be reminded who pays the bills and secures their employment.

Talking It Out

Manager - Good morning, Frank. How's it going?

Supervisor - Pretty good, Mr. Klein. We're right up to schedule.

M. Fine, that's the good news. Now let's talk about the bad news.

S. What do you mean?

M. Customer complaints. I've been getting too many. I just got another one from Mr. Butler. He placed a call two days ago that was never returned. Yesterday Beth Clement, the buyer at Gaffney's, called to say she hadn't received a duplicate invoice she requested. In the past few weeks I don't know how many complaints I've had about late shipments, wrong items, and damaged merchandise. The situation is getting out of hand.

S. (anxious) I'll have to check into it. I've been so busy I've been taking 15-minute lunch breaks.

M. You shouldn't have to do that. If you need more help, let me know. But efficient customer service has to be your first priority. Customer complaints add up to lost customers and lost business.

S. Yes sir, I'll get on it at once.

M. Good. I'm interested to know what you have in mind. What will getting on it at once involve?

S. (frowning) Well, I'll try to pinpoint who's been screwing up and speak to him or her.

M. When was the last time you checked into the complaint situation and took action in response to it? When was the last time you gave your people a pep talk about the importance of good customer service?

S. I don't remember.

M. That's what I thought. When a complaint occurs do you make a record of it?

S. No, I kind of play it by ear.

M. By ear isn't good enough. From time to time you have to make people aware of the critical role the customer plays in the scheme of things around here. You report to me, and I report to Mr. Hopkins, but the real boss—yours and mine—is the customer. Customers call the shots. They pay the bills and write our paychecks. They assure our job security. That's why customer complaints can't be taken too seriously. They should be recorded, periodically analyzed, and tracked down to the source.

S. (nods thoughtfully)

M. Frank, it costs thousands of dollars to open an account and more thousands when we lose one. Customer satisfaction can't be taken for granted. A program to ensure it must be formalized and sustained on an ongoing basis. Just as important, you must create your subordinates' awareness of the critical role customer satisfaction plays in their job security and advancement. We can't afford to take customer complaints for granted.

• • • **TALKING POINTS** Unfortunately, in too many offices and plants, customer service, if not taken for granted, is monitored and organized in a haphazard way. That is rarely the case in top-rated companies. There every effort is made to keep complaints to a minimum. Employees are encouraged to interact positively with customers, to understand and respond to their needs, to record and analyze complaints, and take steps to reduce them. Many companies distribute questionnaires to customers periodically in an effort to pinpoint their particular problems and revise procedures, and sometimes alter the product itself in response. One management consultant's subjects return surveys on what she refers to as the Auditor's Checklist. Its goal is "to monitor performance quarterly on an item-by-item basis."

Dialogue Six

Billing Department Supervisor Jack Hiller doesn't recognize the vital role motivation plays in achieving good customer service.

Talking It Out

Manager - Jack, it's no news to anyone that customer service in this department leaves something to be desired.

Supervisor - I know. We've been getting too many complaints. I wish I knew what to do about it.

M. Okay, we'll talk about that. Let's start with a question: What *have* you been doing?

S. When a complaint occurs I do my best to track down the source of the problem. At that point I try to make revisions or adjustments if it's a matter of procedure. If it's a case where the employee screwed up or was negligent, I take appropriate corrective action, or apply discipline if it's warranted. You may recall that a couple of weeks ago I had to fire Sidney Griffith because too many customer complaints had come in about his being abrasive and rude.

M. Sometimes that has to be done. Your approach makes sense as far as the sticks are concerned. But what about the carrots?

S. What do you mean?

M. Simply this. Attitude is the underlying determiner of peoples' performance and drive. For good or bad, it controls a person's life. Psychologist William James wrote that human beings' behavior can be altered by altering their attitudes. If customer service is anything at all, it is a state of mind. The threat of discipline or job loss can be an effective way to help shape an employee's attitude. But it's only one side of the coin.

S. I'm not sure I know what you're getting at.

M. Just this, I'm getting back to the "carrots"—the strategies and techniques that motivate attitudinal changes for the better.

S. Like what?

M. A good example is a career Brownie point earned as a reward for good performance. This counts in supervisory decisions regard-

ing merit increases and promotions. Do you conduct periodic performance evaluations by which you let your people know where they stand?

S. No, I don't.

M. It might be worth trying. If employees know the quality of their customer service will directly affect their careers, it may make them think twice about the way they conduct business. Another possibility is cash or merchandise rewards for superior service. Incentive plans of this kind are being used in a growing number of companies. One food distributor I know invites customers to cast ballots for employees who render outstanding service. Winners earn cash and product awards. We might consider trying something like that.

S. I see what you mean by the other side of the coin.

M. No question about it. Finally, there's the old sure-win standby of simply complimenting people for outstanding customer service when it's warranted. Franklin P. Jones once wrote in *The Saturday Evening Post*, "The best thing to do behind a person's back is to pat it." You might keep that in mind.

S. Thanks. I will.

• • • **TALKING POINTS** For superior customer service to be achieved, quality performance standards must be set and monitored continuously. On top of that, employees must be given periodic booster shots of motivational adrenaline to keep awareness alive and their attitudes positive. Training programs don't have to be formal. But formal or not, one of the most important elements is to make sure that individuals who are in contact with customers are made familiar with their needs and desires. Remember that whether they fulfill them or not depends in large measure on their *supervisor's* motivational skills.

chapter nineteen

• • • • • • • • • • • • • • •

SAFEGUARDING EMPLOYEE HEALTH AND WELL-BEING

Question: Your employee, Jim Blake, has a back or heart problem. What do you as his supervisor have in common with his doctor?

Answer: Jim's health is your problem as well as his doctor's, for two reasons: 1) Obviously, from a productivity standpoint, supervisors have an interest in the health and safety of employees in their departments; 2) No less obviously, from a moral and human standpoint, safeguarding employee health and well-being is a supervisory responsibility as well. For one thing, you are—or should be—more knowledgeable than your associates and subordinates about everything in your department, health concerns and hazards included. For another, it is a primary supervisory function to provide help and guidance for subordinates in all aspects of the operation, and in the proper use of safety equipment and adherence to safety rules in particular.

DIALOGUE ONE

Warehouse employee Anita Osprey's recent actions and behavior lead her supervisor to suspect that she might have a health problem.

Talking It Out

Supervisor - Anita, do you feel all right?

Employee - Yes, why do you ask?

S. Well, maybe it's my imagination, but you've been acting funny lately. Not your usual self.

E. What do you mean?

S. You don't seem to have the old pep and vigor.

E. (frowning) I have been very tired lately. I may be coming down with a cold.

S. You're sure it isn't more than that? This morning I thought you looked faint, as though you might pass out. And your face was very pale.

E. I don't know. I've been meaning to go for a checkup. I keep putting it off.

S. (reassuring smile) It's probably nothing to worry about. But just to be on the safe side, why don't you go up to the health department and let the nurse take a look at you?

E. (hesitating) I don't know. I'm not really sick. I feel foolish making a big deal over nothing.

S. It's never foolish to make sure about your health. Besides, there's no big deal involved. It will make you feel better to know you're okay. And if you're coming down with a virus or something, you'll be doing yourself, and everyone in the department a favor to find out. The sooner you learn about an illness, the sooner you can get the treatment you need to minimize its effects.

• • • **TALKING POINTS** Employees in your department who don't feel up to snuff constitute a risk to themselves and others in the work group as well. People who are ill perform less efficiently, are more vulnerable to accidents, and if infectious, put co-workers at risk. Smart supervisors become familiar with employees' patterns of behavior to better manage adverse changes. Where warranted by the signs, quick action in the form of recommended medical attention is called for. When employees return from extended sick leave it is especially important to monitor their actions and behavior closely until you are sure they are back to par and functioning normally. All too often returning workers are not fully recuperated, so that too much standing, lifting, or climbing can provoke a recurrence of the health problem to everyone's detriment. Finally, another sign of a possible health problem to be watchful for is frequent short-term absences.

DIALOGUE TWO

Production employee Karl Davis is caught smoking in a no-smoking area of the plant.

Talking It Out

Supervisor - Karl, are you having trouble with your eyes?

Employee - (nervously) No, why do you ask?

S. I was wondering. That sign that reads NO SMOKING, HAZARDOUS AREA, is so large you'd have to be blind not to see it.

E. (morose, no comment)

S. Do you think the sign was posted to deny you the pleasure of a smoke on your rest break?

E. No.

S. Why do you think it *was* put up?

E. Because there are flammable materials in the area. I guess my lighting up was dumb. I'm sorry.

S. Sorry isn't good enough, Karl. Do you have any idea *how* dumb it was? Did you read about the fire in that New Jersey plant last week? One wing of the building burned down. Two people were killed, and three workers and a fireman were severely burned. How do you think you would feel if you were the guy responsible for setting a fire like that?

E. I'd want to kill myself.

S. That would be getting off easy. I don't think there are words to describe what such a feeling would be. I'm going to give it to you straight. Ordinary discipline in this plant usually calls for three chances after an infraction before an employee is fired. But in the case of a safety violation like this an exception is made. One chance is all you get, and that may be one chance too many. But if

you're caught smoking again in a no-smoking area, you're out on the street. Is that clear?

E. *It sure is. It won't happen again.*

S. **Okay, I'm letting you off this time with an official reprimand and a 3-day suspension. But one more time and you've had it.**

• • • **TALKING POINTS** You can't be too tough on a serious safety violation like smoking in a restricted area. In fact, some companies ban smoking anywhere on the premises because of its carcinogenic effects. Other companies refuse to hire smokers altogether, although this is a controversial issue in some states with pros and cons involved. But however you feel on the subject, your supervisory responsibility for employee health and well-being requires you to make not even the smallest compromise with the no-smoking rule in areas where flammable materials or explosive substances might be used or stored.

DIALOGUE THREE

Office Services Supervisor Emily Gross doesn't devote enough time and effort to the promotion of safety awareness in her department.

Talking It Out

Manager - Emily, how is Ben getting along?

Supervisor - He's doing fine. He was only in the hospital one day. They saved the finger; they didn't have to amputate. He'll be back to work on Monday.

M. **That's good news. But I was upset by that accident on the paper-cutting machine. Had the guard been set properly it wouldn't have happened.**

S. *I know. He could run into a workers' compensation problem as a result.*

M. **The compensation problem isn't what bothers me so much as the lack of safety awareness in the department. Promoting and sustaining awareness is one of your primary responsibilities as a supervisor, and I don't think you're giving enough attention to it.**

S. *This is the first accident we've had in months. The office isn't like the plant where all those sharp tools and cutting machines make working a real hazard.*

M. **That's a misconception, Emily. For one thing, even one accident that could have been prevented is one accident too many. That there have been so few accidents in your department can be attributed as much to luck as anything else, and luck is nothing to count on in protecting the well-being and health of your employees. When was the last time you discussed the subject with subordinates?**

S. *(frowning) I guess a long time ago.*

M. **That's what I figured. I have the feeling you haven't given enough thought to the importance of getting the safety message across to your people. Apart from the overriding objective of safeguarding employee health, do you have any idea how many other considerations are involved, such as financial ones, for example?**

S. *What do you mean?*

M. **Well, take training for one. When a person is injured someone else must be trained as a replacement. If the injury is severe enough to require permanent replacement, a whole training program is involved. On top of that, there's workers' compensation and the cost of wages paid for lost time. When an accident occurs it usually generates overtime as a byproduct. Then there's the medical cost borne by the company, and the lost productivity caused by idled equipment, not to mention the cost of damaged equipment that must be repaired or replaced. It goes on and on. Do you want me to continue?**

S. *No. I guess I never thought of it in such depth.*

M. **That's not all. It's true that in many respects a factory environment may contain more potential hazards than the office. But did you know that falling is the most common cause of accidents, especially among older employees? That holds as true for the office as it does for the production floor. All it takes is defective or slippery flooring for an employee to trip and fall. Last week an employee walked into a moving vehicle in the warehouse because he was carrying too many boxes and couldn't see past the stack. An acci-**

dent like that could just as easily occur in the office. Do you have any questions?

S. *No. I'll set up a safety meeting within the next day or two.*

M. Please do. Aside from the safety awareness you may be surprised by the other benefits that will accrue to you personally.

S. *Other benefits?*

M. That's right. Like improved morale because, as surveys show, employees feel better in a workplace with a good safety record and evidence that their supervisor cares enough to promote safety. Not only that, a safe record makes it easier to recruit good employees. It reduces paperwork and gives you the satisfaction of knowing that you are protecting your people.

• • • **TALKING POINTS**   Line and staff workers aren't the only ones who need to be reminded periodically about the importance of safety awareness. Accident prevention doesn't happen by accident. Nor should a safety program be taken for granted. It must be carefully planned, organized, and thoughtfully presented. Many companies offer special incentives for outstanding safety performance: cash and merchandise prizes, annual dinners, departmental banners, and other forms of recognition such as write-ups in the company magazine. But the biggest incentive of all is that of keeping your people productive and out of the hospital.

DIALOGUE FOUR

Receiving Department Supervisor Murray Fink undermines his health with the brutal hours he puts in.

Talking It Out

Manager - Murray, did you ever hear the expression: Work smart, not hard?

Supervisor - Sure.

M. Well, I think whoever dreamed up that axiom must have had you in mind.

S. *(sheepish smile) Yeah, I know what you mean.*

M. **What time did you leave the plant last night?**

S. *About nine.*

M. **What time did you arrive in the morning?**

S. *Eight o'clock.*

M. **Thirteen hours. How long have you been putting in hours like that?**

S. *I don't know. A few weeks, I guess.*

M. **More like months, I'd say.**

S. *I can't help it. I seem to be behind all the time.*

M. **You have two children, right? When is the last time you saw them?**

S. *I see them on weekends.*

M. **More like Sundays, I'd say. I notice you've been coming in Saturdays too. Murray, I'm worried about you.**

S. *Worried? Why is that?*

M. **Do you have any idea how pale you look? And you've been coughing a lot lately. Hasn't Marge said anything about that?**

S. *(hesitates) Yeah, she's been on my back to get a checkup.*

M. **Sounds like a good idea. But you've been too busy, right?**

S. *(resigned look) I can't help it, the job. . .*

M. **Bull! The job's as tough as you make it. You're probably the most conscientious guy in the plant. But conscientious doesn't make you smart, and it won't make you a Senior Vice President either. There are only two sensible solutions for that overload problem: One is more people if you need them to take on part of the load; the other is delegation.**

S. *(nods thoughtfully)*

M. **Murray, there are two things I want you to do: First, I want you to go for that checkup within the next day or two. Then I want you to sit down at your desk and analyze your workload situation, project by project, task by task. Make a list of jobs you plan to delegate, and those you feel you can't delegate. For the ones you think you can't delegate, I want to know why. We'll review the list and thrash that out later. After that, if you feel you need more people I want to know that too, and specifically how they will help. I want**

that analysis by the end of next week—and don't tell me you're too busy.

• • • **TALKING POINTS**   It is the nature of the beast that supervisors are expected to put in overtime, and most of them do. But when a supervisor works overtime on a continuing basis it is a sign of poor planning and management that can be detrimental to the well-being of both the individual involved and his or her operation. Unfortunately, this shoe fits too many supervisors and managers. If you find yourself—except in rare or emergency situations—working 12- and 13-hour days on a regular basis, it may be time to take a hard look at yourself and the way you run your department. Remember, delegate whenever possible.

DIALOGUE FIVE

Young, single, Data Processing Department Programmer Phil Stone, who can't say no to a party invitation, appears to be burning the candle at both ends, and burning himself out in the process.

Talking It Out

Supervisor - Phil, no offense, but you look like something the cat dragged in.

Employee - (bleary-eyed) Thanks a lot.

S. I'm not kidding. What time did you get to bed last night?

E. (grins) Three or four. I'm not sure.

S. How much booze did you consume at that party?

E. Not that much. Hey, I can hold my liquor.

S. I'm not saying you can't. But take a look at yourself. If the rings under your eyes were any bigger I could use them for tires. And you can hardly stand up straight.

E. (indignant) I'm not drunk.

S. No one says you are. But how long do you think you can continue a lifestyle like that without undermining your health? How many parties did you attend in the last couple of weeks?

E. I don't know. I like to party.

S. Sure you do. But do you think you can keep staying up until three or four in the morning on nights when you have to come in to work at eight the next day without its affecting your health?

E. I'm in pretty good shape.

S. I hope you're right. But how long do you think it will continue at the pace you're going? Your body's a machine just like the computer and other machines around here. If you misuse the computer by continually turning off the power without first going to the C prompt, it will eventually break down. If you mistreat your body, the same thing will happen. Tell me something, what kind of exercise program have you set up for yourself?

E. Uh, I jog when I get a chance.

S. How often is that?

E. Not too often.

S. Phil, when I hired you six months ago you said you were interested in eventually getting into systems work. Do you still feel that way?

E. Sure, that's what I'm shooting for.

S. Well, sometimes I get the impression that you're not shooting very straight. When you come to work tired and hung over the way you are now, it stands to reason you can't perform up to your potential.

E. I do my job.

S. Sure you do, but lately I've been noticing some slippage. The other day you were so tired you actually fell asleep at your desk.

E. I wasn't sleeping, I was just resting my eyes.

S. At a quarter past nine? At that hour in the morning you should be alert and raring to go. Let me give you some advice as a friend. You may be enjoying all those parties and late-night carousing. But it may be time to face up to realities. Is it worth jeopardizing your health and career for? Consider the future. Then consider the price.

• • • **TALKING POINTS** Too many young people these days, especially singles, get themselves caught up in a mindless existence where they party and drink until all hours of the morning. If this extends into nights when they have to get up to go to work the next day, the result can be disastrous in terms of job performance, accident risk, and poor attendance, not to mention health problems. Too much loss of sleep coupled with an excess of alcohol make as much sense from a health and career standpoint as moving into traffic might be for a blindfolded driver. As a supervisor, the biggest favor you could do for the chronic party buff, your department, and yourself is to try to open the person's eyes to the consequences of an abusive lifestyle. The performance and behavior of candle burners who fill this bill should be monitored closely with the problem boldly addressed at the first sign of adverse health or work indications.

DIALOGUE SIX

Finishing Department Supervisor Eric Hoffstetter reacts to accidents instead of practicing prevention control.

Talking It Out

Manager - Eric, what did you do in response to Frank Costello's head injury last week?

Supervisor - It wasn't a serious accident.

M. That doesn't answer my question. The accident was a result of horseplay, wasn't it?

S. Yeah. Mel Bostwick threw a spool of wire at Frank and he forgot to duck.

M. Getting back to my question, what did you do about it?

S. I gave both those guys a lecture for horsing around and put official warnings in their files.

M. I can't argue with that. But it was a reaction, not a preventive measure. What concerns me is that if you do no more than react, you're ignoring accident control.

S. What do you mean?

M. Just this: When you simply react to accidents and stop there the root causes tend to be overlooked. Good safety management places a focus on planning with accident prevention in mind.

S. What kind of planning?

M. First, organizing a formal program to pinpoint the causes and conditions that lead to accidents. Then following up to determine what must be done to avoid recurrence.

S. I identified the cause of Frank Costello's head injury. It was horseplay.

M. I know. But what action are you planning to take to eliminate horseplay in the future? Do you see what I'm getting at?

S. I'm not sure.

M. All right, I'll cite other examples. Accident causes range from a failure to use safety equipment such as helmets or guards to slippery floor surfaces and defective tools or equipment. That doesn't begin to scratch the surface. But, whatever the cause, the idea is to dig to the root of the problem. Why does the condition exist? What needs to be done to remove it? For example, let's take an accident that was caused by an employee's misuse of a tool. Why did the misuse occur? Was it the wrong tool for the task? Did the employee know *how* to use it? Did he lack experience? Was he working under stress? Do you see what I'm driving at?

S. I think so. Get to the underlying *cause.*

M. Exactly. The underlying cause is the one too often ignored. It could be sloppy supervision, insufficient maintenance, inadequate training or experience, poor motivation, any number of things. Once you determine the underlying cause you are now ready to put action control into the works.

S. Like what?

M. It depends on the situation or problem. In one case you might schedule more inspections, provide harsher discipline for irresponsible adherence to safety rules, improve training, provide better job procedures, and so on. Whatever the case, safety management implies a great deal more than reaction. It implies a planned and formalized program of accident-cause trackdown and prevention.

• • • **TALKING POINTS** Accident prevention is everyone's business, but as a supervisor it is your business most of all. Reaction to an accident is automatic. You have no choice but to react. But if you stop at that point you avoid the most important half of the job. When an accident occurs, two critical questions arise: 1) Should someone be disciplined for his or her part in causing the accident?; 2) What steps should be taken to prevent recurrence of a similar accident? In management, effective safety control implies safety *planning* with preventive action in mind.

chapter twenty
. . . .
TIGHTENING PLANT AND OFFICE SECURITY

It's a hard world out there, and judging from media reports, getting harder by the day. All kinds of disreputable characters roam the streets. Some are bound to wind up seeking jobs in your organization, and your department. These can include a mixed bag of miscreants from alcoholics and other substance abusers to violence-prone psychopaths and plain everyday thieves. It makes nice people like us shudder to think of it. Equally unnerving is the reality that despite the best efforts of personnel professionals to screen and weed out undesirables, some manage to slip through the net. They might, even at this moment, be employed in your company—or perish the thought—your department. What steps can you take to avoid the physical and productivity perils of unsavory employees in your midst?

DIALOGUE ONE

Accounting Department Assistant Supervisor Ken Putney suspects Joe Torres, a member of his group, of stealing. He goes to his boss, Accounting Supervisor Alan Harris, for advice.

Talking It Out

Supervisor - Why do you think Joe might be stealing?

Assistant Supervisor - The way he acts. The day Charlie's wallet was missing, I saw him sneaking around the locker room twenty minutes before lunchtime. Then, during the lunch hour I saw him go out to the parking lot and stick something in his car. When I asked him what he was doing, he said he was checking the air in his spare. But his face got red as if I had caught him in the act of something or other.

S.   (nodding) That looks like it could be suspicious. Anything else?

A.S. Nothing specific. It's the way he acts. The guy looks guilty.

S.   What you describe as guilty could conceivably be his normal appearance. Are you sure you aren't influenced by the fact that Torres is a Latino?

A.S. No way! I've got nothing against Latinos or any other ethnic group.

S.   I know you don't, but I had to ask.

A.S. He just looked like he had something to hide. I told him some stuff had been missing and I was checking around to see what I could learn. When I asked if he would mind my searching his desk, at first he protested, then gave in.

S.   Did you find anything?

A.S. No. But when I told him I'd like to search his locker and car, he absolutely refused.

S.   (frowning) You're treading on dangerous ground there. In general, employers are legally entitled to check a person's workplace, but they must have a sound business reason. Desks, file cabinets, and the like are one thing. Searching a person's locker and car, or intrusion into rest rooms, lounges, and other places where privacy is expected to prevail is another matter entirely. More concrete evidence would be required for that unless contract provisions specify otherwise. And whatever the case, consistency of enforcement is critical.

A.S. You mean calling for a general locker inspection with sufficient cause might be acceptable?

S.   Perhaps. But singling out one worker with inadequate cause can easily backfire, especially if that person is a member of a minor-

ity group. My suggestion is that you keep your eye on Torres. But do it in a way that doesn't tread on his privacy rights.

• • • **TALKING POINTS**   Privacy experts report that employer monitoring of workers is on the rise. A growing number of companies eavesdrop or otherwise snoop on employees in one way or another. Some hire undercover operatives ("finks") who become chummy with suspect workers and get them to confide past and planned misdeeds, most commonly pilferage. Needless to say, this practice is highly controversial. But some employers are desperate. A growing number are being sued for invasion of privacy with corporate losses mounting. However shameful and unpleasant the subject, it is one no supervisor can afford to disregard.

DIALOGUE TWO

Inventory Project Leader Grace violates inventory control procedures. Her boss, Mr. Pace, wants to know why.

Talking It Out

Supervisor - I just got a complaint from the Controller's Office that too many shortages are showing up.

Employee - I don't know why that should be.

S. Neither do I, so I did a bit of investigating on my own. I checked the on-hand balances of 50 items against the inventory taken this morning. The count was wrong on 7 items.

E. Oh, darn!

S. Grace, every one of the items on that list has two check marks next to it, indicating that they had been double-checked as the procedure requires.

E. (red-faced, no comment)

S. I want you to level with me. *Were* they double-checked?

E. I know they're supposed to be. But on this inventory we were so far behind that. . .

S. That's no excuse. Inventory shortage—or shrinkage as it's sometimes referred to—is a serious problem for a number of important business reasons. For one, it is an indication of possible pilferage or product loss due to some other cause. For another, it's a symptom of possible shipping or receiving department inefficiency.

E. (somber expression)

S. When a company stops order processing and other functions to take inventory it is a very expensive proposition. The direct labor cost is high, and even more costly is the delay in picking, packing, and shipping merchandise. Do you think a company would go to all that expense without a sound business reason?

E. (eyes lowered) No sir, I guess not.

S. Without dependable inventories no company can operate effectively. The Purchasing Department relies on an inventory's accuracy to determine which products and materials it must order for the Production Department. The Sales Department depends on the inventory to tell it which products are available for sale, and in what quantity. And the Security Department is interested because without accurate inventory figures, stealing by employees or outsiders could go undetected for months.

E. I guess I never thought of all those things.

S. Apparently not. Grace, you have a good record with this company and I'd like it to remain that way. If you find yourself behind schedule or too backlogged with work to take a careful and accurate inventory, I want you to let me know at once and I'll arrange to get you the help you need. Taking shortcuts on your own initiative simply isn't acceptable. This time I'm going to settle for an official reprimand. If it happens again you won't get off so easy.

E. Thank you. I'm really sorry, Mr. Pace.

S. Apology accepted.

• • • **TALKING POINTS** Employees tend to take periodical routine events such as taking inventory for granted. It is a common practice when people are backlogged with work to shortcut control procedures, and as Grace's action typifies, seek self-imposed remedies to cut down the backlog. If the motivation for such performance is laziness or indifference, as a supervisor you can't be too firm in your swift imposition of discipline, and with repeated violation a valid cause for dismissal. In the case of normally conscientious employees like Grace, an official reprimand along with an explanation of the seriousness of the violation and its consequences is usually enough to prevent its recurrence.

DIALOGUE THREE

Personnel trainee Frieda Reisch, a recent addition to the department, leaves something to be desired in her screening and investigation of job applicants. Her supervisor sets her straight.

Talking It Out

Supervisor - Frieda, I just reviewed John Thorne's job application. I'm surprised that you approved him for employment in the Shipping Department. Were his references checked thoroughly?

Employee - Yes, they were.

S. I don't see how that's possible. Thorne only applied two days ago. The responses couldn't have come back in that time.

E. Oh, I checked them out by phone. Sam Hawkins says he's shorthanded. He needs people as soon as possible.

S. Don't you know that telephone checks are unacceptable except under very unusual circumstances?

E. Yes, but. . .

S. I know, you wanted to be helpful and satisfy Sam Hawkins's need, but his situation is far from unusual. I've met Mr. Thorne and my instincts tell me there's something fishy about his application. I could be wrong, of course, but after all these years I've developed a nose for this kind of thing. In making those phone checks, were the two companies cited as references familiar to you?

E. No, I never heard of them.

S. Did you look them up in the telephone book to make sure the names and numbers coincided with those on the application?

E. (unhappier by the minute) No, I didn't.

S. Why don't we do that now to be on the safe side.

(They consult the telephone directory together and find that the first company given as a reference is not even listed. The second company's name and number are listed as given. The name of the party given as Thorne's former boss is Pete Haley. The supervisor dials the number and asks for the personnel department while Frieda listens in. The supervisor identifies herself and explains that she is double-checking a reference call made earlier in the day to a party named Pete Haley. "Haley? Let me check. Pete Haley is a packer in the Shipping Department. He's not authorized. . . ." The supervisor says thank you and dials the other reference listed on the job application as Harry Roberts. The response is, "Hello." "Is this your residence, Mr. Roberts?" "No, this is the Edgewood Diner. What. . .?" "Thank you." The supervisor hangs up.)

E. (flabbergasted) I can't believe that!

S. (smiles) It's a big bad world out there. This is one good lesson you usually don't learn in school. I don't know what kind of person John Thorne is, or even if that's his real name. If I had to guess, I'd say he's probably a druggie, a thief, or both. These people hop around from job to job. When they are fired and prosecuted, or more commonly, simply let go, they try and try again until they are able to deceive some other victim. Frieda, you can't be too careful or thorough in investigating references and screening applicants. Another thing you should know is that most companies today don't answer queries about former employees or give references over the phone. When one does, it should serve as an alert for extra caution.

• • • **TALKING POINTS** Extra caution applies two ways. On the one hand, the importance of thoroughness in making reference checks cannot be overstated. On the other, respect for the applicant's privacy rights can't be overlooked. Balancing between the two sometimes means walking a fairly taut tightrope. Above all, this underscores the need for confidentiality when applicant information is obtained. Revealing disclosures about an individual to a third party—on either the transmitting or receiving end of a communication—can result in privacy abuse with serious consequences. Even unwittingly doing so can create problems. In one case, damning information about a job candidate was left exposed on a supervisor's desk. When a snooper caught sight of the memo, the word was quickly circulated. This precipitated a civil suit and heavy damages. Enough said?

DIALOGUE FOUR

Jerry Best isn't a thief. Not exactly. An otherwise well-rated employee, he thoughtlessly helps himself to office supplies.

Talking It Out

Supervisor - Jerry, I'm trying to decide whether to fire you or not.

Employee - (worried) Gimme a break. I didn't think of it as stealing.

S. Then why did you try to conceal the stuff from the exit guard? If he hadn't noticed the bulge in your pocket, you would have passed through with those ball-point pens undetected.

E. (eyes lowered) I'm not a thief, Mr. Rice.

S. (thoughtful) I don't think you are either, Jerry, at least not by nature or upbringing. But what you did was petty theft, to put it kindly.

E. I didn't look at it that way. I figured for a company of this size what difference could a few ball-point pens possibly make? That was wrong. I realize it now.

S. It certainly was. Do you think the company's stationery outlet supplies us with such things as pens, staple guns, paper clips, and memo pads as a complimentary gesture of goodwill? Do you have any idea what the annual cost of office supplies runs us?

E. No sir, I don't.

S. It amounts to thousands of dollars. Those "few ball-point pens" you were caught with cost the company ten dollars or more. Suppose all employees reasoned what difference does it make to a big company and did the same thing? You're good at arithmetic. Figure it out and see what you come up with.

E. I see that now. If you give me another chance I won't do it again.

S. All right, Jerry, because of your good work record, I'll give you another chance. But one more incident of this type and you're through.

• • • **TALKING POINTS** Dishonesty is a state of mind. Where does the petty theft of supply items like pens, pencils, and pads fit into the picture? Should you construe it to be larceny? It depends on the circumstances and the employee involved. Also, on the company's communicated mindset on the subject. In the situation cited above the supervisor was to some extent remiss because had the seriousness of petty theft been made clear to his work group, it's unlikely a conscientious and basically honest person like Jerry would have filched those pens. As a supervisor it makes good security and ethical sense to get the message across to your people that no form of pilferage, however petty, will be tolerated. Some might argue that Jerry, however good his work record, should have been fired on the spot. Whether or not you agree is purely a subjective matter.

DIALOGUE FIVE

When violence erupted in his department, Warehouse Supervisor Vince Todd wasn't sure what to do when the police and reporters came knocking.

Talking It Out

Manager - Vince, I'm glad you came to see me. I was about to call you. I've been in touch with the hospital. Benson is expected to pull through, and from what I've been told, Parker's wound is superficial.

Supervisor - That's right. I just found out they bandaged him up and sent him home.

M. Good. We can be thankful that Rostov wasn't a better shot. It could have been much worse. What made him go off half-cocked like that? How many shots did he get off before being restrained?

S. Five or six. We don't know for sure yet what made him go berserk. The guy's apparently unstable.

M. (nodding his head) He'd have to be. No matter how hard you try to screen out the weirdos, some always manage to slip through. Of course, much as we can do without the publicity, we had no choice but to notify the police as soon as it happened.

S. I realize that, sir.

M. That's what I want to talk to you about. Rostov was arrested minutes after the incident. But we'll be getting another visit from the police within the hour, and probably a bevy of reporters and possibly TV newspeople as well.

S. That's what I figured. What do you want me to do?

M. Very little, actually. Most of all, stay cool and be courteous in response to questions. Don't let the onslaught intimidate you into making hasty or impulsive statements. As you know, it is corporate policy for Security to act as liaison in matters of law enforcement, and for our Public Relations people to field questions from the press and local authorities. Your first step when approached by a police officer, reporter, or community representative, is to request identification. Then refer them to the Security or Public Relations person in charge.

S. If I'm asked a specific question, should I refuse to answer?

M. For the most part, yes, with a few simple exceptions. Just explain that you're not authorized to answer. Bill Hirsch from Public Relations is on his way down to go over with you what you can and cannot say. In situations of this kind, you can't be too careful about statements you make to the police or press. In all the excitement and turmoil it's easy to blurt something out, or agree to an implication that might result in liability for the company.

• • • **TALKING POINTS** A recommended approach when violence erupts is to be truthful and yet intentionally vague. Employee privacy rights, even those of the miscreant in the case of criminal action, must be upheld. Time is usually needed for company authorities and investigators to sort out the issues. In the event a security or other authorized communications official isn't on hand at the scene, your best bet as a supervisor is to be as cooperative as possible without being outspoken. A useful response: "We don't have all the facts yet," or "That matter is under investigation."

Dialogue Six

General office employee Miriam Halstead is found guilty of time-card abuse.

Talking It Out

Supervisor - Miriam, are you aware that Louise left work yesterday at 3:30 without clocking out?

Employee - No, I'm not.

S. I don't think you're telling the truth. Her time card was punched out at 5:00 P.M., the exact same time that you clocked out.

E. I don't know anything about that.

S. I think you do. There's no point in compounding your dishonesty with lies. You were observed by two people punching Louise's time card.

E. That can't be true.

S. I have two witnesses.

E. (face flushed) I, uh. . .

S. That will be all, Miriam. Your final check will be waiting for you in the personnel office.

(Miriam's co-worker, Louise, who had acted in collusion with her friend in arranging the illicit clock-out, was similarly interviewed and fired the next day.)

• • • **TALKING POINTS**   Ordinarily, employees guilty of breaking the rules undergo a procedure of two or more official warnings and suspensions before the ultimate discipline of discharge is imposed. With certain notable exceptions including dishonesty, violence, and in some cases substance abuse. Time-card abuse—involving the employee's own card or that of a friend—is a form of out-and-out stealing. Abusers permitted to get away with dishonesty of this type invite more of the same from co-workers. However unpleasant the task may be, time-card abuse is valid cause for dismissal.

chapter twenty-one

· · · · · · · · · · · · · · · · · ·

TRAINING AND DEVELOPING PEOPLE

Recruiting, interviewing, screening, and hiring people adds up to a heavy investment of both money and time. Most supervisors realize this and in response make every effort to get new employees off on the right foot and functioning effectively. The trouble is that too many supervisors, once new hires are "broken in," forget about them and turn to what they feel are more pressing priorities. This mistake can be costly. "Breaking in" people does not even begin to qualify as a training program. Whoever the employee and whatever the job, training is an ongoing process. It is *teaching,* by means of instruction and example. It is a function that must be continually monitored, reviewed, and tailored to the individual on the learning end. The operational axiom is: If the employee hasn't learned, the instructor hasn't taught.

DIALOGUE ONE

Art Fisher, Section A Supervisor in the Claims Department, is too busy to train and develop his people.

Talking It Out

Manager - Art, I think it's time we sat down and reviewed your department's training program.

Supervisor - I don't have a formal training program. I train people as the need arises.

M. For example?

S. Well, when Eileen quit, I trained Beth to take over her job.

M. What else?

S. When the new word processor was ordered, I sent Tony to school to learn how to operate the machine.

M. What about Joan? How does she figure into your training effort?

S. (frowning) She doesn't. Joan's one of the best people in the department. She knows her job from A to Z. She doesn't need any training.

M. If she's that good, don't you think she deserves a crack at a higher-level job? And if that's so, wouldn't it require some training?

S. Yes, I see what you mean.

M. Eileen was a top performer too. Why did she quit?

S. The reason she gave at her exit interview was to take a job with a better chance for advancement.

M. Had you prepared her for a higher-paying job here, isn't it possible we wouldn't have lost her to a competitor?

S. (thoughtfully) I guess it is.

M. Let me ask you another question closer to home. Are you satisfied with your own job? Do you ever think in terms of advancement for yourself, to Department Supervisor for example, or a managerial job?

S. Sure.

M. Well, if that were to suddenly materialize, who would your successor be?

S. I, uh, I couldn't say offhand. I have a number of good people who might qualify.

M. But no one specific you can name. You have no one in mind worthy of being groomed and trained for succession?

S. Well, no, but...

M. Excuse me for interrupting. As a rule, advancement opportunities don't wait. If you had a good offer tomorrow, how long would it take you to pick a successor?

S. Not very long. A couple of days probably.

M. Just for discussion, let's suppose you picked Mary as your successor. Keeping in mind all those special reports that you run, and the confidential stuff you take care of, not to mention the planning and scheduling, how long would it take you to train her to step into your job?

S. I don't know. At least three or four weeks.

M. That would be quite a feat. But let's say you could do this and chose Bill to take over Mary's job. How much time would it take to train him?

S. Uh, I couldn't say.

M. I'm not surprised. I'm trying to get the message across that training and developing people to take on added responsibility and higher-level jobs isn't a sometime or spur-of-the-moment enterprise. It's an everyday ongoing requirement that takes special thought, planning, and time. Realistically, if a chance for a better job came through tomorrow, it would be long since gone by the time you were ready for it. That might give you something to think about. You owe it, not only to your people, but yourself, to give training and development the very highest priority.

• • • **TALKING POINTS** Failure to provide an effective ongoing training and development program is an unspoken admission of a readiness to settle for the status quo. In today's tough competitive marketplace, the status quo is a career and productivity killer. It sends a message to smart, high-performing employees that they are likely to wind up spinning their wheels if they stick around. It risks leaving the department with an under-supply of good people who end up hating themselves and the company for their lack of courage to quit, and an over-supply of mediocrities who undermine the operation. It puts the supervisor who lacks the foresight to recognize the critical importance of planned, continuing training and development in a wheel-spinning rut as well.

DIALOGUE TWO

Accounts Payable Supervisor Beverly Marcus has job-security fears that keep her from training and developing qualified subordinates.

Talking It Out

Manager - Bev, are the rumors I've been hearing that Elaine is shopping the job market true?

Supervisor - I don't know. I hope not.

M. So do I. She's one of our best people. With her experience, it would hurt the department to lose her.

S. Don't I know it!

M. It wouldn't surprise me to learn that the rumors are true. She's been looking disgruntled these past few months. Any idea why?

S. No. I treat her pretty well.

M. How well is pretty well? Or let me put it another way: What have you done for her lately?

S. What do you mean?

M. As an example, have you signed her up for the Accounting course the company offers?

S. No.

M. Why not? It ties in with her job, and could help qualify her for a higher-level job.

S. (shifting nervously) We've been too busy lately. I can't spare her.

M. Ugh, that excuse again! As a top performer, what kind of attention have you given to her development? Have you delegated any of the work you've been doing yourself? Are you making any effort to groom her for a higher-level job?

S. No. I guess not.

M. It's no wonder then if she's shopping around. Elaine's too smart and ambitious to stay at a job where she sees no chance for advancement. And we both know that "too busy" is no valid excuse for neglecting an employee of her caliber. Bev, let's put our cards on the table. You've been short-changing Elaine because you

view her as a threat to your job security. You're afraid that if she becomes too well-qualified she might take over your job. Am I right?

S. *(eyes lowered, admission enough) I suppose so.*

M. Thanks for being honest with me. As a supervisor you're an important part of the management team and I'd like to set you straight. You're a good and valued employee and a significant investment was made in your own training and development.

S. *(nodding agreement) Yes, I know.*

M. Fine. Then let's take the worst-case scenario. Suppose Elaine was trained to the point where she qualified for your job. What do you think would happen then?

S. *(frowning) Well, I earn over $50,000 a year; Elaine earns less than $30,000. You could give her my job and save $20,000 a year.*

M. And do what? Fire you?

S. *(morose) I guess that's what I was worried about.*

M. (smiling) Let me show you how misguided that reasoning is. What kind of a company would this be if, instead of rewarding our good people, we punished them? What kind of a message would that convey to the rest of the staff and the public?

S. *(thoughtful) I see what you mean.*

M. Now let's look at the situation with your own career and ambition in mind. Don't you ever think of some day advancing to a higher-level job yourself?

S. *Sure.*

M. Well, how could that happen if, at the time the opportunity presented itself, someone like Elaine hadn't been groomed to take over your job? Doesn't that make sense?

S. *Yes, I guess it does.*

M. You don't have to guess. Any way you look at it, failing to train and develop a subordinate for fear she may become skilled and knowledgeable enough to take over, is about as short-sighted and unrealistic as one could be.

• • • **TALKING POINTS** Horror tales can be told of well-paid people, usually executives, being fired and replaced by subordinates earning a fraction of their income. But in the real world such cases are few and far between.

They occur in organizations so disreputable and behind the times, no smart person would want to work there. More often we hear of such cases when they are dramatically portrayed in movies and books. No progressive company worth its salt would penalize people for their skills and achievement. It would be horrendous employee- and public-relations strategy, and it would make recruiting good people a hardship. The potential loss from such a move would far exceed any wage saving that might be gained.

Dialogue Three

Ed Prentiss is miffed because his supervisor failed to sign him up for the company's computer systems training course.

Talking It Out

Employee - It's not fair. I've got 3 years' seniority with good experience as a word-processing operator. Employees with lower seniority and less experience were signed up for the course.

Supervisor - I'm sorry about that, Ed. But longevity isn't the only qualifying factor.

E. *I have a good work record. I'm conscientious and show up on time every day.*

S. No argument there. You're a valued member of this department.

E. *So why didn't I get the break?*

S. Because that training represents a big investment in both teaching cost and time lost from the job while attending the course. You were given the qualifying test the same as other employees who applied for the training. The test results showed you lack the technical potential.

E. *I don't think that's so. Tests always make me nervous. If I took it again, I think I would pass.*

S. Let me check the result again. (checks the record) I'm sorry, Ed, your score was too low for me to give you another crack at the test. Not everyone is suited for every job. You do a good job as a word-processing operator. As long as you continue to do so you'll earn merit increases from time to time, but that's the best I can do.

E. *(disgruntled, but resigned) Thanks anyway for checking it out.*

● ● ● **TALKING POINTS**   Actually, Ed was not only technically unsuited for systems work—and hence the training—he was intellectually unsuited as well. But as his supervisor wisely reasoned, there would have been no point in telling him that, thereby hurting his feelings with the implication that he was mentally unqualified. The fact of life must be faced that, however desirable training may be, as Ed's supervisor stated the case, not everyone is right for every job. Sad as it may be at times, employees must be made to face up to the reality—in the kindest way possible—that an advancement opportunity isn't everyone's cup of tea.

DIALOGUE FOUR

Linda in Purchasing is well-qualified for the company's training course in materials evaluation, but isn't interested in participating.

Talking It Out

Supervisor - Linda, I checked the sign-up sheet for the materials evaluation course and was surprised to see your name missing from it.

Employee - The hours don't fit into my schedule. Maybe if the training was on company time I'd be more interested.

S. I'm afraid that isn't feasible. For one thing the training isn't in-house. For another, you couldn't be spared from the job during the day.

E. Well, thanks anyway for thinking of me.

S. The reason I'm thinking of you is that you're ideally suited for both the course, and assuming you did well, for the job advancement it could lead to. Since this is a college course, do you realize how much money the company's sponsorship would save you?

E. Sure, I know that and appreciate it.

S. Aren't you interested in qualifying for a better job and the increased income it would mean?

E. Yes, I am.

S. But not interested enough to make the sacrifice needed to qualify?

E. (shrugs) I guess not.

S. Very well. Thanks for leveling with me. I'll turn in the approval list without your name.

• • • TALKING POINTS   When a qualified employee turns down a training opportunity that could lead to promotion, a variety of reasons might apply. Your first step as a supervisor should be to pinpoint the reason that applies to the situation at hand. In attempting to do this, Linda's supervisor learned via the grapevine that she was planning to become pregnant and would probably resign within the next year or so. He revised his own thinking and planning accordingly, eliminating Linda as potential promotion material. At other times, a person's rejection of a voluntary training opportunity might be nothing more than sheer lack of ambition or laziness. In a recent case that came to light, the qualified training candidate didn't appreciate her own potential. When her supervisor applied a booster shot of self-confidence the employee changed her mind and performed well in both the course and the advanced job it produced. Each case must be decided on its own merit.

DIALOGUE FIVE

Mike Farrow, a young Production employee, has been bugging his supervisor to train him for job opportunities that don't exist.

Talking It Out

Employee - I've been dead-ended running this drill press for over a year now. How about signing me up for an inspector's course, or maybe training me to operate the automatic screw machine. I'd have no problem breezing through a course like that.

Supervisor - I'm sure you wouldn't. You're a smart guy. You would probably do well. But like I told you before, it doesn't make sense to train someone for a job when no opening is expected.

E. (disgruntled) Even if there's nothing today, it doesn't mean nothing will open up in the future.

S. That may be true, but it's not that simple. One problem is that none of our inspectors or screw-machine operators are old enough to retire in the foreseeable future, and they're all in good health. The other problem is I have enough people on hand who are already qualified to step into both of those jobs should one open up unexpectedly.

E. So what am I supposed to do? Sit on my butt till I'm 50 waiting for a break to come through?

S. *(smiles sympathetically) I appreciate your frustration, Mike. But don't be such a pessimist. You're still in your twenties. I doubt that you'll have to wait quite that long for a break. Still, we both have to face realities. If you receive training for one of those jobs, you'd be twice as frustrated when one didn't come through.*

E. Maybe so, but what am I supposed to do in the meantime?

S. *The only thing I can advise is to be patient. You're a hard worker with a good record. I can't make any commitments right now. But I won't forget about you. Sooner or later a suitable training or promotion opportunity is bound to develop. When one does I'll have you in mind and we can talk about it then.*

• • • **TALKING POINTS** On one hand, few supervisory functions have higher priority than training and developing people to qualify for higher-level jobs and assignments. On the other, a supervisor must realistically keep the consequences of both acting and not acting in mind. Mike's boss's rationale is well taken. It doesn't make good business sense to train employees for a job they won't be able to fill when their training is through. If he acceded to Mike's request the outcome would be predictable: Frustration, followed by either a bitter and unhappy employee, or Mike's resignation, with a good chance that a competitor would reap the benefits of his former employer's training investment. Dealing with an ambitious employee's impatience in situations of this type requires a sympathetic, tactful, and truthful response. Above all, you should level with the person, predicting hope for the future where such hope exists, without making a commitment you're not sure you can keep.

DIALOGUE SIX

Mail-Room Supervisor Doris Lake, too busy to train new recruits herself, is careless in turning over the task to others.

Talking It Out

Supervisor - Ellen, I owe you an apology. You've been standing around twiddling your thumbs for almost two days now. I know how hard this is on a new employee. I've been meaning to sit down with you and break you into the job. But you can see how busy I've been.

Employee - That's okay. I understand.

S. Thanks for your patience. But I can't let you just stand around. Wait a minute. Let me see who's available. Oh, I see someone. Marge seems to be free at the moment. (summons Marge) Marge, say hello to Ellen. She started two days ago. She'll be taking over Jim Keene's desk. I think you know the requirements. Why don't you sit down with Ellen and give her the lowdown. If you have any problems or questions, see me.

(Marge does as instructed. She sits down with the new hire, and the two women chat at former employee Jim Keene's desk. Doris's boss, Office Manager Ceil Blake, passes through the department and notices Marge and Ellen at Jim's desk. She summons Doris to her office.)

Manager - Doris, isn't that the girl you just hired sitting with Marge at Jim's desk?

Supervisor - Yes, it is. I've been meaning to get her started doing Jim's job, but I've been so busy I just can't find the time.

M. So you delegated Marge to do it for you?

S. Yes, I couldn't have Ellen standing around useless until I became free to do it myself.

M. Well, that makes sense. But I can't see the sense of picking someone like Marge for the job. She's a marginal employee. In fact, if I recall correctly you were contemplating firing her a couple of months ago.

S. (frowning) I know. But she was the only one available.

M. I can't buy that excuse. You should know by now that employee training is one of your most important supervisory functions. It is doubly important where new recruits are concerned. The way a new hire is introduced to the job and co-workers helps set a pattern for the person's attitude and performance that, once set, is

often difficult to break. New people tend to emulate and be guided by the person who breaks them in. Do you view Marge as an acceptable role model for Ellen?

S. *No, I guess not.*

M. **You don't have to guess. Assigning Marge runs a risk of creating a clone. In most cases, an employee's supervisor is the best person to do the training. If this isn't practical for some reason, a supervisor can't be too careful in selecting a delegatee with proven qualifications and motivation to handle the job.**

• • • **TALKING POINTS**   On-the-job training can be no more effective than the individual selected for the task. If circumstances prevent you from undertaking the chore yourself as the trainee's supervisor, your best bet—no matter how busy you are—is to take the time and effort needed to select a suitable substitute. Ideally, training should be planned, not arranged on the spur of the moment. Care must be taken to ensure that the person chosen has training experience and the ability to teach. Qualified teachers, whatever their title or rank, should know the job thoroughly, be able to express themselves clearly, possess the patience and rapport the learning process demands, and as important as any other factor, must have the proper attitude necessary to handle the job well.

chapter twenty-two

. . . .

HIRING AND
FIRING PEOPLE

How effectively your department performs depends on three main factors: 1) How effectively you yourself function as a leader and guide; 2) How effectively you hire people; 3) How effectively you act to rid your operation of employees who are irremediably counterproductive. Clearly, the most difficult and unpleasant of this trio is the third—firing an employee who can't or won't meet the mark. No less clear is the reality that if you do a good job on the second factor and hire superior candidates, your trials and tribulations relating to number three will be minimized and will help your efforts to excel as a leader and guide. The ancient adage that an operation is no better than its people is probably the most important of all from a personal career standpoint.

DIALOGUE ONE

Recently appointed Sales Department Supervisor Frank Coleman's interviewing techniques leave a great deal to be desired.

Talking It Out

Manager - Frank, I just got a call from Helen in Personnel that a young lady named Belinda Jones is in her office threatening to sue the company.

Supervisor - (surprised) Because I turned her down for the job? She wasn't qualified.

M. Not because you turned her down. Because of the way you conducted the interview.

S. What do you mean?

M. It seems that some of the questions you asked were either illegal or inappropriate. In addition to being insulted, she accuses you of being prejudiced against her because she's black.

S. That's ridiculous.

M. I know it is, and you know it is, but that doesn't mean the applicant knows it. Helen feels that some of the questions you asked were out of line.

S. I simply wanted to see if she was qualified for the Sales Correspondent's job that was advertised.

M. In that case, what does her credit rating have to do with her being qualified? Or that question about preschool-aged children? Or whether the man she's living with is her husband or not? Helen says you inquired not only about her education, but asked about her parents' education as well. To minority applicants from lower economic class origins questions like that can be construed to be not only insulting and inappropriately personal, but discriminatory as well.

S. (eyes lowered) Maybe I didn't think it through thoroughly enough.

M. You sure didn't. You also didn't read the company's policy manual on interviewing job candidates. It is a well-documented and carefully-thought-out guide that would have spared you this problem had you done so. Frank, Ms. Jones is still in Helen's office. I want you to go in there, apologize to her, and assure her that none of your remarks or questions were intended to be prejudiced or discriminatory. Hopefully, that will get the company off the hook on this matter. Then I want you to crack that manual until you can practically memorize those guidelines.

• • • **TALKING POINTS**   Given Equal Employment Opportunity Commission restrictions and guidelines, interviewing, screening, and hiring job applicants can be a hazardous enterprise. Conducted by the seat of one's pants they are fraught with legal and job-performance risks that could haunt a supervisor for months. In no area of management are supervisory training and savvy more critical. When interviewing candidates, not only *what* you say but *how* you say it can be important. In screening minority applicants, careful objectivity must be applied to avoid questions or statements that might appear to an African-American, Asian, or Hispanic recruit to be culturally biased in favor of Anglo-Americans. As for appropriateness, if an offensive question is asked, even if not illegal, the interview's purpose could be defeated by the candidate's refusal to take the job.

DIALOGUE TWO

Data Processing Department Supervisor Sara Quinn delegates job-applicant interviews she should be conducting herself.

Talking It Out

Manager - (sets employee turnover report on Sara's desk) Have you seen this yet?

Supervisor - (anxious) Yes sir.

M. This is the third quarter in a row that your department's turnover ranks among the company's worst. More employees than ever were either fired or resigned.

S. I know. Historically, I think there's a greater amount of turnover of technical people than others.

M. That may be so, but I don't think that's the answer here. Resignations in the Engineering Department are low. And the Systems Department enjoys one of the company's best turnover records. There must be some other reason and I want to get to the bottom of it. I'm especially concerned when we lose good employees. What reason do most people give for resigning?

S. To seek higher pay or a better opportunity elsewhere.

M. That's a standard response and may or may not be the case. I've been checking the records of several employees who resigned from Data Processing or were fired during the past six months or so, and some disturbing facts emerged. One is that too many people were hired who were only marginally qualified. Another is that a number of candidates were hired who were overqualified. What does that say to you?

S. (somber) Maybe we're not careful enough in our hiring practices.

M. That's my guess. Let's see if we can find out why. Let's review your hiring procedure step by step. When a candidate screened by Personnel is sent to you to be interviewed, what happens?

S. I usually review the person's application blank.

M. Usually?

S. If I'm not too busy or tied up at a meeting, in which case Joe or Harriet looks it over. . .

M. Then what happens?

S. The applicant gets interviewed.

M. By you?

S. Not all the time. If I'm tied up Harriet or Joe might take care of it.

M. (nodding) Thinking back, how many of the accepted applicants are hired by you? Half? One quarter?

S. I don't know. I guess it depends on the time of the month.

M. Take a look at the report. What percentage of the terminated employees listed would you say had been hired by you personally?

S. I guess, a pretty small percentage.

M. (closes report) Do me a favor. Call to mind as many supervisory functions as you can that you consider more important than hiring personnel for your department.

S. (blows out cheeks, remains silent)

M. (smiles) Your answer is right on the mark, Sara. *Nothing* is more important than hiring people, and no one in your department is, or should be better qualified than you to do it. From now on, if you can possibly help it, don't delegate this critical task to a subordinate.

• • • **Talking Points** Hiring an underqualified, overqualified, or otherwise undesirable job applicant, can plague a department and hamper productivity for months or even years. Ideally, with Personnel's help, no one is better equipped than the head honcho to make the hiring decisions. Exceptions do exist, however, such as when a replacement is urgently needed and the supervisor is sick or on vacation. Or perhaps when a subordinate is being groomed for the top job, and under careful supervisory guidance, is given a crack at interviewing and hiring a candidate. It's conceivable that an applicant's qualifications may be too technical for the supervisor to evaluate, and a qualified subordinate is assigned to the task. But whatever the circumstances, a department head should pay close and concerned attention to individuals hired and procedures used in the process.

DIALOGUE THREE

Pete Baxter is a misfit and deadbeat who should have been fired long ago. But Don, his supervisor, finds this a painful task to confront.

Talking It Out

Manager - What's this, Don?

Supervisor - An official warning and suspension notice for your approval.

M. Again! Correct me if I'm wrong, but isn't this the third or fourth suspension for Baxter in as many months?

S. The fourth.

M. And how many warning slips?

S. Six or seven.

M. (scrutinizes notice and reads aloud) "Caught leaving premises for a beer break at a local pub during working hours without authorization. Absent 40 minutes from work station." Isn't that pretty much the same thing he was suspended for last time?

S. Yes, it is.

M. What about the time before that?

S. He was caught asleep in a crate in the storage room.

M. (setting notice aside) How many suspensions do you plan to give this guy before firing him?

S. I told him this was his last chance.

M. Satisfy my curiosity, Don. Why wasn't Baxter fired long ago?

S. I guess I keep putting it off. The guy's got a family. He promised to shape up. I kept giving him another chance.

M. I'm going to tell you a story that may seem like a fairy tale, but it's not. There was this machine operator who kept messing up all the time, always pleading for another chance until he was finally fired. Today he's head dispatcher elsewhere earning twice his former income. He may be a rare exception. I don't know. Some losers will be losers wherever they are and whatever they do. Others change if they find work better suited for them, or a place where they fit. My point is, as much as you want to be a good guy, you may not be doing people like Baxter a favor by keeping them on. Painful or not, when a person deserves to be fired you simply have to bite the bullet and do it. Am I getting through?

S. Yes sir.

M. (voiding suspension notice) Suspension not approved. I want you to fire this guy.

• • • **TALKING POINTS** Hanging on to employees who repeatedly violate rules, fail to perform up to standard, or don't carry their fair share of the workload is a sign of weak supervisory management. It not only hurts other employees, the department and company, but you as the supervisor, and in some cases the employee as well. You wouldn't work in a department that is dirty and messed up with dust, droppings, and scrap. It is no less important to clean up the workplace from a performance and behavior standpoint as well. Employees who don't do the job they are paid for make it more difficult to meet company and personal goals. They have no place in the organization.

DIALOGUE FOUR

Guilty of crisis management, Shipping Supervisor Greg Kirchner thinks in terms of "warm bodies" instead of productive employees and is in conflict with Personnel Manager Alice Schwartz over the issue.

Talking It Out

Supervisor - We're in a bind, Alice, behind schedule with more orders piling in every day. I asked for eight people three days ago. All you sent me was four.

Manager - We're doing our best. We advertised in the local papers and called two agencies.

S. So what's the holdup? You had a lineup of at least twenty applicants in response to the ads.

M. That's true, but most of them didn't qualify. They'd give you more grief than help in the long run.

S. Picking and packing merchandise isn't that hard. If they don't work out I'll let them go before their probationary period expires.

M. That's a self-defeating philosophy. Too many deadbeats are on good behavior while on probation then revert to form afterwards. Others are overlooked in the rush of business, overstay their probation, and by that time are difficult to fire.

S. That doesn't solve my problem.

M. You could have solved it yourself with a little advance planning. You knew weeks ago when the rush season would start. That's when you should have put in your request for extra personnel. We would have had plenty of time to screen and hire all the people you need.

S. I know. I was jammed up with other things and kept putting it off. So what do I do now? Orders are being shipped late. Customers are griping.

M. Those ads are still running, and we'll continue interviewing applicants as fast as we can. In the meantime, I'll call a couple of temp agencies. We may be able to hire a few temps until we can find enough good regulars to fill the bill.

S. Thanks. In the meantime I guess I'll have to keep scheduling heavy overtime in an effort to keep up with the workload.

M. I don't see any alternative. Heavy overtime isn't the best solution. But anything is preferable to hiring "warm bodies" when what you need are quality people.

• • • **TALKING POINTS** How often have you groaned to yourself or an associate: "If I only knew, I never would have hired that guy?" Especially in unionized operations, where chronic losers manage to hang on beyond the probationary period, getting rid of them can be harder than boiling an egg without water. At times, when the unexpected occurs, crash hiring can't be helped. More commonly it's a sign of poor planning. An operation is most vulnerable when order processing and production peaks rivet supervisory attention on getting the work out to the exclusion of everything else. The antidote to mindless hiring is usually simple: advance planning whenever possible. Failing this, try temps, recruiting help from other departments, or if you're in a real pinch, increased overtime. Anything is better than settling for people only marginally qualified.

DIALOGUE FIVE

Joyce, a terminated employee, threatens to sue the company because her supervisor, Ben Smith, failed to follow prescribed procedures in firing her.

Talking It Out

Manager - Sit down, Ben, I want to go over Joyce Cochran's personnel file with you.

Supervisor - (frowning) Why? She was terminated two days ago.

M. I'm all too well aware of that. I just received a letter from her lawyer. She claims she was fired unfairly.

S. She's gotta be kidding. I should have let her go weeks ago. Her performance was consistently below standard. During the past few months her attendance kept getting worse and worse. I had no choice but to terminate her.

M. **I'm not questioning your judgment. What I'm interested in learning is *how* you fired her.**

S. *What do you mean?*

M. **She claims you fired her because you're prejudiced against women.**

S. *That's ridiculous.*

M. **Not according to her lawyer. How, specifically, does her termination notice read?**

S. *Here, I have a copy of it. It states the reason as "Unacceptably excessive absence and lateness despite repeated supervisory warnings." The official warning notices are right here in her file.*

M. **(checks file) I see two notices.**

S. *Right. On the second one she was warned that one more violation would result in dismissal.*

M. **(frowning) I'm afraid she may have a good case.**

S. *Why? I don't get it.*

M. **Let's take another look at that letter. According to her claim, several male employees have had worse attendance records than she, and have not been terminated. She also says most employees get at least one or two suspensions before being fired. That's true, isn't it?**

S. *Maybe so, but none of their records showed performance as substandard as hers.*

M. **Unfortunately, that isn't germane. Poor performance wasn't cited on the termination notice. She was fired for poor *attendance* and that's all that counts.**

S. *(worried) What happens now?*

M. **That remains to be seen. It doesn't look good. I'm as much to blame for this mess as you are; I should have monitored your termination procedure more closely. But let's get it straight right now to avoid any recurrence of this kind: With a few exceptions, such as dishonesty and violence, company policy calls for a system of progressive discipline before terminating people.**

Typically, this would entail three warning notices and one or two suspensions. That might vary slightly depending on the infraction, and needless to say, any reason given for discharge must be supported by well-documented evidence.

S. I have documentation for every one of Cochran's absences.

M. I know you do. But that's only one slice of the pie. Most important of all is to shoot for consistency. That applies to all kinds of discipline. You can't punish one employee after only two official warnings if you give others three or more warnings for the same offense. If one employee is suspended before being terminated, the others are entitled to the same treatment. Finally, you can't fire a person for one thing, and expect other unspecified reasons to apply as just cause in a legal proceeding.

• • • **TALKING POINTS**   No area of the employer-employee relationship is more sensitive than job termination. Where a labor agreement is in force, the issue is doubly sensitive. Care must also be taken to avoid any action that violates statements made in the company's policy manual, or in a contractual agreement with the employee at the time of hire. In union shops in particular, legal mavens thrive. They are quick to seize upon even the slightest evidence of inconsistency in the imposition of discipline. And no matter how conscientious you are in applying discipline, you can't be too conscientious where the person on the receiving end belongs to a minority group. A high proportion of discrimination suits are lodged by African-Americans and Hispanics, and to a lesser degree women, who bring suit against unfair labor practices and sexual harassment in the workplace.

chapter twenty-three

• • • • • • • • • • • • • • • • •

GRIEVANCE AVOIDANCE

Grievances are expensive to process. In addition, whether justified or not, they constitute a barometer of employee morale. Studies show that good morale inevitably goes hand in hand with good productivity. Every company, large or small, union or nonunion, has some kind of formal or informal grievance procedure in dealing with employee disagreements and gripes. But experience proves that the most productive operations of all are those in which good face-to-face communication between employee and supervisor not only helps temper grievances when they occur, but often prevents them from occurring altogether.

DIALOGUE ONE

No grievance articulated, but from John Hudson's actions and behavior his supervisor concludes that something seems to be bothering him.

Talking It Out

Supervisor - (warm, confiding smile) What's the problem, John? I can tell something's bothering you.

Employee - (clearly uncomfortable) No, I'm okay.

S. If that's so, whatever happened to the friendly carefree guy I used to know? You've been walking around with a long face lately. I get the feeling you're frustrated about something, or have a problem on your mind. Is it something connected with work?

E. No, nothing like that.

S. Trouble at home? Are the kids okay?

E. Yeah, they're fine.

S. Marge?

E. She's okay.

S. Good. I'm glad to hear it. In that case, I can assume everything's going well on the job. You feel you're being well-treated. No hassles, no complaints.

E. (frowns, moistens his lips)

S. Uh oh. I smell a rat. Hey, I'm on your side, pal, remember?

E. I don't know; I don't like to be pushy.

S. Getting a problem or frustration off your chest isn't being pushy. It's plain common sense. I won't pretend every problem has a solution, but when you keep a gripe locked up it tends to fester. Maybe, if we pick up the ball and kick it around a bit we'll be able to get it over the goal. Does that make sense?

E. Yeah, I guess so.

S. Good. So let's have it.

E. (takes a deep breath) It's that computer course the company is sponsoring. I put in for it six weeks ago and never heard anything. People with less experience and seniority have been accepted. I've got a PC at home and think I'm better qualified than they are. If you're not satisfied with my work. . .

S. Whoa there, hold up, brother! Whatever gave you the idea I'm not satisfied? Quite the opposite is true. You're one of my most valued employees.

E. Then why?

S. Good question. Let's find out. Wait here. I'll be back in a jiff.

(Leaves office to check it out with the Training Department, returns in 10 minutes.)

S. I think I have the answer, John, and we owe you an apology. I checked the names on that application list. Yours wasn't included.

E. That's impossible. I distinctly remember. . .

S. I know. Two lists were posted, the first was to determine who would be interested. Your name is on that one. The second, two weeks later, was the actual application list. That's the one where your name was omitted.

E. Wait a minute. I must have been on vacation when that list was posted.

S. That's what I figured. But cheer up. We got such a good response, a second course is being scheduled in the near future. I'll make sure you're signed up for that.

E. (bright smile replacing the gloom) Hey thanks, I appreciate it.

S. No problem. Or more correctly, a problem no longer.

• • • **TALKING POINTS** As any experienced salesperson can confirm, sometimes a harbored and unarticulated gripe can be more damaging than a gripe angrily expressed. In the above example, John, an above-average employee reluctant to express his true feelings, might well have found another job and resigned in frustration. Experience proves that often the best way to avoid a grievance is to stay alert enough to the signs to anticipate it.

DIALOGUE TWO

Mary Ann, a financially hard-pressed employee, complains that she doesn't get as much overtime as workers in another department.

Talking It Out

Employee - Workers in Assembly are getting 10 to 12 hours a week overtime. I haven't had more than six hours in the past two months.

Supervisor - Thanks.

E. What do you mean by that?

S. Thanks, Mary Ann, for complimenting me on doing such a good job. Boosting productivity and keeping down overtime is part of my responsibility as a member of management.

E. *That doesn't help my financial situation. I've got two kids at home.*

S. **I'm aware of that. But I think you'll agree that when overtime does become necessary, you get your fair share. In fact, since I'm aware of your problem, when other employees don't object, I will try to give you the preference.**

E. *Yeah, but. . .*

S. **I know, you're still in a financial bind. All right, let's talk about that for a moment.**

E. *(face brightens) You're going to put me in for an increase?*

S. **(smiles) I wish I could. Unfortunately, salary review isn't due for a while. However, there might be another way to increase your income with a little extra effort on your part.**

E. *Like what?*

S. **Like the company's suggestion system. Here, let me show you something. (pulls out a copy of the latest company magazine) It says here that employees of this company earned more than a half million dollars in suggestion awards last year. How much of this bonanza did you take home?**

E. *(ruefully) Zip.*

S. **Okay, that should tell us something. Mary Ann, you're a smart woman and one of the most experienced people in the department. Do you think everything we do here is perfect, that none of our systems and procedures can be improved?**

E. *Of course not.*

S. **Okay, then think about it. A good idea or two could earn you more money than several hours of overtime. It's also a proven fact that no one is better qualified to come up with improvements than the people on the line who process the detailed transactions and do the day-to-day grunt work. People like you, Mary Ann.**

E. *(thoughtful) That's something to think about.*

S. **It sure is, and I'll tell you something else. Another part of my supervisory responsibility is to work with employees like you to help them present their ideas in the best possible light. If your idea is successful it's a feather in my cap as well. So any time you come up with a brainstorm, even if it seems a little wild and far-fetched, don't hesitate to knock on my door.**

E. Okay, thanks.

S. **One more thing. While the easiest place to come up with ideas for improvement is close to home, there's no law that says a suggestion must be confined to the department where you work. So keep your eyes open. A good idea could benefit the sales, marketing, shipping, billing, or production departments—you name it.**

• • • **TALKING POINTS**   Not every grievance can be resolved in a way that will satisfy the complainer; sometimes half a solution is better than none at all. The trick is to listen sympathetically and thoughtfully with amelioration in mind. Fortunately, as in the above case, there is often more than one way to get from third base to home—more than one way to appease a grievant or would-be complainer—to the mutual gain of both employee and company.

DIALOGUE THREE

In an all too common situation, Bill Hardwick, a disgruntled employee, is bypassed for a merit increase or job advancement because of his poor performance and attitude.

Talking It Out

Employee - Joe Corning and Phil Resnick got increases. I do the same work they do. There's no reason I should be passed over.

Supervisor - You were passed over reluctantly, Bill. I wish I didn't have to do it.

E. **If that's true, I would have gotten the raise. You're prejudiced against me. That's why you passed me by.**

S. Prejudiced? I'm surprised you feel that way. But if there's any truth at all in your statement, it's because of your work and your attitude. I can give you my word there's nothing personal involved.

E. **What's wrong with my work and attitude?**

S. (pulling out Bill's file) I'm glad you asked that question. It's important to me that you understand why you were bypassed. Let's look at the record objectively. Take this notation, for instance. On this project last month you were gone from your work station for almost an hour. Your production was way below standard. Here's another example: You missed work on two separate occasions without calling in. And look at this: Last week when we were behind schedule, Joe and Phil worked overtime willingly. You refused. Do you want me to cite other examples?

E. **(lowers his eyes) No, I didn't realize that stuff counted against me. I guess it all adds up.**

S. *It sure does. Jeff, I know you've got what it takes to do a great job for yourself and the company. It's simply a matter of applying yourself and shaping up. You did it before, you can do it again. We all slip from time to time and I don't hold it against you. It would give me great pleasure to see your name approved for a merit increase next time around. Why don't we work together with this goal in mind?*

E. **Okay, I'll try. I'm sorry if I implied there was something personal involved. I guess the problem was me all along. Thanks for leveling with me. From here on out I'll try to do better.**

• • • **TALKING POINTS** When forced to punish a subordinate for unacceptable performance or attitude, act sympathetic, not vindictive. Avoid anger and frustration. Don't make it look as if it is something you enjoy doing. Whatever the employee's grievance, show him or her that *you* harbor no grievance, or personal animosity. You're willing to forgive and forget the past and get off to a new start. Wind up on a positive note. Convince the employee you are ready and willing to erase the grievance or problem from your mind if he works with you toward this end.

DIALOGUE FOUR

Maintenance employee Victor Potok complains he is assigned all the tasks that nobody else wants.

Talking It Out

Employee - It isn't fair. If there's a dirty job around here the odds are ten to one it'll be given to me.

Supervisor - I don't think it's quite that bad, Vic. But let's not forget that you're classified as a utility man. The assignments you get fall within your job classification. I do my best to divide the work as equally and impartially as possible among the utility men.

E. That isn't the way it looks to me! Like cleaning the sludge from those tanks in the lab. I got assigned to that job two times in a row.

S. It couldn't be helped. Pete was on a painting job that was top priority. Joe was out sick, and Charlie was out front scraping the rust from the railings. Would you have preferred that I give you that job?

E. (reluctantly) No, I guess not. That's even worse than cleaning the sludge.

S. (palms up) What can I tell you, Vic? You got stuck with the job because it was work I couldn't postpone, and no one else was available to do it. But look at it this way: You're doing work that has to be done which makes you an important part of the maintenance team and a valuable employee.

E. Yeah, I guess you're right. But I get depressed at times assigned to all that crummy stuff.

S. I can sympathize with the way you feel. I'd be depressed myself. But you're still a young guy, and you're smart. There's no reason you have to be stuck with work you don't like indefinitely.

E. What do you mean?

S. Just this. If you take a look at this plant's personnel roster you'll see there are dozens of job classifications. Since utility man is close to the bottom of the list that means you have no place to go but up if you're determined to do so.

E. You mean promotion?

S. Sure, why not in time if you work at it?

E. What am I supposed to do?

S. Simple. Pick a classification to which you would like to advance. Then determine what you have to know to get there and determine that you will learn it. Take a course, crack a book, whatever. If you apply yourself to your goal, you can't help but achieve it. Think about it, Vic.

E. (thoughtfully) Yeah, I will.

• • • **TALKING POINTS** Every plant and office has its least desirable tasks that must be done by someone. To deal with this problem a supervisor must balance employee preferences and workplace practicalities as fairly and realistically as possible. Another important consideration is the carrot-and-the-stick managerial approach which favors good performers with challenging and interesting assignments, and relegates less desirable tasks to lower-rated employees. At the same time care must be taken not to burden one person with an unequal or unfair share of the grunt work.

DIALOGUE FIVE

Disgruntled after being bypassed for advancement, Peggy in Word Processing, gripes that her seniority entitles her to a promotion.

Talking It Out

Employee - (list in hand) Take a look at this, Mr. Klein. I have more seniority than three of these people who were promoted to Grade One classifications. It's not fair.

Supervisor - I could show you another list, Peggy, a list of all the times you were absent or late during the past six months, or a list of all the times you refused to work overtime when we were in a bind.

E. I'm not the only one who was ever late or couldn't work overtime. I thought raises and promotions around here were supposed to be based on seniority.

S. You've got that all wrong. Seniority is only one factor that influences promotion decisions. Several others are at least equally if not more important. Job performance, as one example, attitude for another, cooperation and attendance to cite others.

E. What am I supposed to do, work overtime if I have a date?

S. That's for you to decide. What's more important, your job or that date? It's not that often that you're urgently needed for overtime, and when you are you get more than enough notice to give you time to reschedule your social engagements.

E. (pouting)

S. Peggy, there are no free rides in the business world. When you refuse to cooperate it makes it tough on me, the department, and your co-workers who have to take up the slack. Sometimes you have to sacrifice your personal desires for the sake of job objectives and needs. I'll be only too happy to put you in for Grade One next time around. All you have to do is earn it.

• • • **TALKING POINTS** Sometimes a supervisor has no choice but to lay it on the line to a griping subordinate. An all too common mistake some employees make is to place undue emphasis on seniority as a promotion or wage-increase entitlement. Others feel their longevity in the department makes them deserving of special consideration with regard to job assignments. If such decisions were based on length of service, or too heavily weighted on seniority alone, mediocrity would prevail and the best performers in the department would be short-changed.

DIALOGUE SIX

Employee gripes get through to Claims Department Supervisor Ron Sedgewick that Section Leader Don Seymour hogs recognition and credit for ideas originated by his subordinates.

Talking It Out

Supervisor - Don, that new voucher system was a good idea. Who thought it up?

Section Leader - I did. Why?

S. I was wondering. I thought Bill might have had something to do with it since it involves his operation most directly.

S.L. He might have mentioned something that touched off the idea. But I was up till two in the morning working out the details.

S. I see. What about the layout for the new claims form? Was that your idea too?

S.L. Oh, sure. More or less.

S. What do you mean by more or less?

S.L. (starting to fidget) Uh, I actually set up the form and finalized it with the forms company rep.

S. Marge had nothing to do with it?

S.L. Uh, she might have had. I'm not sure. I don't remember. Is it important?

S. It's important to Marge. And Bill's suggestion to simplify the voucher system is important to him.

S.L. Yeah, I guess I should have mentioned it.

S. You better stop guessing, pal. I checked into those two suggestions personally and got the lowdown. Bill came to you with the voucher idea; it was *his* idea. Same thing with the claims form revision. Marge thought it up and brought it to you. That was the last they heard about it until it was put into effect.

S.L. (tightlipped, no comment)

S. Don, let me set you straight on this business. Coming up with good ideas is the fastest and surest way for an employee to win management recognition and earn career Brownie points. Working with employees to help hone their ideas and present them effectively is a supervisory responsibility. Giving credit where credit is due is another supervisory responsibility.

S.L. Yeah, I realize that.

S. Do you realize too that denying a deserving person recognition is a cheap and lowdown way to operate? Do you understand what I'm talking about?

S.L. (nods, eyes lowered)

S. There's something else you should know. Hogging credit for a subordinate's ideas or good performance is dumb and short-sighted from a career standpoint as well. One, it discourages creative employees and makes them turn off the idea tap. Two, it makes people bitter, which causes their performance to decline. Three, it encourages your good people to look for more appreciative employers. Four, it has a negative effect on employee attitude and morale. Finally, it hampers your own advancement as well. A key factor when management evaluates supervisory effectiveness is how well or how poorly subordinates are motivated to come up with suggestions. Every time one of your people gets recognition for a good idea, it's a feather in your cap.

S.L. (downcast) I guess I didn't look at it that way.

S. Well, you better start looking, my friend.

• • • **TALKING POINTS** Grievances, expressed or not, have a profound effect on employee morale and performance. Employee gripes about the boss's failure to give credit where deserved are more difficult than most to articulate. All too often, the deprived suggester concludes that racking one's brain to come up with ideas for improvement with nothing to gain for it isn't worth the effort, and stops cold at that point. The smartest and most creative employees are more likely to keep their frustration to themselves and scout the job market for opportunities that will offer them a better chance to gain recognition. The obvious conclusion is that putting credit hoggers in their place is the best departmental therapy a supervisor could administer.

chapter twenty-four

· · · · · · · · · · · · · · · · ·

APPLYING DISCIPLINE CONSTRUCTIVELY

When a company loses customers, makes excessive billing, shipping, and other errors, or suffers from poor productivity, few employees below the supervisory level give it much thought or are even aware of it. Yet when a supervisor attempts to cut down on profit erosion by punishing those responsible for it an uproar often erupts. More employee grievances develop as a result of applied—or misapplied—discipline than for any other reason. Supervisors constantly face such questions as: What punishment is appropriate for this or that violation? How much discipline, and how often should it be given, before applying the ultimate discipline of discharge? When should the rules of progressive and consistent discipline be adhered to, and when can they be disregarded? Such questions are critical to departmental well being, the organization's profitable performance, and supervisory career objectives as well.

DIALOGUE ONE

Production Department Supervisor Sam Hawes suffers from misconceptions about how to apply the rules of consistency.

Talking It Out

Manager - Sam, Gloria Storch is threatening to file a grievance over the official warning notice and 3-day suspension you gave her.

Supervisor - On what grounds?

M. She claims it was prejudicial and discriminatory.

S. That's hogwash. Leaving the plant without authorization and staying out for an hour is a serious offense. If I don't react strongly to abuses like that it will encourage others to commit similar violations.

M. I couldn't agree more. But every case must be decided on its own merit.

S. That's what I try to do.

M. Well, maybe you didn't think this one out thoroughly enough. Gloria doesn't dispute that she deserves to be disciplined. She simply claims that a 3-day suspension is too harsh.

S. Why? Does she think I pulled that figure out of thin air? I checked into the files. She isn't the first one disciplined for unauthorized absence. I can cite at least four others who received 3-day suspensions for the same offense.

M. Maybe so. But let's take a look at those other offenders.

S. (displays the files)

M. (reviewing files) Okay, here's one: Ed Silver. Unauthorized absence from plant, 3-day suspension. Now let's look at Silver's record. Poor productivity, excessive absences, and this was the *third time* he took off like that. Same thing for Rose Genaro. Three-day suspension, three-time offender. Phil Schoen's record is even worse. This all gives a lot of validity to Gloria's gripe.

S. I can see what you mean. But I thought one of the main requirements of discipline was to apply it consistently.

M. No argument there. But consistency applies not only to the punishment itself, but to the performance record of the violator as well. Gloria's overall performance rating is better than average in contrast to these others. Also, this is the first time she was guilty of unauthorized absence from the plant. In applying discipline, you can't do it strictly by rote or by the numbers. Discretionary judgment must be exercised as well. People shouldn't be treated

like robots. A well-rated performer who is guilty of only one violation can't be put in the same category as a poor or marginal performer guilty of multiple violations.

S. *(thoughtful) I see what you mean.*

M. **Good. I suggest that you reduce Gloria's discipline to an official warning notice. At the same time, she should be informed that if she repeats the violation harsher discipline will be imposed.**

• • • **TALKING POINTS**   With so great a volume of grievances and lawsuits triggered by imposed discipline, it is easy for a supervisor to go overboard in shooting for consistency. But as Sam's boss points out, fair and rational judgment must also be exercised when violations occur. Just as, in the nation's court system, the character and reputation of the person charged is considered, and the first offender doesn't receive the same sentence as the recidivist, so must well-rated employees who are infrequent violators be given preference over their lower-rated or chronic counterparts.

DIALOGUE TWO

In sharp contrast to Sam Hawes, Mailroom Supervisor Bev Clark is inconsistent in her application of discipline.

Talking It Out

Manager - Bev, are you aware that Tom Hausner just filed a grievance charging you with reverse discrimination?

Supervisor - I just heard. I don't get it.

M. **He claims that you're much tougher on male employees than you are on females. Is there any truth to his charge?**

S. *Not that I know of.*

M. **Well, you'd better make sure. Check it out and let me know what you find.**

(Bev reviews past history and is dismayed to learn that Tom's charge is not without merit. She reports the disclosure to her boss.)

S. It appears there's some truth to Tom's charge. I'm sorry. I must have done it unconsciously. What do you think I should do?

M. Well, first, why don't you have a chat with him and water down the discipline. After that, I suggest rethinking your discipline policy.

S. I think I've done that already. That I was leaning in favor of women came as a complete surprise to me.

M. (smiling) It takes some careful reflection at times to really know yourself and the way you feel. We sometimes tend to take too much for granted. This can be especially problematical in the imposition of discipline. Experience proves that inconsistency can be an invitation to lawsuits apart and aside from the morale problems it generates.

• • • **TALKING POINTS** Care must be taken when responding to rule infractions to make the process as objective as possible. Permitting one's feelings to dictate judgment is flirting with trouble. We all have our personal likes and dislikes, and sometimes harbor hidden prejudices of which we're not even aware. Supervisors must constantly be on the outlook to make sure disciplinary judgments are not weighted in favor of one person or group at the expense of another. When unsure, the best course is to review the record. Double-check past incidents to be sure that Anglo-American workers haven't been favored at the expense of African-American, Hispanic, Asian, or other minority members. Make sure men and women, young people and seniors, are afforded the same objective treatment. And never forget that a byproduct of favoritism is too often a grievance or lawsuit.

DIALOGUE THREE

Softhearted Accounts Receivable Department Supervisor Mildred Ochs too often stops short when constructive discipline is needed.

Talking It Out

Manager - Millie, what's your definition of recidivist?

Supervisor - A criminal who keeps repeating his crime.

M. Right on. I wouldn't classify you as a criminal. But in a way the term applies to you.

S. Thanks a lot. Why?

M. (smiling) I'm referring to what appears to be your discipline policy.

S. What do you mean?

M. I've been checking the personnel files. Let's take Selma Burke as an example. I noted seven official reprimands for excessive absence from her work station over the past five months: 30 minutes, 40 minutes, 35 minutes. Once she was gone a full hour. If she has a kidney problem she should be sent to the nurse. Otherwise you rate as a recidivist, imposing the same ineffective discipline time after time.

S. (frowning) Oh, I see what you mean. I try to keep after her, but can't seem to get her to reform. If she isn't in the ladies room, she's at the water cooler, or gabbing with someone.

M. With your weak-kneed response you'll never get her to change. Her reasoning is obvious. If all she's going to get are reprimands, why should she reform?

S. I don't know. Selma knows her job and she's a good worker.

M. When she's working.

S. Do you think I should fire her?

M. You shouldn't have to ask me that question. Nine times out of ten the only practical discipline is progressive discipline. Reprimands have their place, but they must be limited numerically. Beyond a point a reprimand has no more effect than a slap on the wrist with a wet noodle. A typical limit is three written reprimands, each one harsher than the one before. At some point, oral reprimands must be replaced by written reprimands. And finally a last chance warning should be stated in clear and unmistakable language. Either shape up or ship out, with that ultimatum enforced where need be.

S. I guess I've been too lax with Mildred.

M. You sure have. She should have been put on a reform-or-else alert a long time ago.

• • • **TALKING POINTS** Just as a parent's repeated admonition to a naughty child has little if any effect unless it is followed by real punishment, so must the same principle apply in the workplace. A sure way for a supervisor to permissively condone unacceptable performance or behavior—and lose respect in the process—is to repeatedly bawl out a worker for infractions without applying the stick in a more tangible way. As a disciplinary measure there is really nothing to measure. The only consequence you can expect is to have subordinates laughing behind your back.

DIALOGUE FOUR

Office employee Al Stockton, a marginal performer at best, bad-mouths the company and its products.

Talking It Out

Supervisor - (unconcealed anger) I just got a call from Mr. Unger. He wants to know what kind of operation we're running if an employee can tell a good customer that one of the company's products is junk and that management couldn't run a hot dog stand efficiently. Am I quoting you accurately?

Employee - (sullen, no comment)

S. Did you say that, Al?

E. *I don't know. Maybe. Something like that. I was ticked off over the raw deal I've been getting around here.*

S. Tell me how that deal justifies your bad-mouthing your employer and damaging the company image and reputation.

E. *I've been here almost three years now. I never once got a promotion or raise. People who have been here half that time are moving ahead. I'm just spinning my wheels.*

S. Has it ever occurred to you why?

E. *Sure. You've got a grudge against me. You had it from the day I was hired.*

S. If that's how you felt, how come you're still here? Lousy company, rotten products, crummy management, supervisor who has a grudge against you. That doesn't make you look too bright, set-

tling for a dead-end job. If I felt the way you do I would have been out of here long ago.

E. (disgruntled) I need the job. I have two kids to support.

S. You'd never know it from your performance and attitude.

E. My performance isn't that bad.

S. That's bull, and we both know it. Any time you're ready we can go over the record: day by day, week by week, year by year.

E. (no comment)

S. I'm going to lay it on the line, Al. You're hanging on by your teeth around here. If you're spinning your wheels it's because your attendance is poor, your attitude is crummy, and your performance is borderline. I probably tolerated it too long already. But what I won't tolerate another day is bad-mouthing the company in general, and to customers in particular. Get this straight, buddy, this is your first and final warning. You're going to get it in writing and it's going into your file. One more time and you're out. Is that clear?

E. (grudgingly) Yeah.

S. Good. Now I'll tell you the good news. This may be hard for you to believe, but I'm a forgiving soul. It's never too late to turn over a new leaf. If I didn't think you were smart and had potential I wouldn't have hired you in the first place. I want you to understand I have nothing against you personally. Prove to me you can do a good job, show up on time every day, dump that negative attitude, and there is hope for you yet. You might even find yourself moving ahead one of these days like some of those other guys you're talking about.

• • • **TALKING POINTS** How do you handle an employee who *almost* deserves to be fired? A double-edged strategy is recommended. First, apply harsh discipline when and where it is needed. Bad-mouthing company products or people, especially to a customer, is a serious offense worthy of no more than one reprieve. Its seriousness can not be made *too* clear to the grousing berater. Some supervisors might argue that firing Al on the spot would have been justified, an argument that may be hard to refute. But, as a three-year veteran his boss gave him a second chance. That's where a second strategy comes into play. A bitter employee is in most cases a nonproductive employee. If Al is to be kept on, an effort should be made to temper his negative attitude with some hope for the future. No employee, not even the presumed deadbeat, is beyond salvation—although with employees like Al, this view might be overly optimistic. Still, it costs nothing to try.

DIALOGUE FIVE

Warehouse employee Sid Smith is caught drinking on the job.

Talking It Out

Supervisor - Sid, I just received a report that you were seen drinking on the job.

Employee - Says who?

S. That's between me and my informant. What I want to know from you is if it's true.

E. It's a lie. The only thing I ever drink on the job is coffee.

S. Then you won't mind going to the nurse's office and taking a breathalizer test.

E. (nervous) I don't see why I should have to do that. It's embarrassing.

S. Let's stop playing games. We both know you've been drinking. You smell like a brewery.

E. (lowers eyes, admission enough)

S. Al, I'm going to lay it on the line. Since this is a first offense, at least as far as I know, I'm going to let you off with an official warning notice. Drinking during working hours is a serious offense. It not only hampers performance but makes you vulnerable to accident. If you're caught drinking again I'll have no choice but to fire you, and you're going to get that in writing on your final warning notice tomorrow. In the meantime I want you to clock out and go home.

• • • **TALKING POINTS**   If a subordinate chooses to spend the lunch hour at the neighboring bar, there's not much you can do about it. But if the employee returns to work under the influence or, worse yet, is caught drinking on the job, it is another matter entirely. You can't be too tough in enforcing the company's no-drinking rule. In some organizations it is grounds for immediate dismissal. The bleary-eyed, wavering, and slurred speech signs of alcoholism are easy to spot. Permitting an employee who is not in complete control of his or her behavior to remain on the job puts not only that person, but the whole department at risk, and can be downright dangerous in the presence of cutting tools and machinery. Swift action must be taken without delay either in the form of getting help where alcoholism is indicated, or in the case of the casual drinker, enforcing the company rule rigidly.

DIALOGUE SIX

Billing machine operator Pat Conrad who works in a unionized company is caught red-handed with her hand in the till.

Talking It Out

Supervisor - I want you to read this termination notice and let me know if any of these allegations are false.

Employee - (red-faced) I can't deny having done it. All I'm asking is for you to give me a break. This is my first offense. Something came over me. I couldn't help myself. It was a moment of weakness. The cash box was open and I was sure no one was looking. I was short of cash, and the temptation was too great.

S. You're not the only one short of cash these days. That's a poor excuse for dishonesty. That you thought no one was looking is an even worse excuse.

E. A cash box shouldn't be left open like that. It's practically inviting a person to steal.

S. You may be right; it was a breach of security. But that doesn't condone your offense. Unfortunately, you were observed taking the money, or perhaps fortunately, if it teaches you a much-needed lesson and will make you think twice the next time you are tempted.

E. It did teach me a lesson. I promise. . .

S. **I'm sorry, Pat, but it's too late for promises. As you know, various items have been missing around here: an expensive watch, a gold bracelet, and other things. In view of this incident you can conclude for yourself who will be suspected of being the thief. Even if I were able to keep you on, it would be uncomfortable working here.**

E. I didn't steal those things.

S. **I'm not saying you did. Pat, the most disagreeable and unpleasant task any supervisor could face is to having to fire someone. Believe me, I don't enjoy doing it. But under the circumstances I have no choice.**

E. I learned my lesson. If you give me a second chance I'll never do it again.

S. **I'd like to believe you, but for certain things there are no second chances. Stealing is one of them.**

E. (setting her chin) Well, I'm going to see what the union delegate has to say about that.

S. **That's your privilege. But I can tell you exactly what will be said: Sorry, there's not a thing I can do about it. Good luck, Pat. Your final check will be mailed to you.**

• • • **TALKING POINTS** It's a sad commentary on the state of values and ethics in America as we move towards the 21st century that incidents such as the one described above are by no means uncommon in the nation's offices and plants. There is very little to discuss in a situation like this. Stealing in the workplace cannot be tolerated, and it would be the rare case where ifs, ands, or buts might be applicable. There is no harder blow for a supervisor to take than the disclosure that a trusted employee is a thief. But as Pat's boss regrettably made clear, and as the company's policy manual made equally clear, where dishonesty is involved there can be no second chance.

chapter twenty-five

$\bullet \quad \bullet \quad \bullet \quad \bullet \quad \bullet \quad \bullet \quad \bullet \quad \bullet \quad \bullet \quad \bullet \quad \bullet \quad \bullet \quad \bullet \quad \bullet \quad \bullet$

DEALING WITH SEXUAL HARASSMENT

An employee complains she was bypassed for promotion because she rebuffed her boss's sexual demands. Work disruption occurs when a supervisor confers favors on a subordinate with whom he is having an affair. A subordinate becomes infatuated and pursues her boss with unwanted advances. Work problems erupt when an affair between co-workers turns sour. Welcome to the real world. In recent years a growing number of sexual harassment and sex discrimination complaints have been plaguing private and public organizations across the U.S. Nor are there indications that the trend will diminish any time soon. So where does that leave you? Often, in the middle of a mess. Your responsibility as a supervisor is to arm yourself with the information and savvy needed to protect your employees' and your employer's best interests and rights simultaneously. This entails sensitive handling of employee complaints without commitment on your part one way or the other before conducting a careful investigation to determine the facts—remembering there are two sides to every case. It also means arming yourself with awareness of the legal ramifications, at the same time keeping in mind that you are not an attorney. First and foremost, your goal must be to expose and stamp out sexual harassment where it exists, and to strive to maintain reasoned objectivity in this difficult and demanding area of supervisory management.

DIALOGUE ONE

Joe Reid, supervisor in a research lab, fails to take complaints of sexual harassment seriously enough.

Talking It Out

Employee - Hank is making my life a nightmare with his sexual advances.

Supervisor - Hey, come on, Alice, you're too sensitive. He's just kidding around. He doesn't mean anything by it.

E. *That's what you told me last time and he's still at it. He sneaks up behind me, makes suggestive remarks, and tries to kiss me in the back of the neck. This morning he tried to grab me. You said you would talk to him.*

S. I did talk to him. He says he's just teasing you. If you laughed it off, he'd get bored and quit.

E. *He won't quit. He's driving me crazy.*

S. Okay, okay, I'll talk to him again.

(The harassment continues. In desperation and holding back tears, Alice goes over Joe's head to his boss who calls the supervisor to account.)

Manager - What the hell is going on around here? Alice just left my office in tears.

Supervisor - Aw, it's no big deal. She's a prude. Hank's been having a little fun with her. I told him to cut it out.

M. You're 20 years behind the times, Joe, and it *is* a big deal. It's always a big deal when an employee makes a charge of sexual harassment. Your attitude and handling of Alice's complaint indicate a total lack of understanding in this area. Employees should be encouraged to come forward in such situations. Instead, judging from the state Alice is in, you callously and insensitively brushed her off.

S. I talked to the guy. What more am I supposed to do?

M. A good deal more. For one thing, casually telling Hank to cut it out counts for little if anything. When a harassment charge is made it's your responsibility as a supervisor to take it seriously, respect the woman's feelings, and investigate the complaint thoroughly. Hank's a married man, isn't he? What did he say when you told him to leave Alice alone?

S. He said he would.

M. Well, he apparently didn't, and judging from Alice's emotional state, instead of clamping down on Hank's behavior your response only encouraged it. It shows not only a disregard and lack of caring for the people in your department, but a complete ignorance of the legal implications as well. What would it require for you to take a complaint like Alice's seriously? Would she have to be raped?

S. (no comment, properly chastised)

M. I want you to write a detailed report of this case, and I want a formal warning inserted in Hank's file with the stipulation that any repetition of his behavior will result in dismissal. And I can tell you this, Joe: If you don't drastically alter your own attitude with regard to harassment you may find yourself hot on his heels.

• • • **TALKING POINTS**   Today, a charge of sexual harassment is often considered valid in the eyes of the law if: 1) It causes the complainant to be upset emotionally; 2) Adversely affects the complainant's job performance; 3) Creates disruption in the workplace; 4) Subjects the complainant to ridicule and embarrassment; 5) Unduly violates a complainant's right of privacy. The Equal Employment Opportunity Commission (EEOC) recognizes that employers are more liable for the conduct of supervisors toward subordinates than that of co-workers toward each other. This applies on two counts: 1) A supervisor's sexual harassment of a subordinate; 2) Evidence of supervisory disregard or mishandling of a subordinate's harassment charge.

Dialogue Two

Order Board employee Marge charges Bill, a co-worker, with sexual harassment.

Talking It Out

Supervisor - I don't think I have to tell you, Marge, this is a very serious charge. We don't tolerate sexual harassment in this company. But I'll have to ask you to be more specific.

Employee - (blushing) He told me I have a terrific body. He said if I went out with him he'd show me a good time. I know exactly what kind of good time he had in mind. I also know that Bill happens to be a married man with a family. I can tell you, I was very upset.

S. I can appreciate the way you feel. But that in itself doesn't constitute sexual harassment. Did he do or say anything more explicitly offensive?

E. (hesitating) He propositioned me. He asked me to go to a motel with him.

S. When was that?

E. Two days ago. I was so angry that, well, that's why I'm here.

S. What was your reply?

E. I let him know in no uncertain terms that I wasn't interested. I told him he should be ashamed of himself and said that if he didn't leave me alone his wife would hear about it.

S. What did he say to that?

E. First he got mad, then he laughed. He said, "You don't know what you're missing, baby." I was so angry I felt like I would explode.

S. Did he bother you any more after that?

E. No, but I thought you should know what kind of person he is. Do you think I should call his wife?

S. I wouldn't advise you to do that. It could cause all kinds of complications.

E. Well, I don't think he should get away with it. I want you to warn him to stay away from me.

S. **I'll talk to him, Marge, and make it clear how you feel if it's not clear already. If he bothers you again, let me know.**

• • • **TALKING POINTS** What constitutes sexual harassment? More to the point, what type of behavior calls for punitive action against the offender? Where unwelcome sexual advances occur, a supervisor must determine: Do they interfere with the employee's performance? Do they create a hostile or offensive working environment? What, specifically is the nature of the unwelcome behavior? How persistent? Marge's supervisor would have violated his responsibility had he dismissed her complaint or pooh-poohed her concern. Different people, men or women, respond differently to unwanted sexual advances. The fact that Marge was upset made intermediary action by her supervisor necessary in this case. Where rebuffed sexual invitations persist, even if they don't meet the EEOC work-related guidelines for hard punitive action, it behooves a supervisor to respond seriously to the complaint and take whatever action he can to eliminate the annoyance and protect the complainant's privacy.

DIALOGUE THREE

Marie, a production employee, is infatuated with Andy, her foreman.

Talking It Out

Supervisor - The woman has no self-respect. She's driving me up a wall.

Manager - In what way?

S. **For one thing, even if I wanted to, I know that from a work standpoint the dumbest thing I could do would be to start up with Marie. I'm experienced enough to know you can hide that kind of thing for just so long. The department would be in an uproar. That's all people would talk about, not to mention its effect on the work.**

M. I couldn't agree more.

S. **Also, I'm married 15 years. I never cheated on Carol and have no intention of starting now. But I also happen to be human. Marie's**

a good-looking woman with a great body. I'd be a hypocrite if I pretended that I was never tempted.

M. *(smiles) I know what you're saying, but let's get into specifics. Exactly how does her infatuation, or whatever you choose to call it, manifest itself?*

S. **The only word I can think of is *blatantly*. Marie's *not* subtle. She rolls her eyes and says we would be wonderful together. When I give her an assignment she rubs up against me like a cat at a post.**

M. *She knows you're married, right?*

S. **No question. She's got an answer for that too. She says man's a polygamous animal and keeps telling me how discreet she is. She says no one would ever know.**

M. *(shaking his head) Some guys would give their eye teeth to be in your shoes.*

S. **Maybe so, but I'd give my eye teeth to be out of them. I've got enough problems without getting tied up with a woman like Marie.**

M. *Andy, I have great respect for your forbearance. My guess is that your persistent rebuffs make you even more attractive to her. To a woman like Marie, you're a challenge.*

S. **Great!**

M. *Do you think she might be playing up to you as a ploy to advance herself on the job?*

S. **I've had no indication of that.**

M. *(smiles) Then it must be your unsurpassed charm and virility.*

S. **Very funny.**

M. *Seriously, what do you think should be done?*

S. **She's not a bad worker, but life would be easier and more peaceful if she was transferred out of the department.**

M. *Exactly what I was about to suggest. If she still bothers you after that, we may have to let her go.*

• • • **TALKING POINTS** Although the great majority of harassment complaints are directed by women toward men, reverse situations such as the above are not all that uncommon. Whether a reversal or not, unwelcome sexual advances, whatever the circumstances, must be dealt with seriously by supervision and management. Female employees at all levels attempt to seduce their supervisors with a variety of motivations in mind: Sexual favors in return for financial reward, choice assignments or increased status, or as in the case of Marie, plain old-fashioned attraction. As Andy wisely points out, one of the surest ways to create departmental disharmony, resentment, and work disruption is for a supervisor to enter into a sexual liaison with a subordinate.

Dialogue Four

Billing machine operator Susan complains she is being held back on the job because of her refusal to sleep with her boss.

Talking It Out

Employee - (clearly upset) Have you got a few minutes, Mr. Griffen?

Manager - Of course, Susan. What's on your mind?

E. I know you're not supposed to go over your supervisor's head with a complaint, but it's Jim Farrow. He won't leave me alone.

M. In what way?

E. (pained expression) I . . . he, he keeps after me. He keeps trying to hug me. When he turns over work he rubs up against me suggestively, and. . .

M. Yes, Susan, what? I know it's not easy, but just let it spill out.

E. He . . . (bursts into tears) He tried to fondle my breasts. He says if I do what he wants he'll see to it that I get a nice raise and promotion.

M. Were those his exact words?

E. Yes. He wants me to sleep with him. He said that if I continue to turn him down I'll be spinning my wheels till I'm sixty. He's got me so crazy I don't know what to do. I want to quit, but I need the job.

M. What did you tell him?

E. I told him I was thinking of quitting.

M. What was his answer?

E. He shrugged and said, "That's up to you, baby." But I'd hate myself if I gave him that satisfaction. It's not fair. I have a good work record and I'm long overdue for a raise. I came to you as a last resort. My father says I should sue. I can tell you something else. I'm not the only one Jim Farrow's after.

M. Oh no? Who else?

E. (hesitates, near tears again) Dottie Kemp and Jo Anne Weiss. Probably others too.

M. (thoughtful) Thank you for coming to me, Susan. Try to calm down. I'll look into this right away and let you know what I decide.

(Farrow's boss investigates the situation. He talks in confidence to Dottie, Jo Anne, another supervisor, and two group leaders. Once assured that Susan's complaint is justified, he confronts Farrow with the evidence. The supervisor tries to deny his role at the outset, but overwhelmed by the weight of the evidence, he confesses his guilt. With the evidence so heavy against him, his boss decides that the best course of action would be to fire Farrow.)

• • • **TALKING POINTS** Sexual misconduct takes on a variety of forms. Its effects on the recipient range from minor annoyance to severe emotional distress. Typically, the courts react more harshly when the accused is a supervisor than if the complaint involves co-workers. Sexual harassment is most actionable when it is linked to such terms and conditions of employment as wage increases, job advancement, and the distribution of work assignments. In the above case, had Susan opted for legal action she would have had an excellent case against the company. Mr. Griffen's response was wise and compassionately sympathetic on the one hand, and sensibly objective on the other. He made no commitment before "looking into" the situation and assuring himself that the evidence against Farrow was airtight and accurate. At this point he lost no time in resolving the problem by terminating the accused whose culpability was too blatant and extreme to warrant forgiveness.

DIALOGUE FIVE

Production worker Gloria complains about being sexually harassed by Frank, a co-worker.

Talking It Out

Supervisor - Tell me about it, Gloria. Exactly how did Frank harass you?

Employee - First, he propositioned me. When I turned him down, he practically attacked me in the locker room.

S. Can you be more specific than that?

E. Sure. I'll give you a blow-by-blow description. He grabbed hold of me, shoved me up against the wall, and said he was gonna give it to me. I'd have to be a moron not to know what he meant.

S. Grabbed you, how?

E. He grabbed my—breasts.

S. What did you do?

E. (grinning) I bit the bastard. Then I kicked him as hard as I could and got out of there fast. He would have raped me for sure. Either that sex fiend gets fired, Mr. Krause, or I sue the company.

S. I'm going to look into this and get back to you. Thanks for coming to me, Gloria.

(Tracking down the other side of the story, the supervisor has a talk with Frank.)

S. Frank, Gloria just came to me with a very serious accusation. She claims you abused her sexually in the locker room and practically tried to rape her.

E. (face reddens) Aw, she's exaggerating. There's no way I would have raped her.

S. She says you grabbed hold of her breasts. Was she lying?

E. I didn't grab her. I tried to turn her around.

S. You didn't touch her breasts?

E. I don't know. Maybe a little.

S. Did you proposition her?

E. Yeah, I guess so. Is that a crime? Hell, she's been asking for it the way she dresses in those miniskirts and tight sweaters, and the way she walks around shaking her butt and making all those provocative cracks. She's the biggest tease I ever saw. You can ask the rest of the guys. I'm only human, Mr. Krause.

S. All right, Frank, thanks for leveling with me. I'll get back to you later.

(Mr. Krause investigates the situation and as he suspects, finds Frank's statements to be true. Co-workers testify that Gloria is a bold flirt who makes sexually provocative remarks to the men. This, coupled with the way she dresses and flaunts her sexuality, influences the supervisor's response to Gloria's complaint.)

S. I'm going to give it to you straight, Gloria. Sexual harassment that is provoked cannot be equated with harassment that is unprovoked. If you don't want male co-workers to make sexual advances, don't encourage them to do so by the way you dress, flaunt your body, and use your sexuality to tease and taunt them. I think we both know what I'm talking about.

E. (lowers her eyes)

S. End of discussion, Gloria. Get back to work.

(The supervisor informs Frank that he is not going to discipline him in response to Gloria's complaint, but to prevent any further "misunderstandings," advises him to steer clear of her in the future for his own protection.)

• • • **TALKING POINTS** Where do you draw the line in deciding what is and is not sexual harassment? When evidence exists that a complainant "asks for it" in the manner described, consideration must be given to the provocation involved. It's not always that simple. The workplace isn't a social club. Not even a bold flirt like Gloria gives co-workers license to exceed prescribed limits of behavior and propriety with regard to sexual advances on the job. Under no circumstances should such actions as the fondling of breasts, pats on the behind, and other repelled bodily contact be tolerated or condoned.

DIALOGUE SIX

Shipping Department clerical employee Betty is offended by the crude obscenities and sexist language of male co-workers.

Talking It Out

Employee - That department is like a cesspool, Mr. Wilson.

Supervisor - In what way?

E. Those men have filthy mouths, every one of them. And the sexist remarks that they make! I couldn't begin to describe them. Four letter words are the least of it. I find it disgusting and offensive.

S. I can't argue with that, Betty, and I can appreciate how you feel. They're a pretty rough bunch of guys. It's not exactly a Sunday-school class.

E. That may be true. But not everyone was brought up on the streets. They should have some respect for the feelings and sensitivities of others.

S. I agree, but you can't change the habits of a lifetime overnight. Did anyone abuse or harass you personally?

E. Well no, but when I asked them to please not use such language in my presence, they laughed. One of them suggested that I ought to wear ear guards.

S. Exactly what would you like me to do about it, Betty?

E. I don't know. I just hate having to work in that environment.

S. I sympathize with your feelings. You're a good worker; I wouldn't want the company to lose you. How would you feel if I could get you a transfer to another department?

E. (face brightens) Oh, I'd really appreciate that.

S. All right, Betty. I'll try.

• • • **TALKING POINTS** Not all harassment-related problems are resolvable. In some cases lines defining degrees of offensiveness must be drawn. In one company recently, workers were ordered to remove sexually offensive photos and posters from walls and lockers in response to female complaints. Controlling coarse and obscene language and behavior when it is not specifically directed at an individual can be tougher than catching a bat with a butterfly net. As Mr. Wilson pointed out to Betty, a rough work crew is no Sunday-school class. Longtime habits are not broken easily. It would not be realistic to expect a crew of stevedores and warehousemen long accustomed to four-letter words and offensive language to suddenly turn chameleon-like and communicate like bank tellers. People unable to tolerate sex-related and other obscenities should not seek work in such environments. Where feasible, a viable response to complaints such as Betty's is a transfer out of the department.

chapter twenty-six

· · · · · · · · · · · · · · · · ·

GETTING NEW HIRES OFF ON THE RIGHT FOOT

New employees can be potentially productive, mediocre, or disruptive. In large measure it depends on how they are indoctrinated and handled during the early weeks of their employment. In the great majority of cases new employees—especially young impressionable new employees—are eager to prove themselves and be liked, serve an important role in the department, and become a productive part of the team. But this won't happen automatically. As a supervisor it's a critical part of your responsibility to work with the new employee to *make* it happen. Your job is to start people off in the right direction from the outset, and during their early formative weeks and months see to it that this heading is sustained. As experience proves, alternate routes can be counterproductive.

DIALOGUE ONE

Office Services Supervisor Helen Bailey devotes insufficient time to new employees.

272

Talking It Out

Manager - Helen, I've been reviewing the Turnover report and came across something that disturbs me.

Supervisor - What's that, Mr. Davidson?

M. A couple of things. For one, out of eight people hired during the last six months, only five passed their probationary periods.

S. I monitor the progress of new people very closely. If there's any doubt at all about whether they will make it or not, I don't take any chances.

M. A policy I strongly endorse. What bothers me is that, since Personnel has an excellent program for selecting potentially qualified candidates and weeding out others, I can't help but wonder why so many recruits are rejected.

S. I wish I knew the answer to that.

M. Okay, then let's have a look at my second concern. I took time to follow up on the progress of those other five people, the ones who did pass their probationary periods. What I saw disappointed me. Only one was rated outstanding. One was satisfactory. The other three were only marginal. I think you'll agree this could be a clue that something is wrong.

S. (frowning, no comment)

M. Helen, I know how busy you are. From what I've observed you don't seem to have a minute of free time during the course of a day.

S. I know. It's the bane of my existence.

M. That's what I'm getting at. Under the circumstances I might hazard a guess that you haven't made much time to give your new people the attention they need. I can't help wonder if you are allowing them to drift too much by themselves.

S. (frown deepens) That may be true.

M. I'm glad you see my point. It's important to help new employees form productive patterns of behavior from day one of their employment. The habits they develop at the outset—good or bad—have a way of hardening and setting in. Keep in mind that if

new hires aren't exposed to positive influences and guidance, their thinking and values are apt to be shaped by negative influences.

S. *Thank you, Mr. Davidson, that sure gives me something to think about.*

• • • **TALKING POINTS** The indoctrination of new employees should be as carefully thought out and planned, starting from day one, as any supervisory function you could name. Think back to your own early days on the job when you were still wet behind the ears. Typically, you were probably a little bit nervous, anxious, and scared. All kinds of questions concerned you. What will your supervisor be like? Will you be accepted? Will you be met with any resentment? Where will you put your personal things? What will the work be like? Will you have trouble understanding it? What about the benefits, working hours, lunch periods, break periods, health insurance, vacations, holidays? When and how will you be paid? From the very moment a new hire appears he or she should be taken gently in hand, welcomed warmly, shown around, introduced to co-workers, made to feel important. Work requirements should be slowly and carefully spelled out, understanding assured. Of special importance during the first weeks in particular, where interaction with other workers is needed, so far as possible the new person should be exposed to well-rated co-workers whose influence will be constructively positive. It bears repetition to stress that values communicated in the early weeks of employment will help shape the new hire's attitude, perceptions of right and wrong, and performance standards for months or years to come.

DIALOGUE TWO

Production employee Ted Panko is miffed because young Bill Cullen has been producing too many units and tries to get him to slow down.

Talking It Out

Supervisor - Bill, your production has fallen steadily in the past two weeks. What's the problem?

Employee - (nervous) I don't know. I'm doing my job.

S. **Sure you are, but you've proven you could do it much better.**

E. *(eyes lowered, no response)*

S. **Bill, let's level with each other. We both know why your output has declined, and the one who knows it best of all is Ted Panko. He's been overheard putting the screws on you. He wants you to slow down. He figures that if you do an honest job it will make him look bad and show him up as substandard. Has he been threatening you?**

E. *(wavering, answer enough)*

S. **Use your head, Bill. You're a good worker and can get ahead in this company. You made a darned good first impression. Don't let a deadbeat like Ted Panko mess it up for you. Do you understand what I'm talking about?**

E. *Yes, I guess so.*

S. **Bill, Ted Panko's a loser. He's a borderline worker with no chance of advancement and a good chance of being out on the street if he doesn't shape up. Is that what you want for yourself?**

E. *No sir, it isn't.*

S. **I didn't think so. Listen, kid, the only way to get any place on the job or in life is through superior performance. You proved you can do it. (gives him a friendly reassuring punch on the arm) Take my advice. Stay away from Ted Panko. If he gives you a hard time, let me know.**

E. *Thanks, I will.*

(Now that the supervisor has set young Bill Cullen straight, he preps for a talk with Ted Panko.)

S. **Ted, if you think I don't know what's going on around here you had better think again.**

E. *What do you mean?*

S. **You know damned well what I mean. The word is out that you've been trying to pressure Bill Cullen into slowing down on the job.**

E. *You've got it all wrong.*

S. **Let's stop playing games. I've got witnesses.**

E. Yeah, like who?

S. Employees who overheard you and feel you're trying to scare the kid and undermine the department. More than one.

E. I was just kidding around. I didn't mean anything by it.

S. Then how come when Bill started on the job three weeks ago he produced 26 units a day after the first week. Since huddling with you his production declined steadily.

E. I don't know. What he produces is his business.

S. Well, it's *my* business too. You may not care about your future and career, but it doesn't give you the right to undermine another person's career. If I hear any repetition of this, buddy, you're not long for this place.

• • • **TALKING POINTS**   Count on Ted Panko stereotypes to taint the corporate scene. Once entrenched, nailing productivity busters like Ted can be difficult. But however tough or unpleasant, they should be firmly dealt with pronto or sooner because their adverse influence on co-workers can be devastating. It is equally important to set things straight for the impressionable, and sometimes frightened victim of their antiprofit crusade. This is especially urgent where the possibility of a "slow down or-else" threat exists. Where such a threat is presumed to be physical, it may be a case for Security to handle.

DIALOGUE THREE

Statistical Department Supervisor Ellen Posner delegates break-in tasks she should be handling herself.

Talking It Out

Manager - Ellen, Ed Fritsche was hired because of his specialized knowledge and experience in the calculation and analysis of technical surveys and tables. And particularly with the idea of turning over the monthly commission entitlement figures. Am I right?

Supervisor - Yes, you are.

M. Do you also agree that the Commission Entitlements Report is one of the department's most complex and difficult assignments?

S. Yes, it is.

M. Then perhaps you can tell me why Mary Evans is training him to do it instead of yourself?

S. I don't know. Mary's a good worker. She knows her stuff.

M. I'm sure she does. But no one in the department understands the complications of that project better than you do. Wouldn't it make good sense to give Ed the benefit of your detailed knowledge and experience.

S. I suppose it would. But it would take a lot of time, and I've been so busy. . .

M. Uh oh, my favorite alibi. "Too busy" rarely holds up as an excuse. In a case like this in particular, the time you save delegating a job you should be doing yourself will come back to haunt you later. The problems you avoid by your superior training will save you all kinds of time in days to come. The better the break-in, the less misunderstandings and errors will result. It boils down to a matter of priorities. Getting a new employee off to the right start should be at the top of every supervisor's priorities list. Mary's a good and conscientious employee, and for most break-in tasks she'd be a fine choice. But she lacks your special know-how and experience in working with the commission entitlements. And she doesn't have your teaching ability. The difference between what Ed learns from Mary and what he learns from you could have a profound effect on his grasp and understanding of the job, and his ability to deal with the tricky problems and decisions he is bound to encounter. I'm a firm believer in the axiom that the more you can delegate, the better. But like most axioms it isn't universally applicable. It's a matter of judgment.

S. I see what you mean. I guess it would make more sense to delegate some of that stuff I'm too busy with than the commission entitlements.

M. It sure would. When work is turned over to a new or inexperienced person, it's important to make sure nothing is lost in the process. There is a vast difference between the delegation of simple routine tasks and tough and complex assignments. On heavy stuff like that a merely good teacher doesn't fill the bill if an outstanding teacher is available. In this case it is you.

• • • **TALKING POINTS**   Getting new recruits off on the right foot is a primary supervisory responsibility on three counts: 1) Setting them straight attitudinally; 2) Defining the work requirements clearly and accurately; 3) Helping to generate self-confidence from the outset. Talented teachers keep these factors in mind automatically and instinctively. They assess the new hire's state of mind and grasp of the subject on an ongoing basis. They encourage questions at the right time and dispel the trainee's fears of appearing slow or dull. They force repetition of key points to ensure proper understanding. They know how and when to boost self-confidence when the employee exhibits a good grasp of a technique or comes up with an innovative idea. Often a break-in chore can be delegated, other times not. It sometimes takes hard and careful thought for a supervisor to determine when to delegate turnover to a subordinate, and when to tackle the task him- or herself.

DIALOGUE FOUR

Marginal employee Al Nelson is approaching the end of his probationary period. Information Services Department Supervisor Mel Green questions Ben Polsky, his assistant, about whether or not to keep him on.

Talking It Out

Supervisor - Nelson has four days of his probationary period left. What do you think?

Assistant Supervisor - I don't know. The guy is certainly trying.

S.   That's a point in his favor. It also raises the question: Is he trying hard enough to make it?

A.S. I wish I could answer that with assurance one way or the other.

S.   So do I. But you're the guy who worked closest with him. That you can't answer with assurance isn't a good sign.

A.S. I know.

S.   Before finalizing the decision, let's have another look at those progress reports.

A.S. (pulls out reports, expression glum)

S.   I don't know, Ben. His potential looks borderline at best.

A.S. Yeah, that's the reading I get.

S.   (sets reports aside) I'd say, unless Nelson shows a startling recovery in the next day or two, we'll have no choice but to reject him. Better safe than sorry.

A.S. I agree. Too bad. Nelson looks like a nice guy.

S.   I know. But you know the expression: "Nice guys finish last." If he's one of those we can live without him.

• • • **TALKING POINTS**   Mel's comment, "Better safe than sorry," says it all. Too often, when a recruit shows a little promise, is likable, and gives evidence of trying hard, the temptation to keep him is strong. But the tough realities of the marketplace must be faced. For one thing, a person who really wants to succeed will never work or try harder than during the probationary period. In addition, some new hires simply have it, others don't. On top of that, experience shows that the recruit who is marginal at the outset will most often remain marginal, or worse, decline further when the probationary incentive is removed. Finally, especially in a unionized shop, getting rid of a marginal or substandard worker who becomes solidly entrenched can be a hard and painful process. Sadly, in some cases a recruit whose potential is borderline as the end of the probationary period nears, will make it if given the chance. But most often, as experience proves, keeping on the questionable new hire will mean saddling the operation with a marginal worker for months or years to come.

DIALOGUE FIVE

Young, recently-hired Stockroom employee Jerry Rich appears to be getting himself involved with the wrong crowd.

Talking It Out

Supervisor - Jerry, in one way a business organization is like a game of craps. Have you ever been to Vegas or Atlantic City and watched the play?

Employee - As a matter of fact, that's where I went on vacation three months ago.

S. Then you know what I'm talking about. If you play the game or just stand around watching, you see soon enough that there are winners and losers. In addition to rolling the dice themselves, most players like to bet with or against the shooter.

E. *Tell me about it. I lost two hundred bucks that way.*

S. (smiling) Okay, follow me on this. Bet with a winner and you come out ahead. Bet with a loser, you lose. Right?

E. *Sure.*

S. Well it works the same way in business with one important exception. In Vegas or Atlantic City the outcome is based mostly on luck. Lucky, you win; unlucky, you lose. Yet on the job in this department, for example, whether you win or lose depends a lot more on how smart you are than on luck. And to a large degree it can depend on whether you back a winner or loser. Do you know what I'm talking about?

E. *Not exactly.*

S. All right, let me clarify. The concept is simple. You have a much better chance of winning if you use your head than if you depend on chance like in Vegas.

E. *I still don't get the point.*

S. The point is this. You're a new employee, recently hired. Are you going to wind up a winner, or loser? You don't know yet. Neither do I. But many of your co-workers have been around for years. Some are winners who advanced on the job and are making a lot more money today than when they started. They're in solid. Their futures are assured. That's one side of the coin. Other employees are losers. They're in the same jobs today, making pretty much the same dough as when they started. They're spinning their wheels. Why? In most cases because they are lazy; their attitudes are lousy; and they feel rules are made for the next guy, not them. They think they're ahead of the game if they can figure out a way to beat the company by goofing off. But only one thing is sure: If they don't change their ways they will remain losers. If you were a betting man, Jerry, who would you bet on?

E. I think I see what you're getting at.

S. Sure you do. Now let's relate it to Jerry Rich and the job. I don't want to name names, but you don't need 20-20 vision to separate the winners from the losers around here. All you have to do to tell them apart is to keep your eyes open and give it some thought.

E. Yeah, I see what you mean.

S. Good. Let's take it a step further. From what I've observed you've been hanging out with more losers than winners.

E. (lowers his eyes) I never thought of it that way. If a guy's friendly, I respond.

S. There's nothing wrong with that, but *how* you respond can make a big difference. If you allow a loser to influence you into thinking that *his* philosophy is the smart philosophy, you're on your way to becoming a loser yourself. If you let him con you into thinking that it's dumb to work hard, or smart to goof off and beat the company, you'll find yourself up a creek without a paddle before you know it.

E. (nods thoughtfully)

S. Use your head, Jerry. You know who the losers are; the guys who never get ahead. Pick your favorite loser and figure it out for yourself. What did that kind of thinking get for him? A better job? More money? More respect? You tell me.

E. Nothing, I guess.

S. You don't have to guess. Now pick yourself a winner. Joe Saunders, for example. He gives a fair day's work for his pay. Joe made Assistant Supervisor after only two years on the job. Or Vivian Mackie. She considers conscientious effort an investment in her career. She's up for promotion to group leader. Or Herb Quigley, another hard worker. He made Grade One in less than a year because of his outstanding performance. Who do you think you should bet on and let influence you: people like Joe, Herb, and Vivian, or some of those deadbeats you've been hanging out with? Whose ideas and philosophies will do you the most good?

E. I think I'm getting the message. Thanks.

• • • **TALKING POINTS**   No one is more vulnerable to being influenced positively or negatively than new employees on the job—young, green employees especially. One of your most important supervisory roles can be compared to that of the seasoned coach on a ball team. Your responsibility to the team, to the new hire, and most of all to yourself is to keep a watchful eye on your "rookies." You can use your proven judgment and maturity to good effect if you steer them down the right path from the outset and teach them how to keep their eye on the ball—not only so far as the work itself is concerned, but just as important, how their ideas, values, and attitudes are shaped. It is up to you to start molding these rookies before the losers grab a hold of them. Keep your eyes and ears open. If you see an impressionable newcomer in frequent contact with a veteran deadbeat, it's a safe bet he or she is being adversely influenced. That should give you a tip-off to act like a pro. Rescue the recruit just as soon as you can—for his or her own good, for the organization, and most of all for yourself.

chapter twenty-seven

. . . .

SETTING HIGH
PERFORMANCE AND
ETHICAL STANDARDS

In the main, the nation's most successful and profitable organizations have one characteristic in common: In their policy statements, conduct, and development efforts, their managements stress the overriding importance of establishing and sustaining high standards of individual performance, product performance, customer service, and ethical behavior. Since the whole is the sum of its parts, to fulfill this objective, the quality credo must filter down from the top executive suite to divisional and departmental echelons. Once again this puts you, the department head, foreperson, or section leader, on the spot. No one is better qualified or positioned to create and sustain quality goals than America's line and staff leaders who are charged with the responsibility for employee guidance and training on operational levels.

DIALOGUE ONE

Several employees in the Data Processing Department seem to take office ethics for granted. Art Foley, the department head, calls his 15-person staff together to talk about it.

Talking It Out

Supervisor - How many of you are familiar with Section 15B of the company's policy manual? I'll give you a tip. It deals with workplace ethics.

(A scattering of employees raise their hands.)

S. Okay, I'd like a volunteer. How about you, Ann? What does an ethics policy mean to you?

Employee - (winces) Some volunteer! (laughter) I don't know. I guess it's about being honest and forthright in our dealings with others.

S. Absolutely right. That's a good start. Who can be more specific? Jim?

E. Employees shouldn't accept gifts from customers or suppliers. It could lead to conflict of interest and it's against company policy.

S. Good. What else? Tony?

E. This business of confidentiality. Certain information and reports are stamped confidential. That designation should be respected. Disclosure of privileged information could lead to all kinds of problems. I remember the old wartime slogan: "Loose lips sink ships."

S. Right on, Tony. Actually, it is the abuse of confidentiality that prompted me to call this meeting. I won't single out individuals, but I was approached by an employee recently who wanted to know why, since a co-worker was earning X-dollars per week, and since he was just as competent, he wasn't getting as much. When I asked him how he knew what the other person was earning, he replied, "Oh, everyone knows." What disturbs me is that it states plainly in the company's policy manual that salary information is confidential, and that the disclosure of that information is a clear breach of ethics. That's one example. Any comment on that?

(Looks are exchanged, but no comments)

S. (smiles) I didn't expect any. I'll give you another example. The other day an employee—we'll keep the name confidential—was overheard by a section head asking another employee to punch

out her time card. That's not only a breach of ethics; it is down-right dishonest. Equally dishonest was her friend's agreement to do what she asked. Do you think I'm being petty and nit-picking? You were about to raise your hand, Myra.

E. *(grins) Not at all. If you're asked to do something unethical you shouldn't even have to think about it. Your refusal should be quick and automatic.*

S. Thank you. Listen, I don't want to preach to you with a holier-than-thou attitude. But it is an unfortunate reality of life in America that ethical and moral standards have declined in recent years. Whether they continue to decline is up to every one of us. The company's code of ethics has been carefully developed with high moral standards in mind. When you're asked by a co-worker or supervisor to do something unethical it might seem at the moment that it's in your best interests to comply. But unethical behavior almost inevitably backfires. It undermines the organization, the department, and most of all your own self-respect. Please give that some thought.

• • • **TALKING POINTS**   We are, each and every one of us, accountable for our actions. How ethical are the people who work for you? Do they run photocopies for their own personal use without getting approval? Do they "borrow" tools or equipment, or use them on the job, without obtaining permission? Do they falsify time sheets or information on reports? Do they lie about the whereabouts of co-workers? Do they disclose confidential information? How permissive are you in turning a blind eye to ethical abuses? Does your company have a published code of ethics? If so, as a supervisor it behooves you to examine and understand it from the context of your own behavior and that of your subordinates. If not, it presents a fine opportunity to take the initiative to help develop one. Proposing this to your boss can only increase his or her respect for you as a human being and innovator.

DIALOGUE TWO

Phyllis thinks she can get ahead on the backs of her co-workers by telling tales out of school.

Talking It Out

Supervisor - What's on your mind, Phyllis?

Employee - I thought you should know, Mr. Green, that some people around here aren't to be trusted.

S. Oh no? For example?

E. Harold Pankowski for one. He called in sick the other day. Well, I over-heard him telling Joe Fried that he wasn't sick at all. He had gone to a ball game.

S. What do you think I should do about it?

E. I don't know. I thought you should know. I'm just trying to be helpful.

S. I see. I wish I knew what to say, Phyllis. Do you think I should reward you in some way for coming to me with this information?

E. (frowning) I'm not looking for any reward. I just thought it was my duty. . .

S. To tattle on your co-workers?

E. (nervousness increasing) I didn't look at it that way.

S. Maybe you didn't—consciously. But isn't it possible that in back of your mind you view this as a way to get in good with the boss?

E. I, I don't think so.

S. Be honest with yourself, Phyllis. Within the past few weeks you snitched on George Collins for sneaking across the street for a beer. The other day you told me Alice spent over a half hour in the ladies room. Before that you informed on Joe Susskind for making a personal call that took forty minutes. You may not realize it, but you've been functioning like a one-woman Gestapo.

E. I was only trying to be helpful.

S. To whom?

E. (sighs) I don't know. Maybe, like you said, I was unconsciously trying to win favor with you.

S. If so, it may be something worth thinking about. I've been check-ing the personnel files recently. Your performance rating is just about average. Your attendance is a bit below average. You're a smart woman, Phyllis. You could probably do better than that if

you put your mind to it. **If you really want to act in the department's best interest, the best thing you could do for yourself—and for me—would be to toe the line more and improve your performance. That's the only way to get ahead in this company.**

E. *(eyes lowered)*

S. **Phyllis, someone once said that to be trusted is a greater compliment than to be loved. Suppose for argument's sake I was the kind of supervisor who encouraged his people to tattle on co-workers. And suppose I rewarded an employee for doing this with a promotion or a raise, for example. Do you think I could trust a person who would betray the trust of co-workers? None of us is perfect. We all stray from time to time. I don't condone such action, but I'm no less human than the next guy. If I stepped out of line on occasion, could I trust such a person not to go to *my* boss and tattle on me, just as you tattled on Harold, Alice, and George?**

E. *(more miserable than ever)*

S. **There's nothing wrong with ambition, Phyllis, if one's ends are gained honestly and ethically. Let's forget this ever happened. But if you're ambitious to advance yourself, tend to your *own* performance, not your co-workers'.**

• • • **TALKING POINTS** One would be hard put to find an organization comprised of employees who don't go off track from time to time. The last thing we'd suggest is for a supervisor to be permissive of the kind of abuses Phyllis exposed in tattling on her co-workers. Your responsibility as the captain is to run a tight ship. But ferreting out and clamping down on offenders is your job and your assistant's. Phyllis's boss makes a potent point in his quote about trust. In most cases trying to get ahead on the back of the next person tends to thwart ambition rather than aid it.

DIALOGUE THREE

Automatic screw machine operator Sam Hertzog is so preoccupied with quantity that he sacrifices quality.

Talking It Out

Supervisor - Sam, I've just been going over the latest productivity figures. Your production is almost the highest in the department.

Employee - (beaming) I try to push the stuff out as fast as I can.

S. I know you do. But before you get a swelled head, listen to the flip side of the coin. Your *productivity* is almost the *lowest* in the department. There's a big difference between production and productivity.

E. I don't get it.

S. You will when you take a look at these figures on the number of rejects you turned out.

E. (crestfallen) Oh, I didn't realize. . .

S. Sam, I know you work hard and try hard, but let me ask you: In grinding out those units, how many cutting tools are involved?

E. Let me see. Six.

S. And what kind of steel is fed into the spindles?

E. Number 42B.

S. That's pretty tough stuff, isn't it?

E. The toughest, and the trouble is it's not always consistent, not even in the same batch at times. One bar may feed through without problems; the next bar may jam or cause chatter.

S. Which tends to knock off the tolerance. Shouldn't that give you a pretty good clue as to why you're producing too many rejects?

E. I guess so. I should mike up the pieces more often to make sure they're holding to tolerance.

S. Right. I'm the last guy to knock quantity, but quantity at the expense of quality can be costly and antiproductive. You're smart and fast, Sam. You could be a top-rated employee. All you have to do is keep closer tabs on your output. A couple of minutes here and there to double check your work more often might mean a few less units produced, but make you a far more productive producer.

• • • **TALKING POINTS** True pride in performance implies pride in quality as well as quantity. To achieve this objective, the focus must be on quality as a primary success indicator. Ideally, quality performance is a team effort between your subordinates and you as a supervisor. It is your job to create and sustain employee awareness. It is your job as well to clearly define problems hindering quality and to provide proper tools of measurement—gauges, testers, whatever. It is the employee's responsibility to check output at predesignated intervals on an ongoing basis. And *your* responsibility to make sure that they do so.

DIALOGUE FOUR

Mailroom Supervisor Blanche Frost's performance expectations are too low.

Talking It Out

Manager - Take a look at this report I just received from corporate headquarters. It's a division by division comparison of departmental productivity. Four divisions, four mailrooms, for example. Out of the four this division's productivity is rated lowest. Any idea why?

Supervisor - (frowning) No, I don't.

M. Do you think the other divisions have a better grade of people than we have here?

S. No way. Most of my people are rated pretty high in character and attitude as well as performance. I think the ratings are well-deserved.

M. I agree. And still these figures don't lie. There must be some other answer.

S. I have no idea what it might be.

M. Okay, let's examine it further. Your department has two main functions: To distribute the incoming mail, and process the outgoing mail. Correct?

S. That's right.

M. All right. Let's look at the functional breakdowns division by division. On a per-employee basis, the other divisions distribute the incoming mail faster and get more mail out the door at the end of the day than we do. Why?

S. *We may have more special mailings which take added time, or more boxes and packages to process.*

M. **That's a good thought, but it doesn't apply, as you can see by the comparison figures here.**

S. *We make very few errors in distributing and sending out the mail.*

M. **No more or less than the other divisions as these numbers indicate. No, I suspect the answer may be in the productivity standards you set.**

S. *What do you mean?*

M. **Simply this. Compare our standards here to those of the other divisions. Mail distribution in particular. Ours are lowest in every case.**

S. *I didn't realize that.*

M. **Neither did I. But now that it's revealed there's only one conclusion to make. Assuming that our people are as skilled and potentially productive as their counterparts in the other divisions, it is the standards we set that makes the difference. Human nature is funny, Blanche. It applies in the Mailroom just as it does in Production. If an employee is expected to produce ten units per hour, that's what most will produce even though they may be capable of twelve or thirteen pieces. As a supervisor, if your performance expectations are too low, the inevitable result will be low productivity.**

S. *That makes sense.*

M. **I'm glad you agree. Let's sit down together and figure out what must be done to upgrade those standards.**

• • • **TALKING POINTS**   The ultimate goal of good management is to motivate employees to produce at their maximum potential. Whether performance standards are developed formally or informally, setting them fairly and accurately requires sound supervisory judgment. A delicate balance must be maintained. Too high can be as detrimental to morale and productivity as too low. Setting unrealistically high standards are almost certain to backfire. Pushing people beyond their normal capability creates unhealthy tension, resentment, and bitterness. Setting standards too low results in low productivity and boredom. Psychological research proves that people are happiest when they are producing at their best.

DIALOGUE FIVE

Customer Service Department Supervisor Fred Kerr fails to track down errors to their root causes.

Talking It Out

Manager - I just got a call from Eunice Stark, the Purchasing Agent at Dunlop & Warfield. Her annoyance was barely restrained. She claims the number of our shipping errors in the past few months is creating a lot of extra work for them, not to mention the aggravation of their stock shortage problems. That's the third such complaint I received this week. What's going on?

Supervisor - I don't know. I talked to Joe Horton about it.

M. And?

S. I assumed he's taking care of it. He's the Shipping Supervisor. It's his responsibility.

M. You're the Customer Service Supervisor, Fred. It's your responsibility too. Let's get Joe up here to my office to see if we can straighten this out once and for all.

(The manager picks up the phone and summons Joe Horton to his office.)

M. Joe, I just got an angry call from the P.A. at Dunlop & Warfield complaining about all the shipping errors that have been coming through lately. As I told Fred, I've been getting similar calls from other customers. He tells me he discussed this with you.

S. He mentioned it a week or so ago.

M. What did you do about it?

S. I got the pickers and packers together and really laid down the law.

M. Specifically, what did you tell them?

S. I told them excessive errors were costly and could lose us customers. I told them to be more careful, and that I was going to get tough on employees who made too many errors.

M. It didn't seem to help much, did it? Tell me something, Joe. Why do you think we're getting so many errors? What's the reason for it?

S. It's hard to say. Carelessness, I guess.

M. That's not good enough. Carelessness is a major cause of inefficiency, but it's too general an explanation. What *causes* the carelessness? There are any number of reasons to explain an excess of shipping errors: Inaccurate picking of merchandise due to poor eyesight; problems with the paperwork that comes down from Billing; faulty arrangement of items in the bins; labeling problems. . . . I'm sure you could add to this list.

S. I see what you mean.

M. Joe, getting your people together and talking to them shows concern. But that alone isn't the answer. And Fred, the same thing applies to you. Passing the complaint buck on to Joe isn't enough. When quality problems exist, whether in the production of merchandise, customer service, or the processing of transactions, there's only one sure way to minimize them. That is to track down the cause of each and every error that exists, and plan action to eliminate the cause if you can to avoid repetition. Sure, anyone can make a mistake, and perfection is an unrealistic goal. But human error is an inadequate explanation for why mistakes occur. Some human error may be unavoidable, but most errors can be avoided if we find out *why* they occurred and take steps to deal with the causes.

• • • **TALKING POINTS** In most efficient and successful operations, supervisory accountability for errors implies a planned and organized system designed to track down the cause of each error committed. Recently, in one office billing mistakes were reduced 70% on the heels of an error-cause trackdown and analysis. The results of the study induced one checker to undergo a cataracts operation, another employee to get her glasses changed, and a third to switch jobs from Checker to Biller. Elsewhere, shipping errors were cut 20% when a billing form used by stock pickers was redesigned so that the sequence of items listed coincided with those stacked in the bins. The beauty of error-cause trackdown is that it triggers all kinds of ideas about how to deal with problems.

Dialogue Six

Receiving Department Supervisor Edith Sokoloff fails to clamp down on mediocre performers.

Talking It Out

Manager - Edith, I'm not going to pull any punches. Your department's performance has fallen into the unacceptable range. You're making too many errors and getting too many complaints.

Supervisor - I'm sorry. We're doing our best.

M. I hope that's not true, because if that's your best, we have problems.

S. (nervous, no reply)

M. (smiling) Don't look so worried. This is nothing we can't solve with a little thought and effort. But first let me show you what concerns me. (shows Edith the current performance report)

S. I didn't realize it was that bad.

M. Okay, let's see what we can do to correct it. Objective Number One is to pinpoint the cause if we can. Do you mind if I make a suggestion or two?

S. Not at all. I can use all the help I can get.

M. Good. To start with why don't we take a closer look at a few of the complaints we've been getting. I indicated some of the most serious ones with an orange magic marker. You have twelve employees in your department. As you can see, three of them were involved in the bulk of the problems. Repeat offenders, you might say. It is clear, for example, that Jeff Mackie doesn't check all the shipments he okays, or if he does, he's half asleep at the time. Same thing for Jean Cartwright. That raises an obvious question:

What steps have you taken in an effort to get these people on the ball?

S. *I talked to them. In Jeff's case I warned him that if he doesn't start toeing the line, it could cost him his job.*

M. **Was this an official warning? Did he get it in writing? Was it inserted in his file?**

S. *Well, no.*

M. **Was this the first warning he got?**

S. *No, I warned him several times.*

M. **What about Jean Cartwright?**

S. *She received a number of warnings as well.*

M. **All oral?**

S. *Yes.*

M. **This sounds like it could be the crux of the problem. Repeated oral warnings have little effect unless they are followed up with action that gives weight to the warnings. When employees repeatedly violate standards or rules, progressive discipline is the only way to keep them in line. It's all right to informally call a worker to account once or twice. But at a certain point tougher and more formal action is needed. This starts with an official written warning or two that goes into the person's personnel file, then a suspension or two followed by a final suspension and warning: Shape up, or else—with the "or else" acted upon in extreme situations. Edith, the permissiveness I see around here is detrimental to all parties concerned. If you allow second-rate performance to persist, second-rate performance is the best you can expect. Understand? The idea is to shoot for excellence, not mediocrity.**

S. *Yes sir, I get the message loud and clear.*

• • • **TALKING POINTS** Lax supervisory follow-up to mediocre performance is an invitation for mediocrity to prevail. Most management consultants who audit performance agree that a major cause of poor productivity is the supervisor who keeps putting off the hard and unpleasant task of confronting employees who don't measure up. The failure to apply progressive discipline where it is called for is a sure way to ensure poor performance throughout your organization.

chapter twenty-eight

- - - - - - - - - - - - - - - -

PROMOTING
HEALTHY AMBITION

On the one hand, properly directed ambition is the most important success characteristic one could acquire. On the other hand, people are judged not by what they attempt but by what they accomplish. The trick is to get both hands working in tandem as a two-fisted team. It's not always easy. Healthy ambition fueled by hard work and a burning desire for knowledge, will advance you steadily towards your goal. But, ambition out of control will hurt your career more surely than thumbing your nose at the boss. This applies to you, and it applies to your people. As a supervisor it applies on two levels: 1) It is your responsibility to carefully monitor your personal ambition to ensure that it is realistically proportioned and manifested; 2) It is also your responsibility to see to it that your subordinates' ambition is applied positively and constructively.

DIALOGUE ONE

Word-Processing Operator Al Stevens is a bright employee who lacks ambition.

Talking It Out

Supervisor - Al, do me a favor. Read this personnel evaluation aloud. It was drawn up at the time you were hired more than six months ago. In fact, it's the reason you were selected over a dozen or more candidates who applied.

Employee - (reads aloud) "Good background, education, and experience. Personable and makes a good appearance. Well-above-average intelligence. Indicates excellent potential for advancement." Hey, is that me?

S. It sure is.

E. So what happened? Why am I spinning my wheels?

S. Good question. Take a look at this *recent* evaluation and read that aloud.

E. (expression changes as he reads) "Borderline performance. Has not lived up to expectations." I see what you mean.

S. Good. That's the first step in the right direction. My impression when I hired you was that you were a smart guy with the ambition, drive, and brains to see it through. Now, it's my turn to ask you: What happened?

E. (frowning) I don't know. At the beginning I was all gung ho. I worked hard and did my best.

S. And your work showed it. Then you started going downhill. You appear to have lost your zest. You don't seem to care anymore. I repeat: What happened?

E. Nothing happened. At least nothing I can put my finger on.

S. When a smart ambitious person stops pushing himself there must be a reason. Did anything occur to demotivate you?

E. (frowning) I don't know. The job didn't turn out to be what I expected.

S. How did you expect it to turn out?

E. I wish I knew. Somehow I'm disappointed, but I can't explain why. I thought the work would be more of a challenge, something I could get my teeth into and show what I could do. Instead it's the same routine day after day.

S. You're bored.

E. Yeah, maybe that's it. I'm bored.

S. Okay, Al, thanks for leveling with me. Now let me level with you. Dull repetition is the bane of the workplace especially for people of higher-than-average intelligence. The problem is a lot of the boring stuff can't be avoided; it's work that has to be done.

E. I know, but that doesn't solve my problem.

S. I realize that. On the other hand, there's a certain amount of work that's more interesting and challenging that I think you'd be able to handle. The problem is you're not the only employee in the department of above-average intelligence, and the way it works is that new people get most of the boring stuff because seniority and experience count in assigning work.

E. Yeah, I guess that's only fair.

S. But maybe we can come to some kind of a compromise. On the one hand, I'm going to give you some of the more interesting assignments. On the other, you'll have to sweat out some of the dull stuff as well. As time goes on, if you're patient and do well, you'll gradually get more and more of the challenging work. As long as you keep your performance-rating high, your opportunities will improve. Does that sound reasonable?

E. It sure does. Thanks for talking to me.

• • • **TALKING POINTS**   Question: What is the most valuable asset on any company's balance sheet? Answer: Employees who enjoy their work. Boredom squelches ambition faster than failing to recognize good work. Keep your eyes and ears peeled for the subordinate you think should be ambitious but isn't, or appears to have lost ambition and drive along the way. Any number of reasons might explain dying ambition from health or family problems to resentment caused by real or imagined mistreatment. But as experience shows, the most common ambition killer of all is plain old-fashioned boredom.

DIALOGUE TWO

The trouble with Anita Held who works in the showroom is that her ambition exceeds her ability to advance on the job.

Talking It Out

Employee - I've been here over a year, Mr. Brown. I think I'm overdue for a promotion to Senior Showroom Representative.

Supervisor - I can appreciate your frustration, Anita, but you're not qualified for the senior job.

E. *I don't see why not. I work as hard as anyone else in the department.*

S. **I know you do and that's an important point in your favor, but your job is** selling **more than anything else. That requires a special talent and persuasive skills in dealing with the customers that come in.**

E. *I do the best I can and I know the product line as well as anyone.*

S. **I can't deny that. But sales personality is very special, and hard to define. Very few people have it. You're a charming person but you just don't happen to have a selling personality, at least not one that qualifies you for a senior position. I'm sorry.**

E. *What am I supposed to do? Hang around when I'm bypassed for advancement, and see others getting ahead?*

S. **You do get periodic increases.**

E. *I'm not willing to settle for that.*

S. **Tell me something, Anita. Do you like what you're doing? Do you enjoy your work?**

E. *(reluctantly) I guess not particularly.*

S. **That's what I thought. You're an introspective person. That's not a bad characteristic. But introspective people aren't always at ease interacting with customers on a face-to-face basis.**

E. *I suppose that's right.*

S. **On the other hand, you have other useful abilities. You have a good understanding of the technical aspects of the product line, and you're good with numbers. You might be happier in another kind of work. How would you feel if I tried to get you transferred to a department where your natural skills would be more applicable?**

E. *I might like that, but wouldn't it mean a cut in pay?*

S. **Possibly. But you would be doing what you like and have a better chance to get ahead. Over the long pull you might come out ahead**

of the game. It's hard to succeed when you're not enthusiastic about your job.

E. *(thoughtful) Could I decide after I see what's available?*

S. **Sure. Let me see what I can do.**

• • • **TALKING POINTS**   Henry Wadsworth Longfellow wrote, "Most people would succeed in small things if they were not troubled by great ambitions." There are few supervisory tasks more unpleasant than having to tell ambitious employees that their ambition exceeds their capabilities. But there's no easy way around this dilemma. When people don't have it, they simply don't have it and no amount of talk will change this reality. On the other hand, never lose sight of the square-peg-in-the-round-hold syndrome. Many employees who can't make the grade in one aspect of the work wind up excelling in another. Explore peoples' interests. Before throwing in the towel, ask them to tell you what they would most like to do and what they think they do well. Their response could be revealing. If you can, give them a chance to demonstrate their unused skills in your operation. Or if this isn't feasible, find out if their abilities can be used elsewhere in the company.

DIALOGUE THREE

Purchasing Department Assistant Mary Regan has what it takes and then some, but lacks personal drive and initiative.

Talking It Out

Supervisor - What's the problem, Mary?

Employee - What do you mean?

S. **I'm not sure myself. It's a feeling I have. You used to have enough spark and energy to light up a birthday cake. Lately it seems to be gone. Do you think you're experiencing burnout?**

E. *I don't know. I do my job. I follow instructions.*

S. **I know you do. But what happened to the pizazz and enthusiasm you used to have?**

E. *(frowning) Is it that noticeable?*

S. Nothing I can put my finger on. I just have the feeling things aren't exactly copasetic, if you know what I mean.

E. I guess I do. Sometimes I feel I'm just spinning my wheels, getting nowhere fast. Other times I feel like a robot. Everything is either assigned step by step or spelled out in the procedure manual. I get no chance to think or act for myself.

S. What you're saying is that you're in a rut.

E. I guess that's right, more or less.

S. Okay, let's talk about it. Do you think you're getting too much supervision?

E. That may be part of it.

S. (thoughtful) That's an interesting observation. If it's true, I plead guilty. You know, there are ten employees in this department. At least half of them need to have everything spelled out for them, every *i* dotted, every *t* crossed. I might have fallen into the habit of doing that for everyone, even people like yourself who are capable of functioning on their own.

E. I can understand that.

S. Tell you what, Mary. I'm going to give you a chance to operate more independently. On the special reports, for example, you'll be on your own unless you need help. All I'll check are the final results. As far as the published procedures are concerned, I won't tell you not to follow them. But keep your eyes open for possible changes that might make the job easier or more efficient. When you spot something, let me know. Procedures have to be revised and updated constantly. I'd like your help in doing that.

E. (face brightening) Thanks. I'd enjoy that. It would make the job more challenging.

S. And give you a chance to make positive contributions as well, which can't hurt your career.

E. Hey, that sounds great.

S. I'm glad you think so. One way or another we'll get that old spark and spirit percolating again.

• • • **TALKING POINTS** Outstanding people like Mary are especially vulnerable to the ancient corporate malady of *rut*initis, a common precursor to burnout. As a supervisor it is in your best interest as well as your subordinates' to spot the symptoms early—listlessness, flagging enthusiasm, and so on—and take action. How? By checking unused talents and skills your superior subordinates might have and taking advantage of them. By boosting their egos with an invitation to act as consultants to help you solve problems. And by granting them increased autonomy if you can as Mary's boss is attempting to do. Less supervision increases self-confidence and helps boost self-esteem. As a status builder it's an ego-nursing strategy as well.

DIALOGUE FOUR

Statistical Department Assistant Supervisor Frank Messner's get-ahead philosophy relies too much on *who* you know and not enough on *what* you know.

Talking It Out

Supervisor - Frank, I'd like to sign you up for that new Windows course the company is sponsoring.

Assistant Supervisor - When is it given?

S.   Two evenings a week, 7:00 to 10:00, Tuesday and Thursday.

A.S. No good. Thursday's my bowling night.

S.   (frowning) That's the third course you turned down for one reason or other.

A.S. I can't desert the guys on my bowling team. They depend on me.

S.   What about the "guys" on your department's team? They depend on you too. I don't have to tell you about the role the computer plays in the job you do. That Windows course is important.

A.S. Okay, okay, I'll read up on it on my own.

S.   That's not good enough. That's what you said about the Accounting course you turned down. Nothing happened.

A.S. (no comment)

S.   Frank, something's been puzzling me. You make no secret of your ambition to get ahead in this company. Yet, when it comes to taking action that will help you do so you cop out on it.

A.S. Oh, I'll get ahead all right. Mr. Williams has his eye on me. And Joe Curran thinks I'm hot stuff.

S. **I'll have to admit, you've made some pretty good contacts around here. Ed Williams and Joe Curran like you. But do you think that's all it takes?**

A.S. Sure, one word from them and I'm in. You know what they say: "It's not what you know, it's who you know."

S. **You've got it all wrong, pal. Let's suppose Ed Williams or Joe Curran recommended you for a promotion. What do you think would happen next?**

A.S. Are you kidding? With their influence, I'd breeze right through.

S. **You're living in a dream world. It's not that easy. They'd have to come to me to find out if you're qualified. I'd have no choice but to tell them you're not because of your lack of interest in increasing your job-related knowledge and skill. I won't deny the value of having good contacts. Who you know may be important in getting ahead. But *what* you know is at least equally, if not more important.**

• • • **TALKING POINTS** Ambitious people are usually smart enough to realize that the right contacts can often account for significant mileage on the road to success. If you are an experienced supervisor you probably know that the more allies you make on the job—line and staff employees as well as fellow supervisors—the better positioned you will be to get your plans and projects accepted. But however much pull one has with the organization's key influentials, unless good ol' dad runs the company, it won't do much good if the substance is missing. The safest and surest get-ahead plus any employee could have, whatever the rank, is to outshine the competition in the know-how department. An old proverb states, "If you have enough push, you can get by without pull."

DIALOGUE FIVE

Evelyn Levine in Marketing has a great deal on the ball, but for one reason or another doesn't participate in the company's suggestion program.

Talking It Out

Supervisor - Evelyn, I won't mention names, but if you'd like I could make a list of at least five employees with less experience, smarts, and know-how than you who earned some nice extra income for themselves this past year as a result of suggestions turned in. I've been wondering why you don't take advantage of this opportunity as well.

Employee - I don't know. I thought about it from time to time, but never seem to get around to it.

S. That doesn't make sense. You're a smart woman. You're in one of the company's most creative departments. You can use the extra money. And you made no secret of your ambition to advance to a senior copywriter's job. I can't think of a more effective vehicle to accomplish your aims than the suggestion program. Napolean Hill once said that good ideas are the beginning points of all fortunes.

E. I suppose that's true. I think what holds me back is that I figure the company pays experts good money to come up with ideas. How can I compete with them?

S. Judging from the score sheet, a lot of employees are doing it successfully.

E. I know. I'll have to give it more thought.

S. You certainly should. The prize money or merchandise you might win is only one aspect of it. The most profitable companies succeed because of the money-making and money-saving ideas their people suggest. Nothing attracts the attention of management faster than a good idea. For one thing, you get acknowledgment in the company publication, which doesn't hurt your career. For another, it helps define your expertise and profit-mindedness.

E. I never looked at it that way.

S. This is as good a time as any to start. There's something else you should know. In one important respect you have a substantial edge over the systems professionals and other experts who are paid to come up with ideas. No one understands the job and its problems and difficulties as well as the person who works at it day after day. That's why the systems people whose job it is to

solve problems and come up with improvements huddle with people like you in an effort to get ideas and put them into effect.

E. *I know. Every once in a while someone from Systems comes around and asks me a bunch of questions.*

S. **Exactly, and to tell you the truth there's no reason at all you can't come up with the same questions on your own and try to answer them. That's how ideas are born.**

E. *(reflecting)*

S. **Give it some thought. And don't forget, any time you come up with an idea that looks promising, even the germ of an idea, I'm right here to work with you to present it to the suggestion committee in the best possible light. When you come up with a winning idea, you may win the award, but it's a feather in my cap as well.**

• • • **TALKING POINTS** Victor Hugo wrote, "Nothing in this world is so powerful as an idea whose time has come." Creative thinking is a habit which, once developed, becomes increasingly habitual as rewards are reaped. In an Ohio consumer products company recently, a veteran warehouse employee, who, after four years of never having turned in an idea, was prodded by his boss to participate in the company's new suggestion program. With his supervisor's help, the first idea he presented won him an $86 award. In the following three years he turned in 28 suggestions, and had 17 of them accepted. He won $11,000 in prize money, and was recently promoted to department head when his boss was upgraded to manager. The biggest favor you could do for yourself and your subordinates is to motivate their suggestion program participation in any way that you can.

DIALOGUE SIX

Advertising copywriter Don Fry knows full well that good ideas are stepping stones to success, and doesn't care *whose* idea he cashes in on.

Talking It Out

Supervisor - Don, I think there's something you should know.

Employee - What's that?

S. **Ed Marcus isn't exactly a moron.**

E. *What do you mean by that?*

S. **When he saw that you got a blurb in the company magazine for dreaming up the special promotion idea, he was really miffed. It wasn't your idea alone, was it? In fact, it was *his* brainstorm to begin with. You simply helped him present it.**

E. *(eyes lowered, admission enough)*

S. **This isn't the first time you tried to hog credit that belonged to someone else. You're smart enough to know, Don, that not only is this practice unethical, it's more than likely to backfire. You're absolutely right in assuming that recognition for good ideas adds up to career Brownie points. But when you claim credit for a co-worker's idea it has just the opposite effect.**

E. *I'm sorry. It won't happen again.*

S. **I hope you keep that promise for your own good more than anyone else's. I'll tell you something else. When you share credit with a co-worker, the payoff is doubled because you are recognized not only for your creative ability, but for your skill as a team player as well.**

• • • TALKING POINTS   Employees with healthy ambition understand the career-boosting role of creative thinking and shoot for profit improvement with this thought in mind. They realize that good ideas submitted and recognized by management are success-building blocks. The employee with unhealthy ambition may understand the same thing, but doesn't care how the recognition is received, or whether or not it's deserved. As a supervisor it's in your best interest to make your feeling in this regard clear to your subordinates. Chiselers who are permitted to get away with credit theft are guilty not only of unethical conduct, but of demotivating the deserving employee who was cheated.

chapter twenty-nine

• • • • • • • • • • • • • • • • • •

Communicating
More Effectively

You have something to say to a friend, neighbor, or relative. What do you normally do? You pick up the telephone, drop over, or send a letter or note. So why is it so darned difficult to communicate on the job? Why is communication so often considered to be the most challenging workplace chore, and the one responsible for so many hassles and headaches? For a variety of reasons. Among them differences: in status and rank of communicants, background and experience, individual needs and motivations, intellectual or emotional mindsets, predetermined influences and beliefs, and so on. It is thus no surprise that because of these and other communication barriers that problems erupt. Still, it would be rare to find a problem that cannot be solved, or at least ameliorated, by talking it out.

DIALOGUE ONE

Warehouse Supervisor George Kahn suspects that John Forman, one of his subordinates, has AIDS. He confides his suspicions to Plant Manager Susan Conrad.

Talking It Out

Manager - What makes you think John has AIDS?

Supervisor - He's obviously ill, seems to be getting weaker, and has been living with someone who, according to the scuttlebutt, recently died of the disease.

M. A guy like that certainly shouldn't be hustling those heavy cases around.

S. Not only that. My guess is that John is afraid to confide his condition because he fears it may cost him his job. I'd hate to see this happen, and I wouldn't want to see him lose his benefits. If I'm right that he has AIDS he's qualified for disability benefits, but I don't know how to get him to admit he is ill.

M. (frowning) It's no simple problem. Tell me something. Does he have any close friends in the plant?

S. Yes. He's very friendly with Bill Schultz. They have lunch together every day.

M. Good, then here's what I'd suggest. Confide the problem and your concerns to Bill. Explain how it will be in John's best interest if he can persuade his friend to confide in the human resources department. They are trained to deal with situations like this.

(The supervisor follows through with the plant manager's advice. John's friend convinces him that his best bet is to confide in the Human Resources Manager who assures him he will not be terminated, and that every accommodation will be made to help see him through this difficult period. The Human Resources Manager then meets with the supervisor to ensure that he understands the company's procedure and policy in dealing with AIDS victims.)

M. I cleared this with John before talking to you. The fact that he has AIDS is confirmed. He likes our policy and is relieved and appreciative that we are trying to help.

S. That's good news. I imagine that one of his greatest concerns is his co-workers' fears of working with someone who has AIDS.

M. No question about it. An important part of the program is the educational aspect. With John's permission, but without John present, a meeting with his co-workers will be set up. A film will be shown explaining that the disease cannot be contracted through casual contact in the workplace. Questions will be encouraged and answered by a doctor from the medical department. I assume you will be able to reassign John to lighter duties in the department.

S. *No problem.*

M. Good. In addition, reasonable accommodations will be made in his work schedule, with the company's attendance policy adjusted to his needs accordingly. As long as he is able to work productively, we will cooperate in this regard. As his condition progresses, we will give him disability leaves as required, and when he can no longer work he will be placed on total disability. That's the best we can do for both John and the company.

S. *It sounds pretty good to me.*

• • • **TALKING POINTS**   It would be difficult to conceive of a more difficult and sensitive supervisory problem than dealing with a subordinate stricken with AIDS. This underlines the importance of a formal corporate AIDS policy, and the understanding of its practical and compassionate aspects by employees up and down the line. "Generally," comments one expert on the subject, "employees with AIDS should be treated no differently than a worker with any other life-threatening illness such as heart disease or cancer. As far as co-worker response is concerned, it must be kept in mind that the most effective antidote to fear is education.

DIALOGUE TWO

Conscientious Sales Department employee Sherry Parker writes correspondence that is too long and verbose.

Talking It Out

Supervisor - How long have you been in the Sales Department, Sherry?

Employee - About four months. Why?

S. I want to thank you for doing such a conscientious job, but if you don't mind I have a suggestion to make.

E. Not at all.

S. Good. I pulled a couple of your letters out of the file to show you what I have in mind. Take this one to Rothman Importing in response to a billing complaint they made.

E. (reviews 3-page letter) What's wrong with it?

S. Only one thing. You have all the facts right, and your ideas are good. But it's too long and wordy. Now, take a look at this letter written by Arlene who was at your desk before you. As you can see, it was in response to a similar billing complaint, but her letter accomplished the same purpose in only a page and a half. Do you see what I'm getting at?

E. Yes, I do. I'm doing a lot of extra unnecessary work.

S. Not only that, it also means the customer has to spend more time getting the message. Here's another example with a similar situation. Your letter took almost two pages, an earlier letter only one. It adds up to lower productivity, and less effective communication.

E. What do you want me to do?

S. Three things would help. First, compare your letters with these other two replies and see if you can spot the excess information in yours. Take a few others from the files and draw the same kinds of comparisons. Next, we'll set up a session or two, and I'll give you some tips on how to make your correspondence shorter and more effective: Succinct instead of long sentences, simple instead of polysyllabic words, less repetition, keeping to the subject, and so on. Finally, I'll sign you up for the next business writing course that comes up. You're a good worker, Sherry. We'll make a good writer out of you as well.

• • • **TALKING POINTS** Management consultant and educator Leonard J. Smith, told a client following a productivity audit, that in his opinion a good educational program for salespeople and word-processor operators could improve productivity in those departments by 40 to 50 percent. If your staff write letters, reports, or anything else, monitoring their communication periodically, and taking steps to upgrade writing skills, can result in substantially improved productivity. As Smith points out, "Business writing is an area of communication where education is urgently needed, and most commonly neglected." If you're not in a position to conduct the training yourself, get someone else to do it, or enroll employees who need help in a business writing course. There is also an abundance of excellent books and other literature on the subject from which both you and your people can derive some helpful tips on how to write more concisely and effectively.

DIALOGUE THREE

Maintenance Department carpenter Al Ruff messes up projects because he is careless and inefficient in turning over the work to his second shift replacement.

Talking It Out

Supervisor - I just got a call from Ed Pierce in Production. They can't use that jig that took almost three days to build.

Employee - What's wrong with it?

S. It's screwed up. For one thing, it doesn't follow the specification sheet. The hinges on the rotating platform are misplaced. The spindles are attached wrong. It doesn't fit on the forming table the way it's supposed to.

E. Tell Ed I'll take a look at it. Maybe with a few changes. . .

S. I already looked at it. It's no good. The whole thing will have to be rebuilt.

E. I didn't position the hinges, and I didn't attach the spindles.

S. I know you didn't. Phil Reboso did. But he got his instructions from you. You're the guy that turned over the job to the second shift.

E. Why blame me? He's the guy who screwed up.

S. That's not the way I see it. I went over the whole thing with Phil. He claims you were impatient with him, that if he asked you a question, you made him feel like a dummy. The story I get from the second-shift supervisor is that you're in such a hurry to get

away at the end of the shift that you're careless about the way you turn over the work.

E. *I'm sorry. Maybe I should spend more time on the turnovers.*

S. **No maybes about it. You're the senior man on the job. You're responsible for the way it comes out. Messing up that jig was expensive and it set Production behind on its schedule. I don't want to hear a complaint like that again.**

E. *You won't.*

• • • **TALKING POINTS**   Careless and inefficient job turnover from shift to shift, or on the same shift where job variety programs are in effect, is an all too common problem in plants and offices. A number of causes may be responsible, not the least of which are poorly written procedures, or the lack of a written procedure altogether. Untranscribed word-of-mouth turnover makes turned-over work vulnerable to misunderstanding and error. Where no written procedure exists—on one-time projects especially—the supervisor should insist that turnover instructions, unless very simple and brief, be written down at the time they are given. This helps prevent errors on the one hand, and establishes accountability on the other. The importance of written procedures cannot be overstressed. Let's assume that on a 12-step project, for example, the sixth step is completed by the first shift person. Ideally, the replacement would begin at the seventh step after ascertaining that nothing happened that might cause any changes in the remaining steps to take place. Such assurance requires good two-way communication.

DIALOGUE FOUR

Bernie Lewin in the Shipping Department sometimes forgets to level with his people.

Talking It Out

Manager - Bernie, I just got an angry call from the Buyer at Millburn Products. Her shipment is two days late. What happened? Millburn's an important customer. Your department should have worked all day Saturday to get that stuff out.

Supervisor - We did work all day Saturday.

M. Three people. Where were the rest of your crew?

S. *The problem around here is that overtime's not compulsory. We could have used eight people on Saturday. All I could get were three.*

M. Why is that?

S. *I don't know. Most of them put in overtime Wednesday, Thursday, and Friday. They said they were too tired to work Saturday. I couldn't force them to work.*

M. I could understand that if heavy overtime was a common occurrence. But it's rare that a situation like the Millburn order comes up. Do you mind if I talk to a few of your people about this?

S. *No. I'd like to hear what they say.*

(Bernie's boss questions a few of his subordinates, then gets back to the supervisor.)

M. I talked with some of your people, Bernie. You're right that most of them don't like to work overtime. But what disturbs me even more is that they feel you didn't level with them regarding the Millburn order.

S. *What do you mean?*

M. They told me you said the order would be complete by Thursday or Friday at the latest and that no further overtime would be needed.

S. *I had to tell them that to make sure I got them to work Thursday and Friday.*

M. Even though you knew you were lying to them? You had to know there was no way a full crew wouldn't be needed on Saturday.

S. *Yeah, I figured I'd take it a day at a time.*

M. It was bound to catch up with you at the end. It's almost inevitable for deceit like that to backfire. It would have been far more effective, and more honest as well, had you leveled with your people, explained that this was a special situation, and you needed their help and support. You usually get much better cooperation by telling the truth. Deceit turns employees off and hinders departmental objectives as well.

• • • **TALKING POINTS** Communication often tends to break down because people don't consider others' feelings in trying to win their cooperation. What you have to say may make sense intellectually. But if it strikes a wrong emotional chord, the message won't get through or be convincing the way you want it to. However clear and direct it might be, the crucial question is: Are you beaming in on the listener's wave length? Nothing can be more off beam than a failure to level with your people and tell it like it is no matter how distasteful the information or news.

DIALOGUE FIVE

Credit Department Assistant Supervisor Marge Reed talks up a storm but doesn't listen effectively.

Talking It Out

Supervisor - Marge, what happened on that $450 return sent back by Capitol Lighting?

Assistant Supervisor - I turned it down. That return wasn't authorized.

S. Why not?

A.S. For one thing, it's nonreturnable merchandise. For another, the stuff was damaged.

S. How did it get damaged?

A.S. You got me there.

S. Maybe it's something you should have checked out. I just got off the phone with the customer. She's furious. She claims you all but accused her of lying.

A.S. About what?

S. She says there's no way she's going to accept damaged goods.

A.S. She's trying to pull a fast one. The stuff was damaged either at the store or in transit on the way back.

S. Do you know this for a fact? The customer claims the carton was dropped by our trucker and was damaged when she received it.

A.S. That's not the way I heard the story.

S. Maybe it's because you didn't listen closely enough, or follow up what you heard. I checked with our trucker. He admits to having dropped the carton.

A.S. (crestfallen) Oh.

S. Marge, Capitol Lighting is a good account. I want you to call that Buyer, apologize for the misunderstanding, and assure her that the credit will be put through at once.

A.S. Right. Will do.

S. And for Pete's sake, the next time *listen.*

• • • **TALKING POINTS** Communication is a two-way street. If only one way is open, the message won't get through or will be distorted. It is a common human failing of some people to hear only what they want to hear. Listening with a closed mind, or in the face of predetermined judgment, can be costly, twice as costly when the person on the other end is a customer. Within the department it can result in missed ideas and suggestions as well. It has been said that we have two ears but only one tongue in order that we may hear more and speak less. The most glib and articulate supervisor will be a poor communicator if he or she listens ineffectively.

DIALOGUE SIX

Product Development Department employee Chuck Machlin thinks his boss is giving him a hard time because he doesn't like him.

Talking It Out

Supervisor - What's wrong, Chuck? You're walking around with a long face again.

Employee - Nothing's wrong.

S. That's not the way I see it. I get the feeling something's bothering you.

E. (no comment, shrugs it off)

S. Come on, what's the problem? Let's have it. Is your health okay?

E. There's nothing wrong with my health.

S. I'm glad to hear that. Trouble at home?

E. No, nothing like that.

S. There has to be something. You act like you've got a chip on your shoulder. Does it have something to do with the work?

E. (hesitates)

S. I thought so. Let's get it out in the open so we can deal with it. What's the problem?

E. Okay, it's the work. You keep pushing all the tough jobs my way. I don't know what you've got against me.

S. Wow, now I get it. Chuck you're one-hundred percent right and one-hundred percent wrong. You're a well-rated employee and I like you. I've been pushing some of the tough jobs your way, not because I have something against you, but because you're a good performer and I'm trying to groom you for a better job with more responsibilities.

E. That never entered my mind.

S. I apologize. The misunderstanding's at least partly my fault. I can't make any commitments at this time, but I should have given you some idea of what I had in mind. However, it's never too late. Let's talk about it.

• • • **TALKING POINTS**   It is an all too common practice for people to reach conclusions based on wrong information or misconceptions. Employees are apt to come to erroneous judgments for any number of reasons: a false assumption; misinterpreted information, true or false; deliberately deceptive information; rumors and gossip; misinterpreted action, as in the above-cited case. Individual characteristics also come into play in reaching conclusions and making decisions. Had Chuck possessed more confidence in his ability and his supervisor's perception of his worth, he might have realized he was given tough assignments for positive, not negative reasons. A shy person may read communication one way, an outgoing person another. It is a mistake for supervisors to automatically assume that what is in their minds is also in the minds of subordinates. It is also important to note that, as in the example above, often what you fail to say can send as strong a message as what you put into words.

chapter thirty

· · · · · · · · · · · · · ·

COMPENSATING EMPLOYEES

A wag once said, "Money may be the root of all evil, but a lack of it is the whole darned tree." Money in business creates an unending contest: Workers try to get as much as they can; owners try to keep as much as they can. Since management is charged with the profit-making responsibility— to make money for the owners—its ongoing task is to get the best materials, equipment, and workers it can for the least possible money. So the contest continues. Where does that leave you as the supervisor? Right smack in the middle as usual. It is no surprise that, as far as employee compensation is concerned, snow falls all year long, even in July. There is much to be said for the ancient adage, "Money isn't the only form of compensation." But neither is it to be sneezed at. The trick as supervisor is to balance the equation as fairly and practically as possible. On the one hand, pay your people what they earn and deserve. On the other, make them aware of other forms of compensation as well—without piling the snow too high.

DIALOGUE ONE

Marginal Production Department grinding machine operator Al Childer complains he's not getting ahead quickly enough.

Talking It Out

Employee - When are you going to put me in for promotion to a Grade One classification?

Supervisor - I'll level with you, Al. When two conditions exist: When a Grade One job opens up, and when you're qualified to fill it.

E. I'm qualified now.

S. You might be if you were the guy authorized to determine who's qualified. But unfortunately for you, I'm the one who has that responsibility, and the way I read it you're still a long way from qualified.

E. I do my job the same as everyone else. You've been working against me from the day I was hired.

S. You've got that wrong, Al. If anyone's working against you it's you.

E. How do you figure that?

S. Simple. Take a look at your attendance record. Take a look at the number of rejects you chalked up during the past six months. Look at the number of times you were reprimanded for unauthorized absence from your work station. Should I continue? I could go on and on.

E. (morose) Come on, give me a break.

S. Give yourself a break. Shape up on the job and I'll be the first one to put you in for that promotion when it opens up. Al, the job is no different from life. Breaks don't come for free. You have to earn them. Work with me toward that end, and I'll work with you.

• • • **TALKING POINTS** It isn't pleasant to deal with disgruntled employees who feel inadequately compensated. But it is no time for hemming and hawing. The bullet has to be bitten. When employees don't measure up, whether they seek advancement or not, no time should be lost in pounding the message home to them. Any strategy you can use to motivate or help a marginally productive worker shape up should be utilized. But more often than not it's the employee himself who must be made to bite the bullet and see the situation's realities.

DIALOGUE TWO

An employee with seniority, Shirley Fox feels she is being ripped off—paid less than a co-worker for doing the same job.

Talking It Out

Employee - It says in the labor agreement that seniority is supposed to be a key factor in deciding wage increases and promotions.

Supervisor - No argument there.

E. Then how come Ruth Dworkin was put in for a 15-cent-per-hour increase and I wasn't? She's making more money than I am now. It's a rip-off. We both do the same job and I have two years more seniority.

S. No argument there either. But it also says in the contract that while seniority is a key factor in qualifying employees for wage increases and job advancement, it's not the only factor. Job performance, for example, is at least equally if not more important.

E. What's wrong with my performance?

S. Nothing drastic, but it could be a lot better. If you compare your performance record with Ruth's you'll see soon enough why she was put in for that raise and you weren't.

E. (disgruntled) I still think it's not fair.

S. I'm sorry you feel that way, but we have to be realistic. As a supervisor, when wage increases and promotions are considered it's my responsibility to take a number of factors into consideration. Performance is one, seniority another, attendance is a third, attitude a fourth, and so on. If you want me to, I can show you the numbers and ratings on each of these factors. In Ruth's case they're outstanding. In your case they're average, and when it comes to attendance below average.

E. (resigned) So what do I have to do to get a raise?

S. That's a good question. Simply try harder. You have the brains, ability, and motivation to do it, and if you put in the effort, I'll help you every step of the way.

E. Okay, thanks.

S. I'll give you another tip, Shirley. As you know, Ruth participates regularly in the company's suggestion program and has turned in

a few good ideas. That helped her earn not only the promotion, but some nice prize money as well. Few things come free in this world. If you want to increase your income, you have to put in the effort to prove you deserve it. Work hard, toe the line, and you'll come out all right. Your income depends on your outcome. You're not the only one who wants to see that raise recommendation; I'd like to see it as well. As your supervisor, the better you do, the better I do.

• • • **TALKING POINTS**   Employees often make a big deal of seniority and it is a big deal. But it must be made clear that it is not the *only* big deal. Number One on the qualifying list for job advancement is the employee's job performance and its effect on productivity, along with the person's rating on such things as attendance, efficiency, attitude, personal initiative, and record as a team player. When compensation complaints based on seniority alone are made, as a supervisor you should have at your fingertips the documented evidence needed to make the griper understand why seniority alone isn't enough. At the same time, encourage the employee to upgrade the other factors involved. Demonstrate your personal interest in seeing the complainant advance. And assure him or her of your willingness to help any way that you can.

DIALOGUE THREE

Softhearted Warehouse Supervisor Ben Goslin recommends that everyone in his department should receive a merit increase.

Talking It Out

Manager - Hey Ben, what are you trying to do, win a popularity contest?

Supervisor - What do you mean?

M. (displays list) Take a look at these recommendations. Are you telling me everyone in your operation is so good that they all deserve merit increases?

S. I've got a great crew.

M. I'm glad you feel that way. But when was the last time you read the company's policy statement on the subject of merit increases?

S. I don't know. I guess not for some time.

M. Let me refresh your memory. (reads from policy manual) "Merit Increases. Semiannual merit increases are awarded to selected employees who demonstrate outstanding performance and above-average effort." The key word is *selected.* Can you truthfully say that every person on this list measures up to this policy standard?

S. I'm not sure.

M. I didn't think so. I've taken the liberty of pulling the personnel folders of the 14 people in your department from the file. Let's go over the names one by one.

(Ben and his boss review the job performance, attendance records, attitude and initiative ratings, team player and cooperation assessments, and so on of the department's 14 rank and file employees. The manager enters an overall evaluation ranging from A for excellent to E for substandard for each worker on a yellow-lined pad.)

M. All right, let's see what we have here. I see three employees rated excellent, six good, two fair, two poor, and one substandard. What do you think, Ben? Do they all deserve merit increases?

S. (glum) No, I guess not.

M. Nine out of fourteen; that's not bad. But I think you will agree that employees rated fair, poor, and substandard don't qualify.

S. (nodding) Yeah, I guess I was trying to be a good guy. I figured if I put them in for a merit raise, they'd work harder.

M. It doesn't work that way. When you give people a merit increase for unmeritable performance the message it conveys is: Why work hard if you're going to get a raise anyhow? (crosses five names from the list)

S. I see what you mean.

M. Good. One further point. Number 14 on the list, Jim Shea, is rated substandard. Not only doesn't he deserve an increase, if his rating doesn't improve he deserves to be fired. Please give that some thought.

• • • **TALKING POINTS** "Good guys" finish last when they reward fair, poor, or substandard employees with wage increase recognition. As Ben's boss pointed out, this is contrary to the message you want to send as a supervisor. Unearned compensation stifles honest effort and encourages mediocrity. Under some labor agreements, periodic wage boosts are automatic. But employees must be made to realize that an inviolable condition of *voluntary* increased compensation is above-average, quality performance. To avoid hassles and arguments, a supervisor must be able to produce documented evidence of *why* some subordinates are entitled to merit increases and others not.

DIALOGUE FOUR

Maintenance Foreman Cal Corning has no choice but to demote Grade One Mechanic Phil Frost to a lower-paying job.

Talking It Out

Supervisor - I've got bad news, Phil. I'm going to have to bump you back down to Grade Two.

Employee - Hey, give me a break. I need more of a chance. I've been Grade One for less than three months. That isn't enough time to get the hang of it.

S. I'm sorry, Phil, in my opinion it's more than enough time. You don't have the skills and experience needed for the Grade One classification. You're also too limited in the tools and equipment you know how to use.

E. All I need is some additional training.

S. You may be right. But it would be too expensive, and would take too long for you to qualify. I can't afford to wait. I need the Grade One skills now.

E. Boy, that's going to hit me right in the pocketbook. I needed those extra bucks.

S. Who doesn't? But you may recall that when you were bumped up to Grade One it was on a provisional basis.

E. Yeah, I know. Does that mean the door is locked so far as I'm concerned, that I can never make Grade One?

S. Not at all. Work hard to develop your skills and experience and you'll have another crack at it some time in the future when the time is right. Meanwhile, if I can sign you up for a training course or two that might help I'll be glad to do so.

• • • **TALKING POINTS** The objective when you have to demote employees who don't measure up to the job is to let them down as gently and considerately as possible. This is not only good human relations, it's good supervisory management as well. Keep in mind that the person will still be on the payroll. Demotion is a serious psychological blow as well as a financial setback. Your goal should be to do everything in your power to keep the worker from losing face with co-workers and, equally important, keep him or her from becoming bitter and demotivated as a result of the unavoidable demotion.

DIALOGUE FIVE

Shipping Department Expediter Liz Larsen protests to her supervisor that she is as well-qualified as Jack Cheskin, and there's no reason she should be paid less than Jack for the same job.

Talking It Out

Employee - If you take a look at the record you will have to agree my performance ratings have been consistently as good or better than Jack's.

Supervisor - I can't deny that, Liz. You're one of the department's most outstanding employees.

E. I also drew a comparison of other compensation factors as well. My attendance record is better than Jack's. His attitude is certainly no better than mine. And when the need for overtime arises, you'll have to admit I can always be depended on. You can't say that for everyone. I'm not saying I'm a better employee than Jack, but I think I'm just as valuable. It's not fair that the only reason he earns more than I do is because he's a man.

S. I have no argument for that, Liz. I'm going to put in a recommendation that your hourly rate be upgraded to the same level as Jack's. I don't have the final word on this and can't make a positive commitment, but I'll do the best I can.

E. Thank you. I appreciate your leveling with me, but I can tell you this. If your recommendation is turned down, I'm planning to sue the company for discrimination on the basis of sex.

S. I hope it won't come to that. But I'll tell the powers that be what you said. Hopefully, it will help to influence their decision positively.

• • • **TALKING POINTS**   It's a new world in today's marketplace. The women's movement has created a drive for fair and equal wage compensation that has advanced a long way. The outcome of an endless number of lawsuits demonstrates that "equal pay for equal work" has government and progressive corporations behind it. What applies to women applies to African-Americans, Hispanics, and other minorities as well. If discriminatory disparities exist in your operation, for the sake of fairness and good human relations, as well as insurance against costly litigation, your best bet as a supervisor is to take whatever action you can toward the cause of equality.

DIALOGUE SIX

Chemical Lab Supervisor Bob Kreissler, must make Sam Lombardo, an outstanding employee, understand that money isn't the only valuable form of compensation.

Talking It Out

Supervisor - Sam, you're one of our best employees, I'd hate to lose you.

Employee - I like working here, Bob, and this department has a great bunch of people. But with three kids, and one starting college in the fall, I'm in a financial bind. If I don't get that wage increase I put in for, I'm going to have to shop around for a job in which I can get a higher income.

S. Before you do that, Sam, you might keep in mind that employee compensation here on the whole is somewhat higher than the general level in the area.

E. Maybe so, but I think I can do better elsewhere.

S. You may be right on the face of it. But let me ask you this: Have you given any thought to the possibility that you might land a job with a higher wage on the outside and still be earning less?

E. What do you mean by that?

S. There are several factors involved in compensation aside from the actual wages you receive.

E. Yeah, I know, fringe benefits.

S. That's only one, but don't knock fringe benefits. Did you know that when you consider the whole package—insurance and other health benefits, holidays, vacation entitlement, special training, sick leave, tuition reimbursement, and so on—this company's outlay runs five to ten percent higher than the industry average?

E. Well no, but when my son's tuition bill comes in I won't be able to pay it with fringe benefits. I'll need hard cash.

S. I can appreciate that comment. With two kids in college I'm in the same spot myself. But did you know we have specialists in the Human Resources Department who can help you plan the best and most economical strategies to use in financing your son's education? I should know because they saved me a bundle.

E. I guess that's something I didn't think of.

S. There's something else you may not have thought of.

E. What's that?

S. That in calculating the compensation you receive, you can't afford to lose sight of the future.

E. The future! Hey, when those bills come in, those companies want their money now, not in the future.

S. That's generally true although in certain situations the company may be able to help there too. We have a very liberal college loan policy. Another fringe benefit. But that's not what I'm talking about. You're still a relatively young guy, not about to retire.

E. What does that have to do with the amount of money I earn?

S. A great deal. I'm talking about the people you work with and for in this company in general and this department in particular. Excuse me if I blow my own horn. But I'm considered to be one of

the foremost experts in this field, and you'll have to admit that I've been devoting a lot of time and attention to your personal training and development. In addition, think about some of the guys and gals you work with—Eleanor, Tom, and Jim, for example. I'm sure you're learning a great deal from them as well.

E. *I can't deny that, and I appreciate the training I'm getting from you.*

S. Another factor to consider is how you *feel* about people you work alongside day in and day out.

E. *I can't argue with that. I guess I'd have to go pretty far to find co-workers more compatible than the group we have here.*

S. I'm glad you feel that way. Sam, you're smart enough to realize that the more you know, the more you grow. It's something to think about. It's true, you may succeed in getting a few bucks more on the outside than you earn here. But if you decide to do that, make sure that in getting more you don't settle for less. As you continue to learn and develop you'll earn more money here. But you can't use your own engine to turn the wheels, if you know what I mean. You'll have to be a little more patient.

E. *Yeah, I suppose I'll have to give that some thought.*

• • • **TALKING POINTS**   Money is and will continue to be an important motivator. But it is equally true that an employee's compensation for good work can't be measured in terms of dollars alone. Nor can the satisfaction a person derives from employment be weighed only in financial terms. Only one disclaimer exists: Such arguments carry little weight in a second-rate operation. Unless those other considerations you claim to be as valid as money honestly apply, employees will see through your attempted persuasion as little more than rhetoric at its most blatant.

INDEX

lack of:
    for co-workers, 168-70
    for organization/leadership,
        158-59
    and performance, 160-62
    and performance, 16
    and supervisor overindulgence of
        subordinates, 156-58
    supervisor's lack of, for partici-
        pants, 154-56
    as two-way street, 152-54
"Ripped off" employees, 127-28
Rumors, squelching, 128-29

S

Security, 208-17
    applicant screening, 212-14
    dishonesty, 214-15
    inventory control, 210-12
    theft, 208-10, 214-15
    time-card abuse, 217
    violence, 215-16
Self-confidence:
    lack of, and resistance to change,
        46-48
    and performance, 16-18
    and problem solving, 176-79
    and repetition of
        instructions/explanations,
        132-34
Self-respect, lack of, performance,
    160-62
Senior employees, and resistance to
    change, 39-40
Sexual harassment, 260-71
    by coworkers, 268-71
    by supervisor, 266-67
    charging co-workers with, 263-64

definition of, 264
failing to recognize/act on com-
    plaints of, 261-62
sexually offensive
    photos/posters, 270-71
    supervisor-subordinate rela-
        tionships, 264-66
Shortcuts, and time abuse, 53-55
"Slow down or else" threats, 274-76
Smith, Leonard J., 172
Status quo, initiative vs., 104-6, 110-
    12
Status-quo advocates, and resis-
    tance to change, 40-42
Stone, Clement, 124
Succession programs, 32-34
Suggestion program participation,
    302-304
Supervisor:
    as line worker, 34-36
    as one-person team, 3-6
    performance of, 15-16
    resistance to delegation, 67-69

T

Tasks, postponement of, 175-76
Tattling/informers, 285-87
Team members, tension between,
    7-8
Teams within teams, 10-12
Teamwork, strengthening, 1-12
Telephone privileges, abuse of, 93-
    95
Theft, 208-10, 214-15
Things-to-do checklist, 76
Time abuse, 49-59
    and employee boredom, 51-53